C000227832

ON NOT BEING ABLE TO SLEEP

Psychoanalysis and the Modern World

ON NOT BEING ABLE TO SLEEP

Psychoanalysis and the Modern World

Jacqueline Rose

Chatto & Windus
LONDON

Published by Chatto & Windus 2003

2 4 6 8 10 9 7 5 3

First published in Great Britain in 2003 by
Chatto & Windus
Random House, 20 Vauxhall Bridge Road,
London SW1V 2SA

Random House Australia (Pty) Limited
20 Alfred Street, Milsons Point, Sydney,
New South Wales 2061, Australia

Random House New Zealand Limited
18 Poland Road, Glenfield,
Auckland 10, New Zealand

Random House (Pty) Limited
Endulini, 5A Jubilee Road, Parktown 2193, South Africa

The Random House Group Limited Reg. No. 954009
www.randomhouse.co.uk

A CIP catalogue record for this book
is available from the British Library

ISBN 0 7011 6977 X

Papers used by Random House are natural,
recyclable products made from wood grown in sustainable forests;
the manufacturing processes conform to the environmental
regulations of the country of origin

Typeset by Deltatype Ltd, Birkenhead, Merseyside
Printed and bound in Great Britain by
Biddles Ltd, Guildford and Kings Lynn

For Suzanne and Christopher Bollas

Contents

Preface

These essays, written over a period of roughly ten years, all share an abiding preoccupation. How to understand the link between public and private worlds, between our collective histories and the inner-most, hidden, components of lives and minds. Whether in the case of the woman writer struggling to transform the most painful aspect of her story into writing, or political actors brought face to face with the worst of their own past, the question is always: how do we negotiate the passage between those parts of ourselves which belong to others by the mere fact of being in the world, and those parts, sometimes too intimate even for us to contemplate, which we yet feel to be most fiercely our own?

The essays were all written for different occasions, some as reviews, some as conference papers on topics such as modernism or the public life of intellectuals in the modern world, some when I was asked to set my mind to something, such as celebrity, which seemed to be in the nature of a general mania of our time. I have chosen to keep the variety of tone and have not added footnotes to those essays aimed at a non-academic audience. Only on putting the collection of essays together did I notice that all the reviews are of women writers, all the psychoanalytic essays are on men. In this collection, then, it is men who struggle with institutions often of their own making, women whose words travel on more unofficial paths.

Different people solicited these essays or provided crucial insight and support while they were being written and after. My thanks to Mary-Kay Wilmers, Richard Poirier, Robert McCrum, the graduate students at the Cornell School of Criticism and Theory in 1997, Biddy Martin, the PhD discussion group at Queen Mary University of London which met from 1999–2001, Moustapha Safouan, Gillian Slovo, Leo Bersani, Adam Phillips, Christopher and Suzanne Bollas, Sally Alexander, Cora Kaplan and Marina Warner. Mia Rose has been present for most of these essays and enriched them all. Once again I have been lucky to have Jenny Uglow as my editor.

Introduction: 'Shame'

Shame requires an audience. Unlike guilt, which can fester quietly inside you, shame only arises when someone knows, or fears, they have been seen. Shame relies on the art of exposure, even if exposure is what it hates most, and most militantly struggles against. Shame has a visceral quality about it – early in his work, Freud listed shame as one of the traumas alongside fright and physical pain. People turn red with shame, are 'flooded' by shame, as though shame – rather like the sexuality it can also cow into submission – brings the body too close to the surface, inner organs and liquids bursting through the dams of the mind. Shame may require an audience, but at the same time it is secret and hidden, not something which as a rule people are in a hurry to share. Only in a moment of the greatest intimacy are you likely to confess to someone the moment in your life of which you are most ashamed. Shame is very precious, but, in a strange tautology, it also seems to be ashamed of itself.

And yet shame is also an action, a transitive verb – to shame – with a very public face. Shaming someone can be a political project. Not just outing, with its complex ethical agenda (it is not of being homosexual but for *hiding* it that the outed public figure is meant to be ashamed), but equally the act of exposing corruption, intended to stop the rot, contains a crucial component of shame. Shaming can be historical and aim very wide. In the 1998 election in Australia, protestors outside Parliament House opposing Howard's Amendment to restrict Aboriginal claims to their traditional lands spelt out 'shame' with a sea of hands (it was commonly referred to as the 'race' election, or as Australia's election 'of shame'). And it can be collective, a part of public contrition when a whole section of a community – the former beneficiaries of apartheid South Africa, for example – are required, and at least partly acknowledge the need, to apologise for themselves. You don't need to have been a torturer (indeed the torturer may be the least likely) to feel ashamed. You can simply feel that you walked away or did not do enough in a hateful world. But shaming is not always effective. Shame can be argued against or simply spurned:

'One might expect that Australia would be shamed by such a damning assessment,' the *Independent* commented in February 2002 on Australia's Human Rights and Equal Opportunities Commission's announcement that Australia was violating human rights in its refugee camps. 'Instead Canberra accused the commission of pursuing an anti-government agenda.' Writing in 2000 on the gap between 'norms and reality' in human rights and humanitarian law in *The American Journal of International Law*, Thomas Meron places his hopes in an education that would lay emphasis on values that lie outside the frame of the law: ethics, honour, mercy and shame.

Shame therefore shunts back and forth, crossing the boundary between our inner and outer worlds. Running through many of the essays of this collection, it is something of a refrain. Written mainly in the 1990s and these past two years of our new millennium, the essays often share a question. What do we gain and what do we lose – whether in the world of public, political, atonement, in the glitz of celebrity, or in the comparative privacy of poetic writing – from living in a world so committed, hooked one might almost say, on people revealing themselves?

Freud famously said that small children are 'essentially without shame' (they show an 'unmistakeable satisfaction' in exposing their bodies). But, in his 1905 essay on 'Infantile Sexuality', he continues almost immediately, 'cruelty in general comes easily to the childish nature' since the obstacle that 'brings the instinct for mastery to a halt at another person's pain – namely a capacity for pity', develops rather late. But if we picture the small, uninhibited child blithely appearing naked to the world (although even this image has become an object of suspicion in the era of child pornography and sexual abuse), the idea of cruelty jars. It is not the characteristic that most readily comes to mind. Perhaps, though, Freud's not often remarked connection has something important to say. What the little child exposes us to is the precarious nature of our ethics – even innocent exposure or self-exposure, Freud hints, contains a dimension of mastery in itself. Both pity and shame are tardy and uncertain arrivals on the scene. It is at least an open question whether it is nakedness or cruelty of which we feel – or should feel – most ashamed.

There is a powerful and shocking moment in Gillian Slovo's extraordinary account of her confrontation with her mother's killers at the amnesty hearings of the South African Truth and Reconciliation Commission, when she realises, not just that Craig Williamson saw what he had done as justified (shameless, he would do it again), but how 'personal' his action had been. In J. M. Coetzee's prize-winning novel, *Disgrace*, which also takes place in post-apartheid South Africa, the central male character, David Lurie, and his daughter Lucy are viciously assaulted by a group of black youths at her farm (he arrives on the farm after a sexual scandal at his university where he was disgraced but refused to be shamed). Lucy says to her father: 'It was so personal [. . .] It was done with such personal hatred. That was what stunned me more than anything else. The rest was . . . expected. But why did they hate me so? I had never set eyes on them.' When her father offers as an explanation he only half believes in: 'It was history speaking through them,' she responds: 'That doesn't make it easier. The shock simply doesn't go away.' People without shame are merciless. Rather like the small child.

Shame, however, brings, no ethical guarantees. In her most recent book, *Hiding from Humanity: Disgust, Shame and the Law*, philosopher Martha Nussbaum argues that shaming, as an arm of the law (public apology, enforced acts of contrition), is always cruelty, always evokes and recalls the most primitive infantile rage. And a culture of shame can in itself bring killing in its wake. In her 1998 report, *Country of My Skull*, poet Antjie Krog struggles to understand the refusal at the amnesty hearings of the Truth and Reconciliation Commission of Winnie Madikizela-Mandela – bar what most have seen as a purely empty performative – to apologise for atrocities committed, if not directly by her, with her blessing and in her name. A colleague at the South Africa Broadcasting Commission explains: 'The essence of this hearing was the collision of two cultures alive in the black community. The culture of human responsibility, human virtue and guilt; and the culture of clan honour and shame [. . .] If she admits to wrongdoing, she dishonours them all.'

The cult of celebrity in the Western world may seem poles apart from these moments of historically forced and traumatic recognition. But celebrity, as the most public form of late twentieth-century self-fashioning, might also lead us to ask what people – both the stars and their watchers – really want from the glare. The lead story for the 1999 Golden Globe awards and the Oscars was Gwyneth Paltrow breaking down in tears. Halle Berry did the same in 2002 but in the name of racial dignity – she was redeeming past shame by her tears. But why does the camera love these moments? It is assumed that what we want from celebrities is perfection: money, beauty, health; no need that can't be met on demand, no flaws, not a single hair out of place, nothing that falters or is weak. Bodies which shine so bright that they blind you to any fear or hesitation beneath the skin. But perhaps the pleasure we take in celebrities, the contract we strike with them is more complex and perverse – crueller – than it might at first seem. Even if there is also empathy, the audience loves the undoing of the stars. The camera lingering on Paltrow's tears – Gazza crying during the World Cup is another famous example – suggests that humiliation, or the potential for humiliation, might be a crucial part of the bargain. Celebrities may inspire awe, but also dread, as well as the excited gasp at the fall (it has become a famous characteristic of *Hello!* magazine that any couple braving its cameras are likely to separate in a matter of weeks). Gods and goddesses with wings of wax who fly too close to the sun. Guilt, it is said, always arises in relation to others; whereas with shame it is your narcissism, the ideal you like to nurture about yourself, that you betray (psychologists describe shame as the only affect which works internally, passing from one to another part of the self). People feel guilty when they violate other people, shame when they fail themselves or the group. In the cult of celebrity, the potential for failure may be the key to success.

Celebrity feeds on curiosity – that much is obvious. But we might want to invert the expected formula – that celebrities are the people we are most curious about – and suggest instead that we create celebrities so as to let a very special form of curiosity off the leash. This violent curiosity feels dangerous to those who go in search of it as much as it does to those on the receiving end. It feels shameful in direct proportion to the murderous frenzy with which it is pursued (the death of Diana would simply be the most glaring instance of the trend). Or in the words of Adrienne Rich, who also appears in these essays, 'Fame slides on its belly like any other animal after food' (from the title poem of her 1999 collection, *Midnight Salvage*). Fame turns all its objects into spoils.

Nor is this just a phenomenon of 'popular' culture. It is not uncommon today for writers to acquire celebrity status, a status which they either court or detest (there does not seem to be a middle way). But for some writers, notably the so-called confessional women poets of the 1950s and 60s – most famously Anne Sexton and Sylvia Plath – something of the complex mix of exposure and failing associated with celebrity appears to have been part of the writing contract which they drew up with themselves. One of Plath's most famous poems – 'Lady Lazarus' – presents suicide as a form of striptease. The speaker taunts her audience with their own tantalisation: 'Do not think I underestimate your great concern'. Uncannily, she anticipates the circus, the mercenary passion, which will greet Plath's own afterlife:

There is a charge

For the eyeing of the scars, there is a charge
For the hearing of my heart –
It really goes.

And there is a charge, a very large charge
For a word or a touch
Or a bit of blood.

The largest charge is for a word, a touch, or a bit of blood. Like blood (thicker than water), writing is the most intimate – and costly – of possessions. But there are other ways of commuting her triad ('a word or a touch or a bit of blood'). However much, however far, Plath exposes herself in her writing, there will always be someone baying for more. It is one of the arguments in the essays to follow that the woman writer – Plath, Sexton, Rossetti – who takes the risk of a letting the reader into part of her body and mind, is likely to find what she does with her language disappearing under the weight of her offering. Her poetry – ostensibly the only reason for the attention she elicits – will never be quite enough. And however closely the critic tries to follow the currents of the writing, she is likely to feel this counter-flow, find herself drifting into her writer's lives, into the inexorable logic of fame. Although only in extreme cases – and in this domain Plath is of course *the* extreme case – will she find herself, as is the topic of one of these essays, charged with shaming her subject, ramming the poetry obscenely into the life, producing interpretations of which she as critic should feel herself ashamed.

'Though terror speaks to life and death and distress makes the world a vale of tears,' psychologist Sylvan Tomkins opens his consideration of the subject in *Shame and its Sisters*, 'yet shame strikes deepest into the heart of man.' In Freud's thought, shame is one of the crucial impulses which lead the child, not just to put her clothes on, but to give some kind of, albeit unconscious, organisation to the confusion and perversion of infantile sexual desires (he once described sleep as an 'undressing of the mind'). Where there is no shame, he writes as early as 1896, before most of his major discoveries, there will be no neurosis (only the male, he states, is likely to be this free). Shame becomes one of a triptych – shame, disgust, morality – which appears as a mantra in the rest of his work, like household spirits who are meant to appear magically in the night and tidy up the mess. Shame almost invariably appears at the start of the list, although the attention he pays to it dramatically declines as the question of morality and guilt become more and more the focus of his concerns. Shame, closer to disgust in terms of gut feeling, gradually refines itself out of the picture. But in the beginning, when some critics would argue Freud was more interested in the pain of lived trauma, shame appears as the very first of distressing affects. On the hysteric, Freud writes in 1895:

> I recognised a universal characteristic of such [repressed] ideas: they were all of a distressing nature, calculated to arouse the affects of shame, of self-reproach, and of physical pain, and the feeling of being harmed; they were all of a kind that one would prefer not to have experienced, that one would rather forget.

Or in the words of Christina Rossetti: 'A shrinking of the memory/ From some forgotten harm'.

Rossetti is the poet who takes this conundrum – a pain so vociferous it must be silenced – and shows how to put it back into words:

> First the shattering ruining blow
> Then the probing steady and slow . . .
> Dumb I was when the rain fell
> Dumb I remain and will never tell.

O my soul, I talk with thee,
But not another the sight must see.

But unlike psychoanalysis, which also aims to speak the unspeakable, Rossetti can carry the dumbness across into her poetry. She can use her poem, which is called 'Introspective', to go on hiding; only the soul will she talk to, only the soul will see. Almost impossibly, Rossetti's poem presents her reader with a spectacle turning its back, as if she were saying to the reader: 'Listen to what I won't be telling you.' The reader cannot help but be filled with the longing to know. But if she tries to follow that path and fill in the silence, she will lose the question – which psychoanalysis in its best moments still keeps open – of how on earth to give shape and voice to what 'one would prefer not to have experienced, [what] one would rather forget'. In one of his boldest articles, from his collection *Forces of Destiny*, contemporary psychoanalyst Christopher Bollas, also the subject of one of the essays in this book, suggests that the trauma of incest is not just the horror of the experience for the abused girl, but the ruin of her capacity for reverie. Thought stalls on an event it cannot bear to contemplate, can go no further. Shame and rage spell the end of mental freedom. The task of psychoanalysis is not so much to undo forgetting, but to put poetry back into the mind.

Forgetting is in any case an infinite task. Really to forget something, you have to forget that you have even forgotten. You have to be 'forgetful of forgetfulness' (the lines come from Rossetti's 'Sappho', in which she imagines herself as Sappho willing her own death). In Freud's early writing, shame is one of the ways we try to forget a part of ourselves, curb our unruly desires, enter the world as it is meant to be. But it can't, surely, be for nothing that shame, as one of the main agencies of this civilising process, is so appalling, something which makes us feel so dreadful that, instead of thinking about it, we would – as in common parlance – rather *die* (or 'I wouldn't be caught dead' to use the other colloquial formula for shame).

Shame and death may be related in other ways. Shame, suggests Tomkins, is not 'unlike mourning'. Unwilling to surrender a love object I feel I have lost, in mourning I become – like someone ashamed – 'exquisitely aware of the self'. In his famous paper on 'Mourning and Melancholia', the focus of another of the essays here,

Freud describes the melancholic as being oddly without shame. Unlike most people who are 'crushed with remorse and self-reproach', and who are filled with shame in the presence of others, he does not behave '*in a normal fashion*'. Instead he is endlessly communicative about his misery, a bit of a boast. The melancholic has lost someone or something he once loved. But whereas the mourner unwillingly, over a long and difficult process, recognises the death as separate, the melancholic draws what has been lost into his ego and then, as his way of holding on for ever, proceeds to flay it alive. Merciless and shameless, he becomes his own torturer. Self-abasement becomes a matter of pride. Writing in the middle of the First World War, Freud is struggling to understand how people let go of their dead, if indeed they can. In the tension between mourning and melancholia, Freud places himself on the side of mourning, of getting things over and done with (just at moments he reads like a general exhorting his troops to move on and up). But the melancholic is stubborn, shameless in the display of his own worthlessness to all. He is there to remind us that, in extreme cases, shame can be a blessing, the heart's desire, something coveted and pursued. Faced with a death too painful to contemplate, there are no limits to which some people will go to torment and degrade themselves.

This is just one moment in Freud's writing where he seems to brush up almost against a limit in his own thought. Or rather against what it is bearable for anyone to think about. There are others, and in these essays I am interested in those instances when Freud seems to trip on the edges of the mind. In what follows, death and sleep appear as vanishing points of psychoanalysis, points when Freud's elucidation of unconscious processes slip, almost inadvertently it seems, into the dark (beyond shame, one might say). In these moments, Freud appears to be telling, or rather showing, us that there are places in our minds and in our histories – in the histories he lived through – which even the idea of the unconscious is insufficient to grasp. Here it is not a question of individual trauma, although the trauma of the war clearly drove much of his thinking after 1914, nor of repression (thoughts tucked away out of sight), but of the furthest, and far more elusive, edges of the mind. Psychoanalysis is often described as casting light on the unknown, but if you follow the trace of sleep and death in

Freud's writing, you can watch psychoanalysis falling out of its own reach, letting go of its own grounds.

At these moments, I suggest in what follows, Freud's writing leaves its even partial allegiance to scientific method and comes closest to writers – often his contemporaries – such as Virginia Woolf and Marcel Proust. But only so close. This is not Freud sharing the insight of the poets, not literature and psychoanalysis mutually congratulating themselves (literature is not being offered as a complement to psychoanalysis, more as a supplement, as in Freud's own suggestion that we should look to the poets when he stalls). There are points in Woolf when she appears to be writing from the place of the dead, in Proust when he pushes the sleeper off the edge of the knowable world. Both of them take Freud even further along paths which it feels as if he was reluctant, or only occasionally willing, to tread. It is a central tenet of psychoanalysis that with the right form of attention, the unconscious, however remote, is somehow there for the taking. Both Proust and Woolf, I suggest here, might disagree. In their different ways they both put flesh on what happens to a mind when it really slips its own moorings or spins too far out of control:

If I can have in and around me so many memories which I do not remember, this oblivion may extend over a life which I have lived in the body of another man, even on another planet. (Proust, *Sodome et Gomorrhe*)

For long spaces of time she would merely lie conscious of her body floating on the top of the bed and her mind driven to some remote corner of her body, or escaped and gone flitting round the room. (Woolf, *The Voyage Out*)

Once you enter this dimension, then bodies, or bits of bodies, can migrate as much as minds. Elizabeth Bowen and the lesser known modernist, Mary Butts, both of whom also appear in these essays, are particularly apt at showing how – beyond all reason – perceptual boundaries between inner and outer worlds can break down: plantlife entering bodies, objects not in front of, but pushing behind, the eyes. In Bowen's perhaps most famous novel, *The Heat of the Day* of 1949, Louie, the first character we meet, leans over a plant during a Sunday afternoon walk in the park in the middle of the Second World War: 'Louie stooped repeatedly to touch petals, her raspy finger-tips being every time entered by her smoothness'; and in Mary Butts interwar novel, *The Death of the Felicity Taverner*, published in 1928, the boundaries of bodies become permeable, as if a body could be invaded by something inside itself: 'something was trying to get out through his eyes'.

Freud rarely goes here, although in my essay on *The Interpretation of Dreams*, I suggest that there is one chapter of that epoch-making book where he does. But the later analyst, W. R. Bion, placed this hallucinatory register at the centre of his clinical work. In his essay 'On Hallucination' of 1967, he writes: 'When the patient glanced at me he was taking a part of me into him. It was taken into his eyes [. . .] as if his eyes could be sucking something out of me.' This is a realm beyond memory, beyond a retrievable selfhood. What each of these writers manage to convey is what it actually feels like not to know what distinguishes you from the objects around you, not to know – in the most concretely imaginable sense – who or where on earth (or perhaps not on earth for Proust) you are.

It seems fair to ask, therefore, to what extent psychoanalysis since Freud has pursued him on these journeys. For Christopher Bollas, the essential unknowability of the unconscious is something that, for the most part, psychoanalysis itself, since Freud, has gone to great lengths to re-repress. And the Egyptian-born, Paris-based psychoanalyst, Moustapha Safouan, whose history of analytic training is the starting point for another of the essays here, believes – in a crushing indictment – that, with the rules for training first laid down in 1925, psychoanalysis was instituted as if 'psychoanalysis had never existed'; as if the psychoanalytic discovery of the unconscious – which should presumably make us suspicious of the idea that psychoanalysis could simply be known and taught – had never happened at all. Behind the stifling bureaucracy of training rules virtually unaltered by the International Association of Psychoanalysts since their inception, we can detect, Safouan suggests, a barely concealed panic. What does the unconscious – notably its murderous, shameful component – do to the idea of legacy (from father to son, for example), to the idea of a smooth transmission of technical know-how involving the perfectly decorous obedience to a set of rules? 'Why such conformity, such a need for respectability or social recognition, if not as an alibi against [. . .] delinquency?' For psychoanalysis, to be a son is to feel guilty, even when there has been no crime. Lineage is a deadly affair. But the history of psychoanalysis charted here is there to remind us that far more havoc is likely to be created – the implications for any group are likely to be more serious – if this is pushed under the carpet, if guilt becomes unspeakable, something of which you have been persuaded to deny because you feel so ashamed.

The story of the institution – the essay 'What makes an analyst?' – is the worst story in this book. It is there to strike a balance, not – as will be clear – in the name of even-handedness, but in order to demonstrate the contrary directions in which psychoanalysis has been, and continues to be, pulled. Rather than casting this as a problem belonging only to Freud's consciousness (a purely personal matter as it is so often represented in the interminable Freud wars), I have tried to follow the different strands of Freud's own thinking into their afterlife and trace their implications for literary and institutional forms – how we write and how, collectively, we organise our professional selves.

In these essays Freud is therefore given two sets of companions. He is surrounded by writers who, for better or worse, take the different pulls of his own writing and commitments, way beyond his founding gesture, and run with them. Towards the 'primary madness', or 'uncommon sense', which Marion Milner in her wonderful 1950 memoir, *On Not Being Able to Paint*, places at the heart of painting (she describes it in terms of ecstasy and terror). The title of this collection is my tribute to her work. Towards a no lesser terror, or petrification: psychoanalysis – in retreat from the danger and exhilaration evoked by Milner – fossilising into a set of transmissible rules. Not that the official voice of psychoanalysis is unaware of the problem: 'Between Chaos and Petrification' was the title of Robert Wallerstein's summary for the *International Journal of Psychoanalysis* of the 1991 5th International Conference on Training; in 1996, Otto Kernberg's 'Thirty Ways to Destroy the Creativity of Psychoanalytic Candidates' was the first article to be published by the *International Journal of Psychoanalysis* on the Internet.

So which of these two destinies should we most fear? If literary departments of universities have been famously more hospitable to the uncertain aspects of Freudian thought, this too – these essays are intended to suggest – has been at a cost. Inside the literary academy as much as inside its own institutions, psychoanalysis has been purged of its extremities – on the one hand, the darkest, most discomforting colours of the psyche (fear and shame); on the other, the more glaring political questions raised by its institutional history (what would authority look like if it acknowledged itself to be driven by the unconscious, instead of seeing itself as more urbanely subject of, and to, its own laws?).

There is always a history to the shape of the mind. The story of psychoanalysis makes that all too clear – its panic and drive for legitimation is inseparable from the after-shock, for its predominantly Jewish community, of the Second World War. In what follows, the collision, or mutual imbroglio, of history and psyche is also a recurrent theme, as war tracks so many of the writers considered here. In a famous meeting between Virginia Woolf and the dying Freud in 1939 described in Woolf's *Diaries*, he gave her a narcissus. When she asked him if Hitler would have existed if Europe had not won the First World War, he insisted that Hitler would have been 'infinitely worse'. No one can of course answer with any degree of certainty a question like Woolf's, which goes backwards, imagining a history that didn't happen. But handing Woolf a narcissus may have been Freud's way, despite the unhesitating confidence of his reply, of agreeing with the spirit behind her question, her belief that the ills and ideals of the ego – vanity, triumphalism, self-idealisation – are the most perilous of all. It was a central belief of one of the most important and influential of her group, John Maynard Keynes, that Hitler may indeed not have arisen if, after the First World War, the German people hadn't been so thoroughly humiliated and shamed.

Like other writers considered here – Mary Butts and Elizabeth Bowen – Woolf's relationship to the unfolding tragedy was complex. Fiercest critic of dictators, she never came anywhere near to slipping into the fascist identification which became, for some of her contemporaries, notably Ezra Pound and Wyndham Lewis, the sinister accompaniment of their experiments with words (her 1938 *Three Guineas* is still one of the most powerful exposés of fascist fantasy to date). Nor did she ever produce anything in her fiction remotely capable of earning the description 'fascist pastoral', as is the case with Butts's *The Death of Felicity Taverner*. But perhaps one of the strangest things she did was to travel with Leonard to Germany for part of their annual holiday in 1935 when the vigour of German anti-Semitism, Hitler's power and at least some of his worst intentions towards England were clear and recorded in her diary ('there is some reason I suppose to expect that Oxford Street will be flooded with poison gas these days'). Five years later, caught in an air raid with Ben Nicholson (who sagely threw himself to the ground), she stood still and lifted her arms to the sky. More sinister, during the earlier trip, suddenly caught in the middle of a flag-waving crown of Nazi supporters shouting 'Heil Hitler', she raised her arms in salute.

If there is something shocking and idolatrous about that gesture, there is something no less puzzling and scary about her wartime embracing of the night sky. What might lead someone, in a state of real potential danger, to identify with, stretch out – yearn – towards the aggressor? What might lead someone to seem passionately to covet what they most fear? Freud, Woolf, Proust, Butts and Bowen are all writers of war. 'It's life itself, I think sometimes, for us in our generation so tragic,' Woolf wrote in a moment of extreme depression after the First World War. It is one of the final arguments of this collection that the intensity of their vision, including the moments when they take writing into the furthest recesses of the mind, is inseparably meshed with, driven by, that history. Barriers inside and between minds start to crumble when the world is falling apart (war in Elizabeth Bowen's words as a 'thinning of the membrane between the this and the that'). Like Woolf, people in wartime behave unexpectedly – the heroine of *The Heat of the Day* falls in love with a Nazi. They do things of which we would expect them – although Bowen's novel issues the strongest challenge to that expectation – to feel ashamed.

There may well be, too, a powerful link between the cult of celebrity, at least in the UK, and such historically specific forms of shame. After all, the royal family – the first of our modern celebrities – came into existence as the Windsors by severing themselves from their German heritage in 1917. The line that runs from Edward VIII's abdication in 1936 to his later Nazi sympathy is famous. Perhaps, in Britain at least, the cult of celebrity is another kind of whitewash; and glitz a way of blinding us to what is not just embarrassing, imperfect, in the humdrum of the day-to-day, but more deeply, historically, shameful, a way of exorcising – however brutally – the ghosts of the past. Could this history be one of the ugly undersides of celebrity? – fame sliding on its belly, to cite again the phrase of Adrienne Rich.

In 'Midnight Salvage', Rich writes, 'I don't know who we thought we were / That our personalities / Could resist the failures of the race'. Even more sanguine:

> But neither was expecting in my time
> to witness this: wasn't deep
> lucid or mindful you might say enough
> to look through history's bloodshot eyes
> into this commerce this dreadnought wreck cut loose

And yet, as I suggest in the essay on her poetry, Rich – one of the mothers of modern feminism and the only survivor of the late 1950s Boston triangle of herself, Sexton and Plath – has not lost her political vision. As I read her, she just believes things have got harder: '*to think, really honestly about your life and other people's lives [. . .] is NOT THRILLING, but often downright nasty. And when it's nasty then it's MOST important*' (citing Norman Malcolm on Wittgenstein in 'A Long Conversation'). The second part of 'Char', dedicated to the surrealist poet René Char, opens with this extract from the journal he kept as a commander in the French Resistance:

> This war will prolong itself beyond any platonic armistice. The implanting of political concepts will go on amid upheavals and under cover of self-confident hypocricy. Don't smile. Thrust aside both scepticism and resignation and prepare your soul to face an intramural confrontation with demons as cold-blooded as microbes.[15]

Before coming up for air – before even beginning to think it might be possible – we have to dive deeper into the wreck (this, finally, was the wager of South Africa's Truth and Reconciliation Commission, with which this collection ends). Declarations of shame can be a front – browbeating is not being promoted here. Nor is shaming as an arm of the law. None the less, perhaps the best way to move forward in the new millennium is to think about the things of which we are most ashamed.

I: WRITING FOR THEIR LIVES

'Faking it up with the truth': Anne Sexton

This piece, a review of Diane Wood Middlebrook's Anne Sexton: A Biography *(Virago, 1991) was written shortly after the publication of* The Haunting of Sylvia Plath. *First published in the* Times Literary Supplement *of 1 November 1991, it carries over to Anne Sexton my involvement with the complex ethical issues raised by biography. Sexton and Plath have become linked through the label of confessional poetry (they attended Robert Lowell's poetry class together in Boston in 1959). And yet, as Middlebrook pointed out when we shared a platform in Manchester about our books, my experience of writing on Plath could not have been more different from hers in relation to Sexton, her difficulty being not a lack of co-operation from those still living and most intimately connected with the poet, but too much. The problem came to a head when Sexton's therapist made available the transcripts of the tapes of their sessions, transcripts which Sexton had made at his instigation. Not surprisingly, on publication of the biography, this provoked a crisis over confidentiality in relation to psychoanalysis in the States. The ethical question here, then, is: what limits should the critic or biographer set around exposure? And does it make any difference if the poet in question is seen, like Sexton, as having perfected the art of exposing herself?*

There is a sense in which Anne Sexton's life story almost defies the telling. 'Maybe', she wrote in one of her early poems, 'there is always another story, / better unsaid, grim or flat or predatory'. For someone best known as *the* confessional poet (indeed she herself insisted that she was the only one), this may seem a strange thing to say. After all, Sexton was – as this remarkable biography stresses from its opening lines – the performance artist of intimacy. Standing before her audience she would, seemingly without inhibition, offer up in her poetry the most private details of her life. It was the great literary roadshow of the unconscious, writing as psychic striptease.

And yet the story told in Diane Middlebrook's *Anne Sexton* is one besides which that process of poetic revelation starts to pale. Incest (father–daughter, mother–daughter), marital violence, seduction by a therapist, violation of professional boundaries and confidences, family friends suddenly claiming to be fathers, lesbian loving – this is a biography which leaves no screw unturned. Only part of this, in fact, appears with any degree of explicitness in Sexton's poetry. Oddly, then, one of the strongest impressions conveyed by this narrative is that performed self-exposure may be one of the best ways for poets, and not only for poets, to hide. As Sexton herself put it: 'I use the personal when I am applying a mask to my face,' or with reference to a veiled poetic allusion to a woman lover: 'I fake it up with the truth'.

Maybe it is the disturbing nature of what Middlebrook has so dramatically uncovered that explains why this is the first biography of Anne Sexton to date – although one might have expected the opposite, given the usual pull, for biographers, of any promise of a slide into sleaze. Producing this biography has clearly been a long and delicate process. One of the most striking things about it is the way that it gets drawn into the vortex of what it describes, the arena of what is appropriate, permissible or bearable to reveal or talk about. If as a biographer you are, exceptionally, given access to everything (most stories about the difficulties of writing biographies point the other way) – the most intimate and disturbing details of the mother–daughter relation, the private tapes of therapy sessions recorded as part of the treatment – how much should you, how much are you then obliged to, tell? Reading this account, it feels as if Sexton has managed craftily to hand on to her biographer the central question of her own writing.

Like the story of Sylvia Plath (her contemporary and friend, and the poet to whom she is most often compared), Anne Sexton's story is at one level banal. A New England WASP, she was born in 1928 into a business family: her father was in the wool trade. Sexton had a writing legacy through her maternal grandfather – he was the editor and publisher of the *Lewiston Evening Journal* which had been founded by his father in turn. With a rigid and formal upbringing (her father never sat down to dinner without a jacket and tie), a public school education (she was the only one of three sisters not to be sent to a private school), finishing school in Boston, an early marriage which was to last more than twenty years, at the age of twenty-seven, she had two children and the reproduction of the ideal middle-class marriage seemed complete, the appropriate expectations fulfilled, the story that of a suburban housewife taking up her socially appointed place.

A year later, Sexton had a breakdown and attempted suicide – the first of a series of mental collapses and suicide attempts which were to colour the rest of her life. In the course of her therapy, as a part of the process of recovery, she started to write about her experiences. The value of her breakdown would, she was told and believed, reside wholly in its communication as writing, an activity that was to last until she committed suicide in 1974. If poetry was a liberation in that it allowed her to move beyond and expose the limitations of the oppressive middle-class home, it also arose out of a partly Puritan injunction to enlarge her sphere of suffering for the good of the world, that is, out of the very form of religious and social coercion she was most furiously trying to escape. Writing as social service – perhaps that explains the tone of public self-flagellation which occasionally creeps into her work.

What did writing do for her? It is the conviction of her biographer, her closest friends and her main therapist that it kept her alive. It also enraged her husband and his family, but inspired countless others, especially women, seeking a new language for a new definition of self. To whom – lover, mentor, doctor, daughter, God – was it addressed? All her life, Sexton oscillated between the painful insight of her close friend Ruth Soter that words never quite take you where, or to whom, you want to go ('Stop thinking you can avoid people . . . or even reach them with your words') and her own lasting, and (for eighteen years) saving, conviction that there was 'an auditor for every tongue'.

It would be misleading, however, to present Sexton's personal and poetic journal as an escape from the straitjacket of an oppressively normal family life. Normality, as this biography reveals so starkly, is most often a myth that families build for themselves. Sexton's paternal grandfather had a serious mental collapse, her father became an alcoholic, his sister attempted suicide at twenty (she killed herself a year after Sexton's death), her beloved great-aunt who lived with the family went crazy, attacked Anne verbally and physically and was taken off to a mental home: 'Anne was now fifteen. "My father was drinking every minute, Nana was going crazy, my grandfather was crazy, Jane (her sister) was having a baby" – the family seemed to be deteriorating all around her.' Sexton never escapes, psychically or physically, from this family history – all her adult life she and her husband lived 'under the watchful eyes of their parents, never more than a short distance from their childhood homes'.

How close can, how close should, people get? – This is one of the key questions Middlebrook's biography provokes. For Anne Sexton, therapy was the great cheat because nothing ever really happened, sex was constantly present but it couldn't actually take place. Sexton was eventually seduced by, and/or seduced, a therapist, Dr Zweizung, with whom she conducted a protracted love affair. It was a violation of professional ethics which underscores one of the central dilemmas of her life – intimacy as what is most desirable and most invasive, at once a fulfilment and a violation of self. As Diane Middlebrook puts it in one of a number of memorable formulas which punctuate her book, desire, especially in the orbit of the family, is something which 'ignites and distances them all'.

So when we read of Sexton's childhood seduction by her father (Middlebrook is immensely careful in stressing that even if this was Sexton's fantasy, it was no less psychically real), and then of her attempted seduction of her adolescent daughter in turn (interestingly here the question of possible fantasied reconstruction on the daughter's part is not raised), or when we discover that Sexton's passage from her first to second therapist was, in a beautiful replica of the Oedipal dilemma which therapy is meant to cure, from a mother to her son (Martha Brunner-Orne to Martin Orne), it feels rather like an inflated version of the basic problem of family life. What are parents and children meant to do for, and to, each other? Not surprisingly, Sexton's daughter deduces from her experience that it is time to separate and draws on her therapist for ammunition and support; only to be confronted by her mother's insistence, similarly backed by her own therapist, that it is impossible for mothers and daughters to be too close. As Sexton puts it in her poem 'Housewife' of 1962, 'A woman *is* her mother. / That's the main thing.'

Out of this knot emerges one part of Sexton's writing which has been of immense importance to women – the bind and inspiration of mother–daughter intimacy and doubling. Desire, writes Middlebrook, in her eloquent discussion of Sexton's third collection, *Love Poems*, 'seeks what has been lost forever, the unsymbolic experience of infant intimacy with a maternal body . . . the immortality of the love burned into the circuits of the body from its first hours of awareness of the body of another'. This yearning for a primordial oneness with the mother has been a hallmark for one recent development in feminism which has seen such a merging as the basis for a new fluidity of being. Sexton's relationship with her daughter might seem to enact that longing, but instead it contaminates it. It spoils the dream by making it too literal, taking the figurative, poetic, dimension away.

There is, however, a very clear feminist story to be told here. Not just because Sexton suffered, refused and exposed the 1950s myth of the ideal woman's role (Adrienne Rich on the dilemma of the mother-poet: 'Two years of raising children and being almost constantly angry'); but also, and perhaps more significantly, because her life raises the issue of how we assess forms of behaviour, the forms of ethical and sexual judgement we choose to make. In her discussion of Sexton's first extramarital relationship, Middlebrook cites Dr Martha Brunner-Orne's comment from her medical notes that Sexton had 'difficulty in controlling her desire for romance and adventure'. Sexton herself saw the situation rather differently – that this was a man who encouraged the best in her, who thought she had a good mind and with whom 'she wouldn't have to talk baby-talk to feel feminine'. As Sexton passes from mentor to mentor (John Holmes, Robert Lowell, W. D. Snodgrass) and lover to lover (George Starbuck, James Wright), she takes off on a dual search for love and what she called 'language' – promiscuity not so much a symptom as body and words on the move.

One of the most impressive things about this biography is the way it manages to recount all this without sensationalism. Middlebrook tells her often shocking story without, apparently, seeking to shock. For the most part, she has managed to write a biography which avoids judgement and steers clear of the twin pitfalls of condemnation or special pleading. Sexton's poetry is presented as both 'egocentric' (Elizabeth Bishop) and as the opposite, 'enobled' by its willing descent into the detritus of a collapsing self (Allen Grossman); Sexton herself emerges as someone of 'inspired, disturbing, associational looseness' and then, rather like the Jesus figure in her poetic sequence 'The Jesus Papers', as 'an often very disagreeable person, disgustingly fixated on the female body, neurotically self-absorbed, terrified of the death for which she has been singled out'. When Sexton unashamedly exploits Snodgrass to advance her poetic career, Middlebrook does not judge her (one can imagine this episode in the hands of a less sympathetic biographer) but turns the moment to her advantage – Sexton spotting the link between poetry and business which most poets deny. For the family of Sexton's husband, on the other hand, she was making 'a bunch of suckers' of them all.

This fine balance cannot, however, survive the weight of the most difficult moments of the book. The affair with the therapist and the episode with daughter Linda are judged unequivocally 'wrong'. In relation to the second, it feels rather as if Sexton has let Middlebrook down: 'It is always disappointing to find that a work of art is wiser than its maker' – a point which echoes Sexton: 'Writers are such phonies: they sometimes have such insights but they don't live by them at all.' Only on the use of the therapy tapes, however, does the book take on a note of defence – not of Sexton, but of the biographer and even more of the doctor who, again in violation of the most basic ethics of his profession, made them available to her. In relation to the potential effects on present and future patients in therapy, it is hard to see how such a decision could be defended. In relation to Sexton herself, Middlebrook echoes the belief expressed by Dr Orne in the foreword that this is something she would have wanted. But how can anyone claim to know? Although, by Sexton's own account, recording the sessions was often a fruitful procedure, the overall impression is that this was a process in which she was by no means wholeheartedly or unambivalently involved. After a year of collaboration, she went through a period when she would pass out increasingly into a state of trance, driving Orne to exasperation, forcing him to end the sessions out of hearing, the tape winding itself on in silence. If the function of the tapes was to help Sexton to remember her sessions, at moments the sense is equally that of the canny wiles of the unconscious driving the process of recording to some kind of defeat.

The use of the therapy tapes has tended to dominate discussion of this biography in the United States. Regrettably, I think, since there is a risk that the fact of the tapes will distract attention from the equally significant issue of *how* they should be read, or, even more, that they will inadvertently acquire the status of a unique form of truth-telling –

hidden but now unveiled – when their existence in fact points all the other way. Designed to help her remember, they are rather a testimony to the disjunctive and contradictory ways in which a self *can* remember, the multiple stories that individuals spin for themselves. What mattered, after all, was the discrepancy between the record of the session, Sexton's recollection of it, the notes she took from the tapes and the events or memories that the session itself was meant to recall. At most, they are one document or representation in a process whose unreliability Sexton herself stressed throughout her life and work: 'the inaccuracy of memory fools us all forever'. Why, indeed, do we assume that in her sessions – as recorded – Sexton was always telling the truth? – 'I have been known to lie and I never let myself down.'

Sexton was a mistress of the 'I' as fiction – the personal as the ultimate persona. This was the basis of her poetic craft. Nor do I think that we should read this merely as pathology, the sign of a false or non-integrated self. Indeed, Middlebrook herself defines Sexton's insanity in terms of her moments of singular, exclusive, one-track vision of the world, her sanity in terms of the mobility of poetic language, words running off in all directions, multiplying significance, releasing the poet from a monolithic vision of herself. If we read the tapes in this way, then this biography starts to tell a very extraordinary and unexpected tale: of how it is the most confessional and intimate of poets who can show us most clearly that the personal is always self-invention and myth. Paradoxically, it is precisely because this biography seems to offer so transparently and flagrantly the secret life that it gives us the tools with which to undo the myth of ultimate revelation, and with it one of the dominant fantasies of biographical writing.

In Dr Orne's foreword, he describes how Sexton said to him at the beginning of her treatment that the only thing she thought herself capable of was prostitution, helping men to feel sexually powerful. One could argue that one of the main differences between therapy and prostitution is that in the former it is the one bestowing rather than receiving the power who pays (Maxine Kumin on Sexton's affair with Zweizung: 'Imagine paying to get laid twice a week!'). For Orne, the value of the tapes is that they reversed the balance and gave a little power back to Sexton: 'Anne made a major step forward when she was first able to show me that I was wrong!' But there is still something uncanny in the way his foreword opens the book giving him a status (and power?) which he clearly held for her during her life, and which he reclaims in his barely concealed suggestion that the loss of him as therapist (together with her divorce) was one of the things that drove her finally to commit suicide.

In a brilliant earlier essay on Sexton's unpublished play, *Mercy Street*, Diane Middlebrook describes the moment when the suicidal Daisy, re-enacting before a priest her sexual abuse as a child, turns to the figure of Christ and 'undaughters herself' in relation to her therapist by 'bringing him a state of mind that resists psychiatric interpretation'. In her poem 'Consorting with Angels', Sexton wrote 'I am tired of the gender of things'. One of the questions this book leaves us with is, not so much what or who Anne Sexton was trying to reach, but what she was trying to get past. Diane Middlebrook has provided us with an extraordinary account of the way one woman, in her passionate engagement with poetry, therapy and gender, powered and disempowered her own life.

'Undone, defiled, defaced':
Christina Rossetti

Again a review of a biography, this time Jan Marsh's Christina Rossetti:
A Literary Biography *(Jonathan Cape, 1994), this piece appeared in the*
London Review of Books *of 19 October 1995. Rossetti presents the
biographer with a very particular challenge because the lushness of many of
her poems contrasts so virulently with the restraint of her life. Rossetti often
tantalises her reader, hinting at something awful in her past which she
never names. In her own poetry she therefore crystallises a tension at the
heart of biography – between revelation and secrecy. What should a
biographer do when a poet seems to have gone to such lengths to offer, but
also veil, her own truth?*

One of the problems for right-wing promotors of ideal family life is
that there is no way of predicting its outcome. It is as if those who
confidently assert that absent fathers spell delinquency for the
children, inadequate mothers addiction, divorce an incapacity to hold
on to relationships or to love in a sustained way, never stop to ask why
it is, then, that the most stable and long-lasting of family unions can
produce offspring who run wild, turn to drugs, contract out of loving,
who seem – often perversely and inexplicably – to be committed to
the extremest forms of pleasuring and/or punishing themselves. The
union of Frances Polidori and Gabriele Rossetti, parents to Maria,
William, Gabriel and Christina Rossetti, was by all accounts
harmonious, affectionate, enduring. Eccentric, not without drama (he
was a poet and revolutionary in exile from Italy), it none the less
offered in terms of devotion, engagement and cultural stimulation a
model that might still pass today as a middle-class ideal of what the
family should offer a child. And yet of the four children, only one –
William – was able to sustain an attachment even vaguely resembling
that of his parents. Maria became a nun, Gabriel the painter and poet
descended, after the suicide of his wife, into drugs and breakdown,

Christina the poetess lived as an ascetic, her religious devotion finally powerless to assuage the self-loathing which seems to have dominated so much of her adult life (according to more than one account, she died raving at her own perdition). 'Why, one wonders,' as Jan Marsh puts it, 'did the four siblings have such difficulties when their parents' marriage was so happy?' Or, on the diametrically opposed nature of Maria and Christina's religious experience (respectively utmost contentment and utmost pain): 'Why two sisters, growing up in the same environment, should respond so differently to the same religious influences is a question not easily answered.'

A different way of putting the same questions would be to ask instead, not why are the members of the same family so different, but what it is that they are carrying for each other? It is hard reading this story not to be struck by the similarities with other such creative family sagas (the Jameses most obviously), where it feels as if one member suffers so that another can write, or that one collapses at home so that another can be a citizen of the world, or one starts to fail at the very moment when another begins to recover and achieve. Gabriel was Christina's closest mentor – encouraging, editing and promoting her work – but he started his decline into paranoid mania the year after she began to surface from one of her most debilitating periods of illness. 'Thus,' writes Marsh, 'with something approaching normality, the worst period of her adult life closed.'

Typically and immediately, the most striking of such distributions is sexual. Christina and Maria both lived a life of cloistered virtue (literally in Maria's case). In the formula of Victorianist, Angela Leighton, the faith of the women redeemed the doubt of the men. Place the sisters alongside Gabriel, and the contrast could not be bolder between 'virtue' and 'vice'. But Christina, in the words of Virginia Woolf, was no 'pure saint'. As a poet, she used her writing to examine what was unbearable, even unreasonable, about her own restraint. If, therefore, the brother carries the renegade part of the family on the surface, the sister bears her share of it in the heart. It is arguable, finally, whether Gabriel, all fire and fury, or Christina, locked into apparently seamless piety, was the most powerful spokesperson for the unconscious of their age.

In her earliest story, 'Maude', the heroine says to one of her cousins: 'Have you been very gay lately? I begin to acquire the reputation of an invalid; and so my privacy is respected.' Rossetti shared the condition of invalid with Elizabeth Barrett Browning, the predecessor to whom she felt she owed so much. As with many Victorian girls, the debility began seemingly without warning or explanation in her teens. Maude's remark, however, hints at the extent to which physical weakness could be a cover: a parody of the requisite female passivity which created a hermetically sealed, imaginatively untrammelled, space for a woman's mind. In that space, Rossetti could explore the lives she never lived, the pleasures she refused, the cost of her own severity, the oppressive, even sadistic, face of the deity to whom she was so devoted. It is because the writing is in such fierce tension with the lived decorum that she is now increasingly recognised as one of the major poets of her time. But that tension makes the task of the biographer particularly difficult. To write this life, it is crucial not to take the surface day-to-day narrative at its word.

At moments, reading this story is rather like reading one of Freud's and Breuer's early case studies. Like Anna O, who opens *Studies on Hysteria*, Christina found herself as an adolescent girl bound to the care of an invalid father, seemingly without protest, until her body – registering its objections – starts to speak: chest spasms, constriction, feelings of suffocation, palpitations, extreme weakness, lassitude: 'as if,' she wrote, 'my body were not such as others are'. Fifteen years later, Maria is struck down with erysipelas (an inflammation of the skin associated with 'violent passions or exertions of the mind'). In a sense Christina's suffering is the subject of this biography, as much as her writing or how she passed her days: 'What,' Marsh asks, 'made the younger Miss Rossetti so distant and her poems so mournful?' But it is also her secrecy. Described by her brother William as a 'fountain sealed' (her own expression in 'The Heart Knoweth its Own Bitterness'), Christina returned repeatedly in her poetry to a form of suffering which seemed to call out for understanding while stubbornly refusing to be named:

Weep, for none shall know
Why sick at heart thou weepest . . .
For none shall guess the secret
Of thy griefs and fears.

Would there be any cause to weep, these lines seem to ask, if anyone understood why?

On this basis, and explicitly drawing on the Freudian analogy, Jan Marsh argues that Christina Rossetti was abused by her father as an adolescent girl. Ageing, debilitated, demoralised, what – she fairly asks of her own hypothesis – could this father actually have done? (Mutual masturbation is her suggestion.) No one would argue that the weak are incapable of abuse – it may be their only form of affirmation; but if your framework is victim/aggressor, it is none the less a problem when the reputed aggressor is so manifestly, as in this case, in the process of losing all his powers. Marsh is, however, supported in her speculation by the theme, unmistakable in the poetry, of something traumatic, invasive, phallic even, which broke Rossetti's quiet, shattered her life and which, above all, can never be told:

> First the shattering ruining blow
> Then the probing steady and slow . . .
> Dumb I was when the rain fell
> Dumb I remain and will never tell.
> ('Introspective')

And again:

> If I sleep, he like a trump compels me
> To stalk forth in my sleep:
> If I wake, he rides me like a nightmare;
> I feel my hair stand up, my body creep:
> Without light I see a blasting sight there,
> See a secret I must keep.
> ('Nightmare')

Marsh's theory has been dismissed and even mocked by some reviewers. Strangely, what gives her theory – that something traumatic happened – its plausibility is not something dramatically offered by the poetry, but the opposite. Beyond memory and consciousness, something is being withheld: 'A shrinking in the memory/ From some forgotten harm.' Thus Freud, before discarding his seduction theory, answered those of his early detractors who insisted that only his suggestion led his hysterics to believe they had

once been abused by arguing that what convinced him was the pain
with which the memory emerged, the tenacity with which they held it
back. Rossetti's poetry works over this patch with enough regularity
to make me feel that Marsh is on to something.

Were I to speculate along similar lines, however, I would have gone
for Gabriel, given the kind of desperate, at times self-defeating
attachment that seems to have bound them to each other. 'I have gone
through the same ordeal,' she writes to him in the year of his death. 'I
have borne myself till I became unbearable to myself' (this is
empathy, clearly, but it could also be read as tracing for his
remembrance a pain or burden which she is suggesting they might
share). And even without a theory of abuse, it is worth noting the
peculiarity of passion, by no means untypical at this time, which tied
the members of this family to each other. At the age of forty-five, in a
poem dedicated to her mother, Rossetti declared herself her 'least last
valentine' (the last child left at home, she cared for her mother until
her death).

The problem with this line of reasoning is, however, rather
different: not whether something happened to Christina, but what the
hypothesis does to the writing – Rossetti's and to the process of
biography itself. It was this problem that led Freud, one might say, to
discard his early hypothesis of abuse to concentrate on the fantasy
world of his patients (he has been wrongly accused of disbelieving
them, whereas it is more that he shifted his focus on to something else
which offered him, and his patients, more options, more places to go).
If a poet has (perhaps) been abused and then goes on to write, what
are we doing when we run the poetry back into the trauma? Or to put
it another way, if the poetry tells us about the trauma, what, if
anything, can the trauma tell us about the poetry? Rossetti's writing at
moments suggests something momentous and awful took place; but
look again and it has as much to say about thwarted, sensual, longing
('I long for one to stir my deep'); about, not just the pain, but the
teasing pleasure of secrecy; about just how far writing can take you if
there is something in the life you want to transform or even leave
behind. Abuse and secrets are perversely connected in another way:
one forces on you what you don't want; the other makes you want
what it won't let you have. Critics agree that Rossetti was the mistress

of tantalisation; it is the theme of her most famous poem, 'Goblin Market'. These are the opening lines of 'Winter: My Secret':

I tell my secret? No indeed, not I:
Perhaps some day, who knows?
But not today; it froze, and blows, and snows,
And you're too curious: fie!
You want to hear it? well:
Only, my secret's mine, and I won't tell.

Writing this life in terms of a secret to be uncovered, Marsh picks up the bait, responds to the poet's lure. You could say that she is being oddly faithful to Rossetti's project, although at times the density of rhetorical questions goes way over the top: 'Was it a real dream or half-waking vision, or an actual experience of fear, graphically rendered? Why did William's rhyme words – verses written to a prescribed rhyme scheme – prompt such a macabre scene? What was the pitiful monster with its clammy fin, and why did it so frighten her?' The trouble with the theory of abuse is not just that it closes the door on its own questions (having first so dramatically set them up), but that it takes the pleasure out of the writing.

Reviewing two 1930 biographies of Rossetti in her essay, 'I am Christina Rossetti', Virginia Woolf had this to say about biography:

The old illusion comes over us. Here is the past and all its inhabitants miraculously sealed as in a magic tank; all we have to do is to look and to listen and to listen and to look and soon the little figures – for they are rather under life size – will begin to move and to speak, and as they move we shall arrange them in all sorts of patterns of which they were ignorant, for they thought when they were alive that they could go where they liked; and as they speak we shall read into their sayings all kinds of meanings which never struck them, for they believed when they were alive that they said straight off whatever came into their heads. But once you are in a biography all is different.

Something about the disparity between the minimalism of Rossetti's life and the intensity of her achievement brings into particularly sharp focus the way biography creates meaning out of nothing, compulsively filling in the gaps and silences between words (abuse could in this sense be seen as the natural trope for biography, instead of as a shocking surprise). But it might also be because one equally crucial strand of Rossetti's poetry runs so keenly across the surface of suffering – 'self stabbing self with keen lack-pity knife' – that reductive explanations, even if they are correct, seem finally so out of place. Why – to reply to Marsh's question with a question – must there always be a reason for suffering? Although she allows on the very first pages of the book that sorrow can come from nowhere, and later that many of Rossetti's symptoms remained without explanation, the whole pull and drift of the biography goes the other way. If dissatisfaction can be 'unfocussed' when 'powered by indefinite or inadmissable cravings' – the reference is to 'The Heart Knoweth its Own Bitterness', one of Rossetti's most desolately yearning poems – why must pain be given so much more tangible shape? 'The meaning of the verses,' Marsh comments of 'A Pause for Thought', 'lies precisely in the not-naming of the thing desired, which thus stands for all such hopes.' As if desire can be left empty, but pain must be filled. 'Death hangs, or damage, or the dearth of bread' – you don't have to choose; in these lines suffering is out looking for its mate. Or to put it another way, if suffering is not always within reason, it is because suffering has reasons all of its own. 'Only the heart', writes Rossetti, 'its own bereavement knows.'

By her own account, and following a well-trod religious path, Rossetti was a miserable sinner. The spiritual burden which the Puseyite tradition she adhered to placed upon its followers was immense. In a wonderful moment, Jean Ingelow writes to Rossetti: 'Surely it is a fine thing that we are never satisfied with ourselves'; no need for so much 'compunction and contrition', since 'it is agreed we are nothing' – 'Let us cast this care too upon him' (this would be to make our sense of unworthiness His problem, so to speak). But Rossetti's spiritual and psychological journey took her deeper and deeper into her own 'evil'. It was a relentless pursuit: 'I pursuing my own evil from point to point find that it leads me not outward amid a host of foes laid against me, but inward within myself . . . It is I who undo, defile, deface myself.' In this context, to deprive Rossetti of her own spiritual accountability would be an affront to her belief, not least because this 'susceptibility to sin', in Marsh's phrase, releases the poet into her artistic freedom, her ability to identify whatever the circumstances with God's creatures in the world. When Gabriel objects to one of her poems on illegitimacy, Rossetti replied:

> while it may truly be argued that unless white could be black and Heaven Hell my experience (thank God) precludes me from hers, yet I don't see why 'the Poet mind' should be less able to construct her from its own inner consciousness than a hundred other unknown quantities.

This is to issue another caution to the abuse theory. Poetry, she is arguing, has no necessary connection to a life. It allows you to make everybody else's life – above all the lives you would never dream of living – your own. To 'read incest for illegitimacy', as Marsh suggests, is to miss this point. Nothing, it turns out, need have happened; this God will 'visit you for an unholy thought as much as for an unholy deed'.

Jan Marsh is best on Christina Rossetti's religious poetry and beliefs, especially in the later part of her life. Partly because this period – often dismissed as her final flight into wretched poetry – is, as Marsh convincingly argues, where Rossetti came most fully into her own: 'I am not what I have nor what I do / But what I was I am, I am even I.' Paradoxically perhaps, it was within the confines of religious spirit that Rossetti could most widely, and as a woman assertively, extend herself. Early on, Marsh notes the way she would use the female mode of humble submission to get somewhat different messages across ('Meek compliances veil her might'). But when Rossetti asserts that Christ and even God was made in woman's, not man's image – 'one of the tenderest of divine promises takes, so to say, the feminine form: "As one whom his mother comforteth, so will I comfort you"'; when she hands Eve the moral victory ('a feminine boldness and directness of aim combined with a no less feminine guessiness as to means, her very virtues may have opened the door to temptation'); when she defies warnings against independent witness by publishing her prayers, she is doing far more than laying claim to the Protestant tradition in which 'each woman could be her own theologian'. Though dotty at moments, she is also oddly perspicacious: 'Did [the serpent] stand somehow upright? did he fly? what did he originally eat? how did he articulate? . . . Fix the botany of Jonah's gourd.' This is Rossetti as spiritual guide without apology, pushing self-authorisation to the limit, throwing her own sexual-political cautions to the wind (she had refused to sign a petition in support of women's suffrage).

It may be, however, that Jan Marsh is best on Rossetti's religious writing because it was in this sphere that Rossetti herself issued what we might read today as the strongest warning to the literal-minded biographer. It was in her commentaries on religious texts that she made her most explicit bid for hermeneutic freedom, her boldest defence of readings that follow the heart: 'If some points of my descriptions are rather flights of fancy than lore of modern science, I hope that such points may rather recall a vanishing grace than mislead from a truth.' And, she continues, should anyone object that 'if I have fancied this another may fancy that . . . till the whole posse of idle thinkers puts forth each his fresh fancy, and all alike without basis; I frankly answer, Yes.' In a much earlier poem, Rossetti wrote:

> I loved and guessed at you, you construed me
> And loved me for what might or might not be.
> (Sonnet 4, 'Monna innominata')

Love lies in the guessing, in granting your loved one the greatest possible freedom, the widest imaginative and spiritual reach. That she famously let both her suitors go and died a spinster could perhaps be read more positively in some such terms. But it is not clear how one would go about writing a biography in such a spirit.

'Go, Girl!' Adrienne Rich
and Natalie Angier

Adrienne Rich, completing the circle of Plath and Sexton (the three were together in Boston in the late 1950s), offers in the collection reviewed here – Midnight Salvage: Poems 1995–1998 *(Virago, 1999) – a meditation on what can be salvaged from her own feminist, political past. In this review, first published for the twentieth anniversary issue of the* London Review of Books *of 30 September 1999, I place her alongside Natalie Angier whose* Woman: An Intimate Geography *(Virago 1999), by charting a geography of the female body, challenges feminism to enter into a positive dialogue with science. What is the relationship between science and poetry? What are the most fruitful vocabularies for a feminism trying to move into the new millennium? Can there be a reckoning with feminism's earlier Utopian dreams without discarding its vision?*

Survival of the human species may not be guaranteed but the language of survival has always been fundamental to feminism. Germaine Greer seems to be convinced that the species is heading for extinction: 'When, far in the future, the human race has exterminated itself,' she concluded a 1997 article in the *Observer*, what ghastly ritual, she asks, will intelligences from other galaxies landing on our planet deduce from the scars on the bodies of women of the west? For a while at least, Adrienne Rich believed that what was destroying itself was patriarchy, as in these comments from her 1971 essay 'When We Dead Awaken': 'The creative energy of patriarchy is fast running out, what remains is its self-generating energy for destruction.' Women's task in advancing its end was simple, brutal and clear: 'As women, we have our work cut out for us.'

For Rich, feminism has always been a 'struggle for survival', a phrase she often used. More recently, she has described writing poetry: 'I feel as though it's for my survival, first and foremost ('Interview', 1991). But in the early poems which accompanied these statements, Rich was not so much exhorting feminism – a role at which no one has been better – as setting it a question. In 'Waking in the Dark', a poem from her 1973 collection, *Diving into the Wreck* – her latest, *Midnight Salvage*, can be read at least partly as its reprise – she asks: If 'Nothing can save this', if nothing can preserve a world which masculinity has made 'unfit for women or men', then what can be salvaged, what will be left for the survivor other than to wander lost and dazed, or else to dive shining the beam of poetry into the wreck? And if we are, as we seem to be, talking survival, with its barely muted Darwinian echoes, then can anyone – indeed can feminism – exempt itself from the failures of the race? *Diving into the Wreck* was in fact Rich's seventh collection of poetry (her first appeared in 1951), which means that already in 1973 – most often identified as the very beginnings of the second wave of twentieth-century feminism – she was in a position to look back:

I don't know who we thought we were
That our personalities
could resist the failures of the race

Lucky or unlucky, we didn't know
the race had failures of that order
and that we were going to share them
('From A Survivor')

Surviving is an awkward business; Rich's writing can be read as a continuous exploration of the difficulties this poses for feminism. If patriarchy is hurtling towards extinction, then what does it mean for feminism to join in, to complete the job, as it were? If the energies of patriarchy are so overwhelming, then how can anything in the world, including the inspired fierceness of our own enterprise, even our own dreams, not be contaminated by the fierceness of men? 'When I dream of meeting / the enemy, this is my dream: / white acetylene ripples from my body' ('The Phenomenology of Anger', from *Diving into the Wreck*). Can you destroy something well? No survivor ever feels wholly benign. No survivor, surveying the wreckage all around her, ever feels simply entitled to survive. One of the – appropriately millenarian – questions being put today both by feminists and, for very different reasons, their critics is how far feminism has in fact survived itself. Feminism, one might say, is uniquely poised to ask the question – recalcitrant and yet germane to any politics – of how to endure one's own rage. Perhaps, too, the refrain of survival suggests a closer connection between feminism and Darwinism than has sometimes been thought. If, as Rich would have it, feminism is a struggle for survival, are women, or the species, to be saved?

The bonobo is a female-centred, egalitarian primate species, of which only a few thousand still exist, virtually inaccessible to humans, in the dense remote forests of Zaire. *Aggressive Behaviour*, the official journal of the International Society for Research on Aggression, introduces a review of Frans de Waal's *Bonobo: The Forgotten Ape* somewhat apologetically: 'Although most of this journal is devoted to papers on aggressive behaviour and violence, it is worth remembering that its mandate also includes the study of peaceable alternatives.' A 'tragic and optimistic species', the bonobo exceptionally uses sex to resolve clashes of power rather than the other way round. 'As these intelligent creatures gaze from the photographs,' writes the reviewer, 'it is virtually impossible to avoid responses of anthropomorphic delight.' Natalie Angier shares this delight and in *Woman: An Intimate Geography* offers the bonobo, if not quite as a role model for women, at least as an alternative primate lineage, another history we can wrench from biology in order to build a better future world: 'We humans have within us a polychromatic phylogeny, a series of possible paths.' 'Our lineage,' she says citing *Bonobo*, 'is more flexible than we thought.'

On the face of it, Angier has written a book about science. Although it can be seen as being in some ways critical of Darwinism (a critical review by the neo-Darwinist Helena Cronin is reported to have been spiked by the *New York Times*), it in fact opens with a defence. Feminism has repudiated scientific arguments about the female body at too high a cost, severing the mental from the sensual substrata of our lives. If Germaine Greer devotes chapter after chapter of her book, *The Whole Woman*, to the monstrous inflictions and mutilations enacted on women's bodies, mainly at men's but sometimes at women's own behest, Angier comes at the same problem from the other end. 'This book,' she opens, is a 'celebration of the female body'; woman is an 'evolutionary masterpiece'. Science, including

Darwinian science, can be mobilised in the service of seeing how and why women's bodies – so miraculously – work. *Woman: An Intimate Geography* is a kind of conjuring act. Angier knows just how hard it can be for women to enjoy, as one might say, or take pleasure in themselves. She knows that celebration is close to incantation, like warding off demons in the dark. 'I have made it a kind of hobby, almost a mission,' she wrote in the introduction to her previous book, *The Beauty of the Beastly* (1996), 'to write about organisms that many people find repugnant.' Angier, one could say, is a writer who honours her own loathing. *Woman: An Intimate Geography* is not the first feminist ode to joy which feels as if it has been – at least partly – snatched from the jaws of fear.

Do women love women? Feminism – uniquely perhaps among political movements – has always had to wrestle with what its main protagonists are feeling and thinking, not only about their opponents, but about each other and themselves. In part because it assumes that one of the things patriarchy does best is drive wedges between women, feminism has been spared the delusion of believing that harmony and shared political interest are necessarily the same thing (or that the second can be comfortably relied on to breed the first). In one of her most famous essays, 'Compulsive Heterosexuality and Lesbian Existence', Rich called on women to reject what she defined as the forcing house of heterosexual intercourse and turn instead to women – for love, for sex, for contact. Angier is firmly on the side of heterosexuality and even marriage (in one bizarre twist, she argues that monogamous women – precisely 'married, conservative, Christian women' – have especial orgasmic capacity, or rather claim to have when questioned, which might make us wonder who exactly this group of women were aiming to please). But if the bonobos are crucial, it is because they seem to suggest that there are no heights of solidarity which women cannot reach, that they do love each other, or in another species' existence at least once did. 'The original adult deep bonding,' Rich wrote in her essay, 'is that of woman for woman.' The bonobo is the best living example we have of a gynocentric, primate world.

Gynocracy may not, however, be an idyllic affair. Whereas Rich spoke of 'empowering joy' between women, Angier is more cautious. Bonobos are not 'goo–girls, and they fight, and they're hierarchical and greedy, and they can be murderous towards each other'. A whole chapter of *Woman: An Intimate Geography* is cheerfully devoted to a spirited defence of the aggression of little girls (a resolute cheerfulness, or 'chirpy wellness', to use Angier's own self-ironic expression, is the main spirit of the book): 'the hyena girls, the leopard girls, the coyote and the cow girls . . . the living, seething, aggressive girls who are the only girls I have ever known'. After the bonobo, the spotted hyena comes close to being Angier's next heroine. Not so much for her undisputed bad behaviour – 'the hyena soul is pure fury' – but for demonstrating, contrary to the first scientific investigations into the matter, that her aggression is not attributable to the high testosterone levels to which both male and female cubs are exposed in the uterus. In which case aggression immediately ceases to be the prerogative of the testosterone-charged male: 'the studies which link testosterone to aggressive or dominant behaviour are not pretty. They are a mess.'

None the less Angier would like aggression, or one kind – our kind – of aggression to be a good thing: 'women-centred, harsh and intimate'. This takes some doing. One of feminism's greatest talents has been to turn such psychological posers into its best trick, but this one might be the hardest of all. If we do not like aggression in men (not the same thing as saying all men are always aggressive), but we like the myth of our sweet passivity even less, then where should we look? If there is, as Angier puts it, an 'aggressive need for female alliance', are you sure you will be able to tell the aggression and the alliance apart, keep the aggression out of the group? (You might say that groups or alliances are only ever cemented through the aggression they direct to the outsider, in which case what here, if anything, is new?) Angier recognises the problem but still believes that on the matter of aggression, there is no limit to what women, if they only set their hearts and minds to it, can achieve: 'We are free to salvage aggression and do with it as we please. We can rehabilitate it and recode it. We can share it.' (How exactly without – as it were – losing it, can aggression be *shared*?)

Angier describes her book as 'liberation biology'. In this she is oddly close to Greer – 'a woman's body is the battlefield where she fights for liberation' – but light years from Camille Paglia ('that most noisome and anti-feminist of self-proclaimed feminists' as Angier describes her), despite Paglia's claims in the issue of *Women: A Cultural Review* devoted to feminism now that she has been vindicated by the return of hormones and biological sex differences to the agenda. (Is it in fact a biological argument to suggest that women's disgust at their own menstrual blood can be traced to our 'evolutionary revulsion from slime'?) With considerably greater precision, Angier is in fact unapologetic in raiding the pantry of scientific findings for her own ends – she also calls her book a 'scientific fantasia'. Criticism of her book as scientifically unsound seem therefore beside the point. She prefers bonobo to chimpanzees, who have dominated our myths of ancestral lineage to date, but when appropriate the chimpanzee also has lessons to teach us of her own. Half her offspring, it turns out, have not been sired by the resident male. Female promiscuity is species-efficient and canny: 'The females of the group didn't rely on "sex" finding its way to them; they proactively left the local environs, under such conditions of secrecy that not even their vigilant human observers knew they had gone and became impregnated by outside males.' There is no relationship for women between monogamy and building the nest.

Angier is at her best in debunking this type of conservative sexual myth. For example: who ever claimed that women are closer than men – that is genetically, biologically, naturally closer – to their mothers?

A son may rightfully be thought of as a mama's boy: he has her X chromosomes alive in every cell of his body. He has no choice – it's the only X he's got, and every cell needs it. Thus he has more of his mother's genes operating in his body than he does of his father's, thousands more . . . If you do the calculations, your brother works out to be about 6 per cent more related to your mother than your father, and he is 3 per cent more related to your mother than you are, because half your cells, on average, have all the mother chromosomes turned off, while all of his remain turned on.

In other words, there is more of the mother in the boy than in the girl. 'We are all of us strange little quilts, patches of father-tone in some of our tissues, shades of our mother in others.' On this basis, and against the boast of her father that men contained greater genetic variety, Angier can claim that women have a more complex and interesting phylogenetic inheritance than men: 'It is the woman who is the greater mosaic, a patchwork of her past [. . .] We are more motley by far than our brothers.'

'This book is not a dispatch from the front lines of the war between the sexes,' Angier writes in her introduction, 'it is a book about women.' But is this a viable distinction? Especially when as here, and as for many feminists, it is your father who you are arguing with inside your head. 'I have resisted this for years, writing to you as if you could hear me,' Rich opens one of the several addresses to her father which punctuate her 1986 collection *Your Native Land, Your Life*. It is not your body, Angier concedes in a rare moment, but lived experience which will allow you to recognise the type of your father – 'cold, aloof, angry, hyper-critical and infinitely alluring' (compare Rich: 'the cruelty that came inextricable from your love') – in your sleep and 'keep your eyes and nose and hormones far, far away'. Fathers and patriarchy are not, although they may sometimes seem to be, the same thing. Rich:

> For years I struggled with you . . . After your death I met you again as the face of patriarchy . . . there was an ideology at last which let me dispose of you . . . It is only now . . . that I can decipher your suffering and deny no part of my own.

Surprisingly perhaps, it is Rich rather than Angier who seems to be suggesting that you might – just – be able to struggle against patriarchy, and lay down your arms before your father at the same time.

Out of the elaborate armoury of anecdote and counter-myth which Angier brings to her battlefield, perhaps the most powerful story, however, is this one. Jane Carden suffers from AIS (androgen insensitivity syndrome), which means that although she has a boy's chromosomes, her body failed to issue the last-stage instructions for the building of male genitalia, leaving her, in defiance of her chromosomes, in every respect a girl. 'Being androgen deaf, Jane's body took the course that a mammalian fetus will in the absence of androgens: it chose to go girl' – and later to go woman, flush with all the insignia of feminity which, for one line of evolutionary thinking, is there simply to attract a reproductive mate. Carden, however, will not reproduce. She was lied to as a young girl that she had had twisted ovaries at birth; she was wretched at puberty until discovering the truth about her syndrome freed her into the complexity of her history. Now she revels in her ability to appeal to and enact both sides of the divide ('she has balls when she needs them'): 'I'm just like my mother, an aggressive, obnoxious human being. I'm the daughter my mother created. I am the woman I was meant to be.' Clearly mothers are the ancestry to lay claim to, fathers the spirits to be conjured away in the night. Angier calls this chapter 'The Mosaic Imagination' and comments: 'The healthiest and most womanly of women are . . . a rendition of Amazon queens, self-possessed and self-defined, women whose bodies have an enviable integrity and a fleshy non-replicative beauty that razzes Charles Darwin.' For Greer, in *The Whole Woman*, these are 'failed women', 'spurious females', and the chapter in which they appear along with mainly male-to-female transsexuals has the title 'pantomime dames'.

We might, however, pause at that 'self-possessed, self-defined'. Not just because it is so immediately countered by Carden's own insistence that she is her mother's creation, but because of the oddly self-sufficient and controlling vision of human subjectivity which the phrase implies. 'Can a woman have too much self-confidence?' Angier asks at one point, as if, just for a second, a flicker of suspicion at her own powers of praise – at the powers of and for women she is invoking and praising – had crossed her mind. After all, nobody creates or defines themselves. It is, in a way, the strangest of ideas that anyone could, or could want to, be complete (one might express the same reservation about the title – *The Whole Woman* – of Greer's book). For the neurobiologist Gerard Edelman, who has done most perhaps to ground our mental apparatus in biology, to put the mind 'back into nature' (there is no mind/body dichotomy not even in relation to fathers), it is at the point of our engagement with others – our 'social, effective, and linguistic interactions' – that science has to withdraw. Once you are in language, 'consciousness is *not* self-sufficient and beyond doubt . . . it is always in dialogue with some other'. This, he argues in *Brilliant Air, Brilliant Fire*, is one of a number of reasons why, in relation to human subjectivity, science finally fails. 'Science fails for individual histories':

There is no more mystery to our inability as scientists to give an explanation of an individual consciousness than there is to our ability to explain why there is something rather than nothing. There is a mystery, perhaps, but it is not a scientific one. If one stays solely with one's own mind, the mystery rests in imagining how that particular mind arises with regard to its own history.

'I don't know how to measure happiness . . . there is no other issue to think about politically, but I don't know how to measure happiness,' George Oppen wrote to June Oppen Degan in 1970 (an extract from his letter is the epigraph to *Midnight Salvage*).

How then should women see themselves? As mosaics, fractured with the lines of putative and possibly regraspable pasts; as fluid, and open – like the clitoris in Angier's most lyrically enthused chapter – to 'multiple interpretations' (multiple *interpretations?*); or bounded by confidence, self-possessed, self-defined, invincible? Do we in fact want to feel divine? (American doctors, as Angier says, are a dab hand at making women wonder why they are feeling 'fatigued, crampy, not quite divine'.)

We are getting perilously close to the image of the 'liberated Western woman in her pumps and smart skirt, toting a laptop en route to the airport' whose planetary distribution via the Internet Angier offers in the last chapter of the book, without a trace of irony, as one of the positive by-products (for women) of globalisation. Just how much should feminism borrow from the American dream? That globalisation works to the detriment of a majority of women in the world is one of the subjects on which Germaine Greer is most convincing and eloquent. For Adrienne Rich, in the poem from which *Midnight Salvage* takes its title, globalisation is the blindspot, the failure of vision to be put at the heart of feminism's reckoning with itself:

> But neither was expecting in my time
> to witness this: wasn't deep
> lucid or mindful you might say enough
> to look through history's bloodshot eyes
> into this commerce this dreadnought wreck cut loose

Do we really want to start the celebrations when one half of the world of women, and not only women one might add, is falling into the wreck? On the other hand, there is something self-defeating in believing, as many now seem to, that feminism must choose between the language of celebration and lament. Perhaps it is because this is in fact a false distinction – the two are bloodsisters – that they are so mutually provocative with the more optimistic feminists often sounding like cheerleaders staving off a dirge (five of the fourteen essays in Natasha Walter's collection *On the Move: Feminism for a New Generation* are called: 'You, go girl! – young women say there's no holding back'). As Brecht once famously put it in relation to capitalism: every time a man struggles for his family another one falls into the gutter. Struggling can be a very cruel affair. Can we envisage a world in which we could be sure that ' "doing well" by one, or some, was immiserating nobody'? (from the closing poem of *Midnight Salvage*). Here we might take an unlikely tip from evolution which, as Angier points out, does not strive for perfection: 'It does not strive at all.' Woman may be an evolutionary masterpiece, but we must not make the mistake of believing that 'everything that is is for the best':

> I don't know who we thought we were
> That our personalities
> Could resist the failures of the race

In fact, as Angier proceeds she herself draws more and more limits around scientific knowledge. It is one of the ways *Woman: An Intimate Geography* most interestingly doubles back on itself. For one persona, the aim is to redress the existing imbalance between myth or metaphor and the facts (for example, on the breast: 'a few ounces in facts a few tons in metaphor'). In order to make real choices about our bodies we need to be informed: 'Let us examine lactation in the cold light of morning'; 'Let us overthrow the lore, the idiocy, and the Paglian prissiness about menstruation and found a myth on reality. How and why do we bleed?' This is an ethos which has been central to feminism. To correct the lore, to insist on the damage, to bring up from the wreckage the 'book of myths / in which our names / do not appear':

> the thing I came for:
> the wreck and not the story of the wreck

the thing itself and not the myth
('Diving into the Wreck')

But there is a second persona which is deeply suspicious of this very impulse. When we pitch good against bad science, we need to remember, this voice cautions, that all science is bad science if it goes almighty, if it thinks it can be sure. On the uterus:

> In truth, we know remarkably little about the purpose of various opiates, chemicals, hormones, and hormone precursors that the uterus secretes with such vigor . . . When the endometrium ceases to wax and wane, does the secretory program of the uterus likewise lapse into quiescence? Some experts say yes, some say no, all should probably settle with 'don't know'.

On the breast: 'In sum, we don't know what makes the aesthetic breast . . . [Scientists] are baffled by breasts and they should be.' On the relationship between pheromones and ovulation: 'We don't know. We can only speculate. We must expand our imaginations backwards, forwards and outwards.' On whether the female hormone androsenedione causes aggression: 'Maybe or maybe not. We don't know.' On oestrogen: 'We don't yet understand it. We can't quite control it . . . It doesn't control us, and its favorite word is *maybe*.' On hormones in general: 'A hormone does not cause a behavior.' Perhaps it is the problem, rather than the solution, that 'we want to explain ourselves to ourselves'.

For this second voice, which becomes louder in the course of the book, it is not just that science has hitherto been used against women, dressing up unenlightened self-interest as truth. It is the very claim to knowledge which stands in the way of our freedoms. We are after all subjects in language. 'We ascribe meaning wherever and however we choose.' This turns things round considerably. Instead of fighting myth with reality, we should concede that we are all, unavoidably, in the game of interpretation: 'Hold on to the fire of alternative interpretation.' Angier's call to found a 'myth *on* reality' already suggested the problem. After all, it was through poetry that Rich claimed to seize the thing itself. Ascribing meaning – or even letting oneself adrift in language – might be the first and most important choice of all. Angier's book can be read, finally, as a plea for poetry (like Rich she has a predilection for images drawn from under the sea); or even better, for a science that does not shy away from poetry, science that is not ashamed of its own limits as science. Another opposition to add to the many false binaries (male/female just being the most immediately obvious and pressing) which feminism likes to skew.

Recent feminist debates unavoidably bear all the signs and scars of generational struggle – Greer vs. Walter is perhaps only the loudest and most highly publicised. Rich herself, who was born in 1929, can of course be seen as the feminist great survivor – a term with special resonance if we remember that she is the only survivor of the late 50s Boston poetic trio she formed with Sexton and Plath. What is most striking and powerful about this new collection of poems is the commentary it provides on the passage, for feminism, for any politics, through time. These are poems which are ruthless in retrospect, generous in memory and self-critique. (Memory, it might be worth noting, is where Edelman locates the singularity of identity and the failure of science.) It is an illusion of so much contemporary feminist polemic that you either move forwards or back. *Midnight Salvage* is, to use its own phrase, 'a long throat, casting memory forward'; these are poems written in a future perfect tense – 'Sometime looking backward / into this future'; poems which pace the past – 'straining / neck and eyes I'll meet your shadow' – in dialogue with generations to come:

> you who will want to know
> what this was all about
> *Maybe this is the beginning of madness*
> *Maybe it's your conscience*
> as you, straining neck and eyes
> gaze forward into this past:
> what did it mean to you?
> ('A Long Conversation')

On first reading, *Midnight Salvage* may not seem to be a feminist collection, or not perhaps of the colours most famously associated with Rich. Its central question seems to be how to be, or rather whether it is still possible to be, a radical in our time (it also appears to be the collection in which Rich definitively takes her leave of the university: 'Could not play by the rules / in that palmy place: / nor stand at lectern / professing anything at all'). If not quite addressed to men, it repeatedly cites and opens up conversations with men; the last long poem – 'A Long Conversation' – contains extracts from *The Communist Manifesto* as well as quoting, among others, Coleridge to Wordsworth in 1799: '*I wish / you would write a poem / addressed to those who, in consequence / of the complete failure of the French revolution / have thrown up all hopes / of the amelioration of mankind.*' One poem writes the memory of a paraplegic GI and ends with a fantasied sexual encounter; one possible if unexpected answer to Rich's own earlier question from the 1950s: 'What is the connection between Vietnam and the lover's bed?' ('Interview', 1991). In the past, Rich has argued that feminism's revolutionary energies should not be reduced to Marxism. Here, in the face, I suspect, of its apparent failure, or rather of those rushing to celebrate its demise, Marxism, along with Brecht and the surrealists, is restored to its place on the page, given the poetic time of day (anyone convinced of the redundancy of Marxism could do worse than to read this book).

This is not a collection that brings good news ('you won't get quit / of this: the worst of the new news'). Rich has never had any illusions about how much, how much of the time, is being destroyed, about the random horror of the at once deregulated and perfectly controlled systems of the modern world ('this commerce this dreadnought wreck cut loose'). The tone here is cautious and determined; Rich writes just this side of despair – in this she could not be further from Angier who wants to rouse us, through our bodies, to hope. Salvaging has become unmistakably harder; the world has become more, and more casually, brutal since *Diving into the Wreck* – birds are salvaged from an oil spill, Midnight Salvage is the name of a yard where an old craftsman was accidently, carelessly, run down. Rich is not ready – in this she might seem to come down emphatically on one side of recent feminist argument – to rejoice: 'Had never expected hope would form itself / completely in my time'; 'Accomplished criminal I've been but / can I accomplish justice here?'

None of this stops her from scavenging, however, from building up a future out of the debris of her past. In poem after poem, she invokes her radical predecessors, often using the second-person pronoun (nearly every poem is an address). Against all the odds, against the temper of the time (Coleridge to Wordsworth: '*an almost epicurean selfishness, disguising the same/under the soft titles of domestic attachment/ and contempt for visionary philosophies*'), she calls up the inheritance to which she insists we can still – those of us who want to – lay claim. 'Crane hallucinated Edgar Allan Poe in the New York subway,' she writes in a note to the poem 'The Night Has A Thousand Eyes'. 'I conjure Crane, Miles Davis, Muriel Rukeyser, Julia de Burgos, and Paul Goodman, or their descendants.' Poems are dedicated to René Char and Tina Modotti. On the page, the poems are mosaics of quotes, all the voices running to and from each other (the poetic equivalent, one could say, of Angier's patchworks, mosaics and quilts). Surviving, moving forwards through time, depends – these poems suggest – on how you layer your past identifications, on who is there for you to seize and conjure into your mind. The truly unsalvageable is a city without memory where 'nothing's forgiven . . . but almost everything's forgotten' and where a woman, crammed with memory which no one else wants, lies 'scabbed with rust' (the poem is called 'Rusted Legacy'), her tale untold: 'no one left / to go around gathering the full dissident story'.

You can, Rich seems to saying, build your lineage (compare Angier: 'our lineage is more flexible than we thought'). Inheritance, for the purposes of argument, is not just in the genes. Once you are in history, ancestry ceases to be a given: 'it's the layers of history / we have to choose'. Memory is not exactly the site of freedom, but the layering of identity and memory is the only basis for moving forward through time (perhaps flimsy foundations can be a good thing). There is, of course, a limit and that limit is language or poetry itself. The last poem of the collection, 'A Long Conversation', ends: 'charred, crumpled, ever-changing human language / is that still *you*?' (language is the final addressee of the book). Like language, memory is, and should be, finally beyond your control. Taking possession – as say, taking possession of our bodies – might be impossible (both the first and last thing feminism should do). If we can see that language is circumscribed by doubt, is there a way of placing that insight at the heart of our politics? Keeping language, and time, open: 'It's not the déjà vu that's killing / it's the foreseeing' ('Letters to a Young Poet').

We should be suspicious of our drive to quantify, and callibrate ('I don't know how to measure happiness').

If, then, Rich is crafting her political and poetic past, there is always something in language that arrives uninvited or escapes: 'All kinds of language fly into poetry, like it or not' ('A Long Conversation'). This last line fairly describes the overcrowding of these poems, all the carefully chosen voices jostling to speak. But Rich is not, as I see it, using poetry to qualify the political will (a time-worn opposition); she is giving us the sketch for a form of politics which would allow the unpredictable shape of language its place. Feminism might take much from her vision of resoluteness and randomness combined. Why are the two always seen as somehow compromising each other? What would a politics look like which accepted both at the same time?

In one of her earliest and most famous poems, 'Snapshots of a Daughter-in-Law', Rich wrote: 'a thinking woman sleeps with monsters'. Though not exactly monsters, it is none the less something frightening and unpredictable which, in this last collection, she conjures up from the deep (although Angier's underwater images are almost invariably more lyrical, she also writes at one moment of the 'deposition of dreck and pain'). Remarkably, Rich can do this, while also making a plea for historical accountability. To argue, as many have, that the layering of the poetry mutes or mellows her political statements seems, therefore, to miss the point – nothing softens here. Contra some recent voices, feminism is no more at the end than it is back to the beginning of its task (on the matter of time we can surely do better than this). Feminism should go on asking for too much, or rather for things which have often been deemed politically incompatible, even by feminism itself. To struggle for justice, go into the dark and hold on to the immeasurable nature of happiness.

Sylvia Plath – Again

'This is not a biography'

In memory of Sandra Lahire

This essay, published in the London Review of Books, *of 22 August 2002, was first delivered at the Poetry 92Y Center in New York in November 1992, the epilogue as it were to the difficult process of publishing* The Haunting of Sylvia Plath, *which had met with the fiercest opposition and disagreement from Olwyn and, especially, Ted Hughes. That the dispute between us should have finally centred on biography gives a further twist to the questions addressed in the previous essays on Sexton and Rossetti. Why is it so hard – perhaps especially in the case of the woman writer, and especially the women writers considered here – to hold writing to its own place? What price does the writer pay when her words are, without reprieve, trailed back into her story? Why is the critic of Plath always assumed by her legatees to be prying? In this instance, these questions turned out to be carrying the weight of a sexual politics, unspoken as far as we know in the now ghostly exchange between Plath and Rich in the 1950s (Plath reputedly asked Rich whether it was possible to have children and write), but which have been central to Rich's feminism.*

The piece is dedicated to the gifted film-maker Sandra Lahire, the creator – among many other films – of Living on Air, *a film trilogy based on Plath, whose death in 2001 brought her own unique writing on Plath's relationship to surrealism and contemporary feminist experimental film to a premature end.*

(Following the essay are two shorter reviews from the Observer *of 1 February 1998 and 2 April 2000, of Ted Hughes's* Birthday Letters, *and of Sylvia Plath's* Journals *which appeared for the first time in Britain in a new uncensored edition in 2000, as the finale – hopefully – to this saga.)*

How *not* to write a biography of Sylvia Plath? We could put this bizarre question another way. What is the relationship for a poet between writing a mind and writing a life? Does self-revelation (or confession, to use the famous label for Plath and her contemporary Anne Sexton) lead us, not just into the inner recesses of the poet's thought, but through the veils, behind the closed doors of her past? Do we enter the room, see the knife slit the finger, catch the raised voices, watch the vase shatter, hear the baby cry? Plath's language is sensuous, evocative enough to bring all this, and a great deal more, to life. But the question still remains. How much *do* we know? And is the point to try and find out? Are we meant to be sleuths, piecing fragment upon fragment until the picture is spread before us? There she is! Sylvia Plath – nothing hidden. The true story told. Isn't that why she wrote in the way she did? Isn't that what she would have wanted, after all?

Biography loves Sylvia Plath. There have been so many and there will surely be more. When I first ask students what they know of Sylvia Plath, they almost invariably reply that she killed herself and was married to Ted Hughes. Occasionally they run these two snippets together as if the second was, in some mysterious not wholly formulated way, related to the first; as if together they add up to something that leaves nothing more to be said. I watch this story shut down around her, clamping her writing into its hollow, wooden frame. Death and marriage may have fed and fuelled her writing, but – posthumously at least – they cramp her style.

According to Freud, the act of suicide always involves more than one person. Maybe that is one reason why suicide is classified as a crime. Maybe, too, that is why biographies of Plath always take on the aura of hunt the culprit, not because, as is most often assumed, someone – usually Hughes – must be held accountable for her death, but because there is an unacknowledged crime calling out to be uncovered, another death, another body to be found. Suicide, as everyone knows, casts a shadow over all those it leaves behind. In my conflict with the Estate of Sylvia Plath (more below), I often felt that I was not the real quarry, more like a diversion, that I was duelling, hit and miss, in the dark. Although they have often denied it, the defensiveness of the Plath legatees is notorious. But perhaps the fervour with which they have warded off incursions from the world outside has been part of a deeper struggle. To kill the killer. Even though she is already dead. It is a paradox about suicide that the murderer, who lives on for ever, is the one who didn't survive.

It has become a commonplace to say of biographies of Plath that they take sides. Loving or hating Plath – biography reveals its true feelings. In *The Silent Woman*, her openly partisan study of Plath biography, Janet Malcolm insists that this is an unavoidable part of the state of the art: 'As the reader knows, I, too, have taken a side.' One flyer for her book states: 'A writer finds Ted Hughes innocent but biographers as a group guilty', which suggests the process is interminable and that, as a form of writing, biography has the capacity to indict itself. No biography, no act of writing can be neutral, but something far more serious, indeed deadly, seems to hang in the balance when biographers of Plath dispute whether or not she was bearable, whether she was disliked or liked by her friends. Out of the mire, a banal but chilling proposition starts to emerge – that we decide on the innocence or guilt of a plaintiff according to whether we like them or not. Legality, our conviction in the rights and the wrongs of the matter, trails our desires (whether the reverse would be preferable is not clear). Whenever I read biographies of Plath, I always have the suspicion that someone or other is being criminalised simply for being who they were.

In the case of Plath, the subjective component of all biography therefore takes on a special edge. Someone has to be guilty. Someone is to blame. And if someone is going to be guilty, then someone else – the person telling the story – has to be sure. Plath biographies are remarkable for their rhetoric of conviction. We are in a court of law. The biographer is mounting her case. Beyond the normal demands of biographical discovery – the search for the crucial detail, the painstaking reconstruction of every facet of a world (biographies, as we know, are getting longer and longer) – incriminating evidence is being gathered. Plath biographies tend to answer each other, shouting like opponents across a legal gulf, each one insisting that she or he has a greater claim to the truth than the one who went before (why otherwise write a biography at all?). The greater the fervour, the fiercer the claim. In the case of Plath, truth is not just subjective, it is mortal. To die for.

Perhaps the link to pursue, then, is not the one between passion and truth, but between truth and death. Between being so knowing, and touching on the one thing which – as the cliché puts it – no one can ever *know*. Something untellable, but which has to be told, enters the frame when the subject of biography dies by her own hand, when death arrives too soon. And if that subject is a woman, then there is always the risk that femininity will take on a deadly hue. In Freud's reading, Cordelia – the 'most excellent' of the three sisters – becomes, in her dying moments, the 'Goddess of Death'. In Lear's arms, she is in fact carrying him, bringing him to the point where he will 'make friends with the necessity of dying'. Such is the pull of the woman, never more deadly than when so perfect, so innocent – like Cordelia – of any crime. Once the link is made, it is something of a no-win situation for the woman. Plath's story offers us the same combination of elements, but more nakedly as we might say. Let the dead woman carry the can. What, it seems fair to ask, is being exorcised in the seemingly endless, punishing, scrutiny of Sylvia Plath?

It is not therefore that biography is irrelevant or inappropriate in thinking about Plath. If anything the reverse is the case. We are dealing not with a deficit but with a surplus (biography overspilling itself). In relation to biography, Plath is a type of Russian Formalist, whose famous objective was to 'lay bare the device', show things as, however bizarrely, they are. To defamiliarise, you take something all too familiar – doesn't biography try to make us feel at home, show us round the house? – and make it *strange*.

But if biography is relevant to the work of Sylvia Plath, this does not for me make the work biographical. On the first page of *The Haunting of Sylvia Plath*, published just over a decade ago, I wrote: 'This is not a biography.' This was partly at legal prompting – such a declaration seemed otherwise unnecessary – but it also, as I saw it, went to the spirit of her writing. When biography reads the lines from 'Daddy' – 'The black telephone's off at the root' – as a reference to Plath ripping out her phone after a call from her husband's lover, they do her, it seems to me, a disservice, jam her wires. They deny the transformative potential of her art. Plath has taken an act of rage and turned it into a moment of recognition. The speaker realises that she has reached the end of the line with a father to whom no language travels because he can no longer – perhaps never could – be found. Something insufferable at the time, to which the only possible response could be an action, has become bearable by making the passage into words. And they take the politics out of the poem – what is the legacy after the Second World War of a German-speaking father for an American girl? Biographies of writers have to move obstinately in the opposite direction from their subject, going back over the ground, filling in the space – the one pulled open on the page – between writing and its source. They have to wrestle with the fact that, for the writer, the lived life was the point of departure rather than the place at which, unlike the biographer, they are desperately trying to arrive. At worst it is a kind of insult – don't think that this life, for all your efforts, will ever be anything other than the thing you truly are.

Similarly, 'Parliament Hill Fields' has been read with reference to a miscarriage that Plath suffered shortly before writing the poem. Here the issue seems more complex, but goes even more to the heart of what writing, specifically poetic writing, is capable of:

> On this bald hill the new year hones its edge.
> Faceless and pale as china
> The round sky goes on minding its business.
> Your absence is inconspicuous;
> Nobody can tell what I lack.

In these opening lines, the speaker seems to me to go to some lengths to make it very hard indeed to know what she is talking about. This is a form of language refusing to identify itself: what is absent is inconspicuous and what is missing to the speaker cannot be told. Although it becomes clearer in the course of the poem – 'Already your doll grip lets go', 'The blue night plants, the little pale blue hill / In your sister's birthday picture starts to glow' – these are shreds and hints which take on the aura of something that slips and fails. Even here it is not unambiguously a miscarriage, since these could equally (or more so – 'doll grip'?) be allusions to a dead child. Plath is confusing and overlaying time registers, refusing the distinction between a child who dies and one who was never born. If anything, after the first, as it were, concrete allusion – 'Already your doll grip lets go' – the uncertainty increases:

The tumulus, even at noon, guards its black shadow:
You know me less constant,
Ghost of a leaf, ghost of a bird.
I circle the writhen trees. I am too happy.

Who is letting go of whom? 'You know me less constant' suggests that
it is the speaker who has relinquished whatever it is that she has lost.
Something fades; the speaker herself is inconstant; it is not clear – lost
one or speaker – who is the ghost.

Plath writes a poem in which what is biographically loss – loss of
the unborn child – loses itself in turn. She offers the experience as
something which can only be reached indirectly, which the speaker
can only circle in words. To name the event as if that is what the
poem is 'about' arrests this process. Not knowing, we as readers
undergo a radical uncertainty about what language can and cannot do.
What in the world can language grasp when the world itself has not
been entered?

A year later Plath returns to the theme in her poem for three voices,
'Three Women'. Three women in a maternity ward offer to the reader
a distillation of their different experience – one gives birth to a boy,
one miscarries, one abandons her baby girl. These voices overlap and
counterpoint each other; in experience they are crucially distinct
(there is no doubt that the second voice miscarries); but in voice they
are uncannily and progressively alike. This time, Plath does name
what has happened to each of them but only as a starting point. As the
poem continues, the voices blur. By doing this, Plath raises a question,
central to biography, but troublesome if the aim is to get back from
the words to the poet's life – to what happened to her and to her
alone. Is any experience, even the most terrible and/or life-defining,
especially if you are a woman, simply your own?

When the BBC issued the script, it named the three voices as
'Secretary', 'Girl' and 'Wife', the last as the woman who keeps her
baby, whereas in fact the only one of the three women who alludes to
a husband is the one who miscarries (a classical 'slip' which deems
either that a woman with a baby must have a husband or that only the
woman who has a baby is worthy of a husband, or indeed both). By
merging and blending the three voices, by refusing to name any one of
them, Plath offers her caution. Do not recognise, differentiate,

identify too fast. Do not fix a history against the grain of the words. Do not rush to judgement. In this the poem becomes an allegory for the perils of biography. Outside poetry, language is expected to make certain things unequivocally clear: who exactly is who and what are they all up to? Poetry leaves the connections wide open.

'This is not a biography'. Perhaps, however, it is not so easy. For it is not just Plath's own writing, but writing on Plath that is inexorably sucked into her life. In this, critical activity shares the same dilemma, runs the same risk, as poetic writing. My opening question: 'How *not* to write a biography of Sylvia Plath?' could be rephrased: 'Is it possible *not to have written* a biography of Sylvia Plath?' Clearly the Estate of Sylvia Plath thought not. Any writer on Plath who has sought permission to quote from her writing will testify to the pressure exerted on them by the Estate (many have). But in my conflict with Olwyn and Ted Hughes, the issue sharpened as a dispute about biography and forms of interpretation, about how a poet can or should be read.

On 22 January 1991 I received a set of comments from Ted Hughes on *The Haunting of Sylvia Plath*. Five months previously Virago had received a twenty-page document from Olwyn Hughes listing her objections to the typescript, to which I had responded lengthily and in detail. The timing in itself felt strange, like the delayed – and more effective – late appearance of the chief character in a play. At issue was the distinction, central to the book, between fantasy, as the realm of poetic exploration, and reality or the lived experience of Sylvia Plath, a reality I claim to know little, if anything, about. For Freud, fantasy refers to a psychic domain, no less important – indeed no less real – than the world we live and move in; but it is distinguished from that world by the fertility, the potentially endless transformative capacities of the mind. We use fantasy, conscious and unconscious, to explore things that have not happened and never will, to see in our mind's eye worlds out of reach. In fantasy, we are capable of thoughts, often terrifying and exhilarating, which we never dreamt we had ('I wouldn't dream of it' is, for psychoanalysis, the classic instance of denial, our way of partially recognising something we can only bare to acknowledge as a dream). If asked to express them consciously, we would never dare. More simply, to focus on fantasy in the life of a writer, say Sylvia Plath, is to pay tribute to what a mind – to what *her mind* – is capable of. As if to underline the point, one correspondent writing to me after the book was published suggested that I should perhaps have used 'phantasy' to avoid the connotations, which often attach to 'fantasy', of 'just' or 'only' or 'mere'. Plath, she suggested, should be seen as a painter: 'I remember a quote by Picasso,' who, she continued, 'said he only painted what he saw.'

If this is worth spelling out here, it is because my conflict with the Estate turned on these terms. Almost without exception, Hughes has deplored biographies of Plath. And yet in his exchange with me, in a strange repetition of the biographical move, he ground all talk of fantasy back into his own past. Grant fantasy a reality of its own and it crosses the barrier into the real world. There can, he argued, be no distinction between fantasy and a life. This is not the argument that, however mediated, fantasy will always include the kernel of the world from which it departs. There is no mediation. I was 'surreptitiously rewriting the real history of Plath's relationship to Hughes', replacing it with my 'own fantasy', imposing an 'invented identity' on Sylvia Plath. In doing this, I was 'depriving' Hughes of his 'real history', imposing on him, no less than on Plath, my 'invention.' This was, Hughes concluded, 'too elusive for the LAW' (his capitals), but 'immoral', and given that this was an educational work, 'corrupt'.

No fantasy, then, except mine. And no fantasy in the writings of Plath. Facing each other across an unbridgeable divide, the reality of Hughes's (and Plath's) history, and a lie. There is only the life. Fantasy does no work; it has no life of its own. Critics of Freud have argued that, as soon as he introduced the idea of fantasy into his work, he proceeded to neglect the reality of his patients' lives. Hughes's is the stronger case, as it were. Any talk of fantasy is a front, an act of bad faith. It is always, finally, the life that is being talked about. 'I supposed he was suffering from Korsakov syndrome,' Aunt Fini comments of Ambros Adelworth in W. G. Sebald's *The Emigrants*, 'an illness which causes lost memories to be replaced by fantastic inventions.' It is as if writers on Plath have a version of this syndrome. Except that, in Hughes's diagnosis, it would operate transversally: his memories, the critics' – deluded – inventions.

The dispute came to a head over my reading of these lines from 'The Rabbit Catcher':

It was a place of force –
The wind gagging my mouth with my own blown hair,
Tearing off my voice, and the sea
Blinding me with its lights, the lives of the dead
Unreeling in it, spreading like oil.

I tasted the malignity of the gorse,
Its black spikes,
The extreme unction of its yellow candle-flowers.
They had an efficiency, a great beauty,
And were extravagant, like torture.

I comment:

> The sexuality that [the poem] writes cannot be held to a single space –
> it spreads, blinds, unreels like the oil in the sea. Most crudely, that
> wind blowing, that gagging, calls up the image of oral sex and then
> immediately turns it around, gagging the speaker with her own blown
> hair, her hair in her mouth, her tasting the gorse (Who – man or
> woman – is tasting whom?), even while 'black spikes' and 'candles'
> work to hold the more obvious distribution of gender roles in place. If
> we pass to the next stanza, the uncertainty intensifies as we are given
> what can only be described as a symbolic geography of (the female) sex:

> There was only one place to get to.
> Simmering, perfumed,
> The paths narrowed into a hollow.

> If we read the first line of the poem as referring to the rabbit's
> predicament, lured without option, and if we then read that as the
> dilemma of the woman, then we have to notice too that what draws her
> on unfailingly, are nothing other than the most recognisable clichés of
> femininity itself (simmering, perfumed, hollow).

My question then, as now, is: if Plath uses an image, rabbit catcher,
which so obviously calls up a feminist reading – woman trapped like a
rabbit by marriage and man – and turns it sexually around in her
mind, what is she doing in the process? For if the trap starts to look
(sound, smell) like the body of a woman, then there can be no easy
accusation. Readers have rushed to see this as a moment – literal,

biographical (Olwyn Hughes: 'The poem is based on an actual incident') – of rage against Hughes. Instead, Plath makes the reader go through a set of such strange and discomforting contortions that you no longer know who, or where, you are. Danger slips in and out of the trap that has been set for it. Plath can be seen as issuing a warning: for a woman, danger resides not just outside in the man who stalks her, but, no less powerfully, within.

And if Plath winds the moment up with sexual pleasure, then we can surely also ask what is being conveyed about women's relationship to the forms of violence which feminism has most powerfully protested against. It is the peculiar genius of Plath for me, part of her abiding importance for feminism, that while laying her charge against the institutions of patriarchy, she can manage also to say that it is not only men who trap rabbits. It takes two. Fantasy and sexual ambiguity are the two sides of one coin. Take a story – let's say an event from a life (Olwyn Hughes: 'there are hollows and dells as described') – and blow words into it until it twists and distends to breaking point. 'I am surprised,' I wrote in a subsequent communication with Ted Hughes, 'that at no point does Mr Hughes [the third person was used throughout our exchange] allow that I use the poem to offer a critique of a too easy association of the rabbit catcher with himself.'

For Olwyn Hughes, this was 'the most damaging attempt at character assassination in the whole book', the 'precise insinuations' 'defamatory' to Hughes and Plath, and 'by extension' to Carol Hughes 'and to any woman TH has had a relationship with'. Hughes commented: 'The gross insult on Sylvia Plath's sexual identity made in this interpretation is totally INADMISSIBLE [his capitals]. [. . .] This must be cut or totally revised.' In response, I added to the text: 'For Freud, such fantasies, such points of uncertainty, are the regular unconscious subtexts – for all of us – of the more straightforward reading, the more obvious narratives of stable sexual identity which we write.' In reply, I had written to Hughes:

> I do not consider my reading of 'The Rabbit Catcher' to be a 'gross assault' on Sylvia Plath's sexual identity. That writing can be a place where ambiguity of sexual identity can be explored is an idea that follows, creatively for me, from the psychoanalytic questioning of the too rigid assumption of sexual normality that is part of our 'civilised'

life. Crucially, however, this is a reading of a poem and therefore, once again, implies absolutely nothing about Plath's lived identity as a woman.

The political consequences of this seemed worth spelling out:

> But it might be worth saying here that the idea that sexual identity can be unconsciously unstable is an argument that has been used by that same form of feminism, to which I myself belong, which questions a too rigid assumption about what men and women are (that men for example are the sole source of violence) or about the relationship between reality and fantasy (that if something appears in a fantasy it implies that that is what is inevitably going on). This is not unrelated to Hughes's own critique of overliteral interpretations of Plath's poetry.

Hughes replies that, even though I call my book an 'interpretation', what is in fact involved is 'speculation about what went on in the heads of Plath and Hughes', a 'licence', regardless of my intentions, for 'rampaging reinvention' and 'gossip'. Interpretation transmutes itself back into facts. No question. It is the inevitability of this process, its unstoppable nature that Hughes insists on, as if all readings were powerless against the drift. In this world, all statements are propositions, all poems bear the scars of vulgar (mis)understanding almost before they have been read. One vulgarity leads to another. In direct proportion as the life is, not crushed *out of*, but forced *back into* the poem, so the offensive, now dangerous nature of sexual ambiguity, increases in pitch. I was asked to imagine the effects of my reading on Hughes's and Plath's children:

> In what she calls the 'sexual normality that is part of our civilised life' [the scare quotes around 'civilised', there to suggest some scepticism about the term, have gone], the sexual identity of mothers is a very delicate topic – presumably because it is internalised in such a vulnerable way in the sexual identities of the children. Ms Rose will surely agree with this. After all, there are still countries where speculation about somebody's mother's sexual life is grounds for homicide.

To which he adds: 'Ms Rose thought that she was writing a book about a writer dead thirty years, and seems to have overlooked, as I say, the plain fact that she has ended up writing a book largely about me.'

Gossip transmutes itself into fact. The plain fact is that I *have* written a book largely about Ted Hughes.

This is not, however, the end of the story. In 1992, a dispute broke out in the pages of the *Times Literary Supplement* about the pressure which writers on Plath feel to be exerted on them by the Estate. In reply to a letter from Olwyn Hughes, justifying such intervention in terms of the 'forests of fantasy' that have grown up around Plath ('I knew nothing, when I took the job on, of the snippets of vindictive and unjust rage in Plath's letters and comments'), I described the pressures, notably in relation to 'The Rabbit Catcher', to which I felt I had been subjected by Olwyn and Ted Hughes. Ted Hughes's reply, which opens by describing our dispute as a 'corrosive misunderstanding', is worth extensive quotation. After stating that the interpretation of 'The Rabbit Catcher' 'distorts, reinvents etc. Sylvia Plath's "sexual identity" with an abandon I could hardly believe – presenting her in a role that I felt to be vividly humiliating to Plath's children', the body of the letter turns on the question of interpretation and its effects. The emphases are mine:

> What happens when [these speculations] leave her head, and start up a life outside her control, inside other people's heads? Don't they, at that point, cease to be speculations and become – nine times out of ten – facts? Or at least, quasi-facts – that do influence ideas, if only in a fluctuating, provisional way?
>
> [. . .]
>
> I asked her to imagine her 'interpretation' in the context of small-town gossip. Here, Ms Rose's *shocking 'fantasy'* about the controversial public figure Sylvia Plath would follow the course familiar, I thought, to all. By the third step, that is, it would no longer be 'interpretation' or 'fantasy' but plain fact [. . .] As part of the teaching of Sylvia Plath's poetry world-wide, a *titillating 'revelation'*, for almost everybody taught, a kind of 'fact'.
>
> [. . .]
>
> While almost all students and all but the most sophisticated readers will find it interesting to jump to the conclusion that Sylvia Plath actually was, or possibly was, *like that*, only the rarest reader, I think,

will apply Ms Rose's interpretation to their own mother. Why should they? The very idea is ridiculous. Sylvia Plath is only a dead, peculiar person in a book – the connection would never be made.

Only when one of those students or readers meets Sylvia Plath's actual children will the connection be made: this is the son or daughter of *that freaky woman who was like that.*

[. . .]

That, as I say, is the first humiliation: to know that the world (since they can't put limits on the possibility) *has been told this* about their mother. [. . .] I tried to jolt Ms Rose into imagining their feelings, seeing her book (as I have seen it) in a friend's house and assuming instantly that their friend now thinks about their mother the thoughts Professor Rose has taught them *with eyes sharpened by that particular bizarre high point* in her book. At that moment, clearly, Ms Rose's 'interpretation' takes its second step – not just into reality this time.

[. . .]

I did not see how Ms Rose could fail to have full and instant knowledge of the peculiar kind of suffering such a moment induces – the little dull blow of something like despair, the helpless rage and *shame* for their mother, the little poisoning of life, the bitter but quite useless fury against the person who *shot this barbed arrow* into them just to amuse herself.

[. . .]

I was *so strenuously locked into beating at her door*, as I have described, *simply to wake her up* – it never dawned on me that all she could feel is *threatened* [Hughes's emphasis].

'Freaky', 'like that' – what I am imputed as attributing to Plath's lived sexual identity cannot be named. Hardening into fact, it travels the world. Before the term gained the currency it has today, it *globalises* itself. Interpretation loses its provisionality, becomes speculation (guessing at a secret) and revelation (exposé). And yet the shriller the sound – 'shocking', 'that particular bizarre high point in her book', 'titillating revelation' – the less it can be spoken. Which puts this writer an impossible position. I did not name Plath as a lesbian (to use the word) – as the reading of 'The Rabbit Catcher' hopefully makes clear. I did not name her identity at all, but chose to follow the 'fluctuating', 'provisional' (to use Hughes's terms) movements of sexuality through the language of the poem. I would still argue that you cannot deduce her life from these words and that poetry is a place, like dreaming, where the unlived as much as the lived can be explored (the most that could be deduced would be an unconscious bisexuality which, as often as not, never sees the light of day). But not to name lesbianism here, since this so clearly became the centre of my dispute with Hughes is, it seems to me, to accede to a prejudice. It is in fact a kind of naming or branding; it names the lesbian as unspeakable.

I cannot comment on Hughes's children, although in the letter I wrote in reply to Hughes, but did not finally send to the *TLS*, I asked why more pain would be caused them by a continuous celebration of Plath's writing than by a biography such as Anne Stevenson's *Bitter Fame*, which was written with the full co-operation of the Estate. Not to mention where such condemnation of sexual ambiguity would leave, say, the author of the *Sonnets*. Far more crucial, or within reach of what I am able to read in the letter, is the extraordinary link which it demonstrates between representation and ethics. For it is only if the poem is literalised – if the gap is refused between writing and identity, between fantasy and a life – that Hughes's ethical objections stand. Only if poetry is read as reference can its exploration of sexuality – of anything – become a *slur*. Hughes may indeed be writing about what happens all too often to interpretation in our culture (shaming as a central component of celebrity). On that much we agree. But, as I see it, that is not a reason for less interpretation, but more. It is a reason for anyone involved in the interpretation of writing, Plath's writing, to struggle harder to keep open the space where language works.

An early draft of 'The Rabbit Catcher' contains these lines:

Snares
Without apparent motive, the paths
The paths narrowed into this hollow from many directions,
Narrow without apparent motive.

They burned in the hot sun [Simmering, perfumed]
They had no [without] apparent motive
The snares grew from the border grass [effaced themselves]
   in the air, little loops of emptiness
But significant, they had a significance.

Most of this makes it into the final version, except for 'without apparent motive' and 'But significant, they had a significance'. Hidden markers of a poem which retain, I would suggest, their colour, these words place the act of writing in a realm between uncertainty and meaning. How much room, in the biography which Hughes saw me as having written – in most biographies – is there for that moment of suspension in space and time? No writer has suffered as much as Plath from the biographical imperative. Finally, the issue is not one of freedom of interpretation, of how much the writer on Plath is permitted to say. The dilemma is better put in the form of a question. To what forms of uncertainty – of language, sexuality and knowing – do you have the right?

Birthday Letters

Ever since Sylvia Plath's death in 1963, there has been an argument as to who was responsible, whose fault it was – Plath's or Ted Hughes's – that she died. On the face of it, *Birthday Letters*, Hughes's extraordinary poetic sequence to Plath, might be seen as another stage of that quarrel. Or else, and far more productively, these poems might serve to bring that futile process of recrimination – of accusation and counter-accusation – to its end.

On the jacket of *Birthday Letters* is a painting by their daughter, Frieda Hughes, of volcanic red and yellow smothering a dark background through which patches of blue barely glimmer. The book itself, the rest of the dust jacket, and above all the name of the author, picked out in a lighter shade, are all blue. 'Red,' he writes in the last poem, 'was your colour', but – and this is the line on which the whole collection ends – 'the jewel you lost was blue':

Blue was your kindly spirit – not a ghoul
But electrified, a guardian, thoughtful.

One way of reading these poems, then, would be to say that Hughes is painting himself into Plath's best colour. These poems are not, however, a defence, an argument in Hughes's own service as they will no doubt be accused of being, or, as many have been suggesting over the past weeks, a reply – at last – to his critics, to those who have accused him of hard-heartedness, and worse, in relation to Plath. To read them in these last terms seems to me to do Hughes no favours, and in fact weakens their peculiar quality and deprives them of a large measure of their force.

These poems offer their readers an account of a failure. Written after – and some, clearly long after – Plath's death, they circle round a missing centre, trying to find a reason for why she took her own life. If they are at times assertive and confident – knowing, even – they are just as often questioning and unsure (the number of question marks in the poems actually outstrips the number of poems in the book). These poems gather strength as they lose their conviction. The question – why did he fail her? – comes through finally much more loudly than the question to which, at moments, Hughes seems to offer some kind of an answer – why Sylvia Plath was bound, long before he ventured half-blind on to the scene, to die.

On first reading, there does seem to be a narrative of explanation that can be lifted out of these poems: that Sylvia Plath was doomed by the eight-year-old girl inside her who failed to grieve a father who dies too soon; that her whole project – 'trajectory perfect as if through ether' – was to get back to that father in his grave (whereas Hughes had 'no more purpose in me than my own dog which I did not have'). This leaves Hughes no option but to go seeking for them both: 'a big shock to meet me face to face in the dark adit where I have come looking for your daughter' (this, one of the only two poems not addressed to Plath, comes near the end, as if Hughes was left with no other place to go). According to this story, from very early on, Plath was heading inexorably to her death, and Hughes was a helpless bystander. If Hughes's earlier poetry often reads as a tribute to a nature in excess of his own mastery, this would then be the first time that such a force, at which he also marvels, so utterly defeats him.

But precisely because what Hughes is writing about is a form of energy with a strength and will of its own, no attempt – if indeed this is the attempt – to hand it over to Plath alone, to her distressed and haunted selfhood as he sees it, can work. Lines like these, often cited over the past two weeks, are almost too easy to lift out of the poems: 'auditioned for the male lead in your drama', 'I was a fly outside on the window pane / of my own domestic drama', 'Your life was a liner I voyaged in', 'Inside your Bell Jar / I was like a mannikin in your eyeball'. But they only tell half, if indeed that much, of the story. For every one of these seeming explanations we get another which makes it impossible to see this tragedy as Plath's fate, as her doing, alone. Something of cosmic proportions 'billions of years in anonymous matter', enters the house searching for a place to land: 'Who's here? That's the question: Who's here?' In this poetic journey – whose pronoun is no longer 'you' but 'we' – they are in it together: 'We caught each other and fell in a heap', 'fate assembled us', 'the myth we sleepwalked into', 'we had no idea what we were seeing'. Try working out, for example, whose is the blackness in these lines:

> I folded
> Black wings round you, wings of the blackness
> That enclosed me, rocking me, infantile,
> And enclosed you with me.

Even if you read this as Hughes as protector, this is hardly self-exculpation. Ironically, the more he convinces us that this was his role, so the felt dimensions of his own failing become that much more brutally clear. One of the most striking things about these poems, especially on second reading, is how engaged, active, participating, Hughes is as protagonist of this tale: 'I was focused, / So locked into you, so brilliantly.' And just how much, indeed, he accuses himself:

> I brought you to Devon, I brought you into my dreamland.
> I sleepwalked you into my land of totems.

(This poem is called 'Error'.) He hews her a writing table out of coffin elm; when she smashes his table top, it is he who exhorts that energy into poetic words: ' "Marvellous!" I shouted, "Go on. Smash it into kindling. That's the stuff you're keeping out of your poems!" ', only to ask what he has done: 'Deep in the cave of your ear / The goblin snapped his fingers. / So what had I given him?' In what is bound to be one of the most controversial poems, 'The Rabbit Catcher', which comes like many of these poems in reply to Plath's of the same name, Hughes lays out the violent terms of their difference:

> I saw the sanctity of a trapline desecrated

You saw blunt fingers, blood in the cuticles.

But then he asks:

> Had you caught something in me,
> Nocturnal and unknown to me? Or was it
> Your doomed self, your tortured crying,
> Suffocating self?

It is as if these poems at once enter the fray and call a halt: 'Let the blame hit the olive trees.' This is poetry, as 'a combustion of the stuff of judgement'.

What makes this collection so powerful and convincing for me is that its poems seem to be telling us just how pointless it is to try to give a definitive answer to their own question. Running through these poems there is another question. What makes – and breaks – a marriage? What happens when sexual euphoria, its often giddy sense of rebirth, walks straight into all those other occupants and attachments with prior claims, ghostly fragments of any life, who have already taken up their positions inside your heads? What happens when a shared and uplifting passion, for, say, poetry, hits the reef of the domestic day-to-day? What happens when two complex, contrary, cultural legacies collide? Violence, these poems also hint, is familiar, domestic, at home. There is something excessive but also chillingly commonplace about what they describe.

Nothing has ever evoked Plath like this; the way these poems summon her ('real, warm, lucent'), celebrate her ('a great bird, you / surged in the plumage of your excitement') is, above all else, what overpowers. But they do also present the reader with some puzzles. One is their view of Plath's own poetry. In Hughes's previous writings, he has seemed to date the birth of her best creativity from 'Poem for a Birthday', the long sequence which she wrote in 1959 (this, I had assumed, was one of the meanings hidden in the title of *Birthday Letters*). But in this collection, Plath's poetry seems to be sprung from a bad and dangerous place. In more than one poem something not quite Plath, something wreaking havoc, brings the words – 'like entrails' (used twice) – on to the page:

Who caught all
That teeming population, every one,
To hang their tortured eyes and tongues up
In your poems?

If this is true, then her readers are dupes. All they have is 'the empty masks' of her genie; or gloves from which 'the hands have vanished'. Or worse, they are the guilty party to the crime:

In the wilderness
Between the locusts and the honey
They demanded it. Oh, no problem
If that's all you want,
You said, and you gave it.

And this is not to speak of the image, in the penultimate poem addressed to his children, of those who have written about Plath's work:

Let them
Jerk their tail-stumps, bristle and vomit
Over their symposia.

The appearance of *Birthday Letters* has been used to produce a caricature of feminism as always pitying Plath and blaming Hughes as a man with no heart to speak of. As if there was not also another strand to feminism, one which has precisely learnt from Plath the uselessness of this opposition, admiring her for her brave and agile capacity to berate both the world and herself. It seems pointless and invasive to speculate on why Ted Hughes has chosen to publish these poems today. But there is a question that can be put. If these poems have been published they cannot be addressed to Plath or their children alone. They must be calling for a response. Of understanding? Of sympathy? Why then does Hughes once again represent with such unremitting anger those who have responded to Plath's writing, or who have been inspired by what she wrote to write words of their own? Perhaps the success of *Birthday Letters* could also help to bring this battle to an end. So that the continuing love of Sylvia Plath, by those who have only her words to go on, might no longer be seen as the death of her.

The Journals

Sylvia Plath's journals, never published in England before, released in a heavily censored version in 1982 in the States – with, as the editor then put it, their 'intimacies' and 'nasty bits' removed – appear here more or less complete for the first time (*The Journals of Sylvia Plath, 1950–1962*, ed. Karen V. Kulkil, Faber & Faber, 2000). We still don't have the journals of her last two years, one of which disappeared and one of which Ted Hughes by his own account destroyed shortly after her death: 'I did not want her children to have to read it (in those days I regarded forgetfulness as essential to survival).' Not surprisingly, given this history, the publication of the surviving journals is being heralded as an event of unique literary significance, Plath speaking without interference in her own voice. But although Plath was desperate to be published (that despair is a constant refrain in these pages), and no diarist writes without an invisible audience, of all Plath's writing, this is the one which was never intended for publication. When she was not winding her life into these diaries, Plath spent most of her time busily and determinedly transmuting their contents back out the other way into her art. Reading them we become eavesdroppers. Given the intensity and rawness of the writing, at moments it feels like walking straight into someone else's dream.

It is however, I think, a mistake to see these journals as giving us access to some new or previously hidden 'truth' about Sylvia Plath. One way of rendering herself in writing, they offer in fact no solutions to previous mysteries, no definitive answers to the questions which, with an interest bordering on – indeed crossing over into – the obsessive, her life has so often provoked. Plath appears here as someone with, in her own early phrase, 'so many little lives': 'my writing, my desire to be many lives'. Many little lives, not like the proverbial nine lives of the cat, although her first failed suicide and eventual death too obviously invite that comparison, but as something she could use her writing to be, a way of ceaselessly shifting herself across different psychic territories, across different and often contradictory ways of experiencing herself. If the journals are cause for celebration it might be, bizarrely, because evidence can be found within them to support every single theory that has ever been produced about Sylvia Plath – the never recovered child of the dead father, the woman oppressed by the small suffering psychic landscape of her mother, the woman trapped in a domestic life unredeemed by a feminism which arrived too late on the scene, the woman nursed by her husband out of pain into burgeoning creativity, the woman betrayed. They are all here. With each one so vividly and insistently present, and each one just as immediately countered by the energetic presence of another, it becomes clear that none of them, that is, none of them on their own, will in fact do.

When the journals were first published, an editorial note introducing the section in which she rails against Hughes for suspected infidelity told us that the 'real source', as Plath 'notes eight months later', is 'her father'. Without that interference this time, we are thankfully spared having to judge anything here as less or more 'real' (although this publication should not be used to repress the history of past censorship of Plath). In fact, we do Plath the greatest disservice, these journals can teach us, when we read her as aiming with determined and singular purpose for the tragic denouement waiting in the wings. Effervescent – 'I can't stop effervescing' – the writing here fires in all directions at once. If it also displays a relentless and controlling logic, a 'will working back to hack out its own happenings', we should, however, note that plural ('happenings') – one will, but many disparate events. We should note too how, with phrases like that, Plath takes responsibility for everything in her own life. As you read, you can almost hear Plath issuing her advance warning against the single-track interpretations, all the attempts at blame or redemption, to come: 'I know pretty much what I like and dislike; but please, don't ask me who I am. "A passionate, fragmentary girl", maybe?'

The serialisation of the journals over the past weeks, both here and in the States, have predictably enough selected those extracts which are most sensational – Plath's erotic life (her first sexual experiences, her first meeting with Hughes now uncensored, her marriage) and her inner psychic turmoil (her therapy with Ruth Beutscher, one of the sections of the journals sealed until 2013 and then unsealed by Hughes before he died). It is not hard to see why. Plath's sexual life is rendered here with such intensity – 'Such good fuckings', 'pants wet with the sticky white filth of desire' (the 'filth' is presented as her mother's imagined disgust) – that it is as if there are no barriers between her body and the page on which she writes. Writing for Plath is a form of internal assault: 'what a poet I will flay myself into'. Almost before you have had a chance to register the violence of the first sex with Hughes ('washed my battered face, smeared with a purple bruise from Ted'), and to note how far she goes to embrace it ('Consider yourself lucky to have been stabbed by him'), you can watch it racing into poetry: his – 'I lust for him and in my mind am ripped to bits by the words he welds and wields'; and her own – 'where are my small incidents . . . the blood poured from my shoes'. Among other things, the journals offer us perhaps one of the most extraordinary records of sexual energy on the move: energy spilling and transmuting itself – but by no means always willing or able to do so – into words.

In her therapy with Ruth Beutscher in 1959, Plath rages without let or inhibition against her mother (Beutscher had also treated her at McLean's hospital during her previous breakdown in 1953 and supervised her electric shock treatments). This is therapy as catharsis. Plath's father was the one who died, but her mother appears here as the haunting figure, the one who, in order for Plath to find her voice, must be placated: 'How can I get rid of this depression: by refusing to believe she has any power over me, like the old witches for whom one sets out plates of milk and honey' (the phrase is uncannily resonant of Plath's last gesture of setting out plates of milk for her children before she died). In a way, however, this is the weakest part of the book. Because it is so repetitive, because against the grain of everything else in her writing, it suggests – as indeed the therapy itself seems to have suggested – that there might be one cause of Plath's anguish, her 'mental fear', one solution, therefore, to her distress. As we watch the increasingly smothering closeness of Plath's relationship with Hughes start to move in and suffocate them both, 'as if I were living with one eyelash of myself only', 'Dangerous to be so close to Ted day in day out . . . must strike out on my own', it is hard not to start asking whether the euphoria and intimacy which Beutscher offered weren't also a trap. More repetition than cure: 'If I "cure" no one else in my whole career,' Beutscher wrote in an unpublished letter to Plath just months before she died, 'you are enough. I love you.'

For anyone reading these journals, it is perhaps ironic to reflect that in writing them, whatever the inner dialogue, Plath was above all writing for herself. That there was no one there watching or loving, suggesting topics for poetry, or interpreting her dreams ('Ted claims this is the rebirth of my deep soul'). This might be finally the most important thing about them. If they should be read as revelation, it is not so much for the life as for the writing – what she asked of it, what it did for her, where it failed. As well as, despite or rather deep amid all the drama, for the banality of the details and anxieties she so meticulously describes. For that reason alone, no potential writer trying to haul themselves from bed or drudgery or distraction into writing should miss them. Like all journals, these rent the veils of the very privacy they most fiercely protect. They ask to be read cautiously, going but also respecting the distance.

Virginia Woolf and the Death
of Modernism

Virginia Woolf once wrote that all accounts of a life are misleading because states of non-being are impossible to describe. In this essay, written in 1997, I try to trace the work of death in her writing as her way of making non-being palpable on the page. In a famous encounter, Woolf met Freud just before his death on the eve of the Second World War. Mourning was the topic of Freud's most cited paper 'Mourning and Melancholia'. Did Woolf, in what she allows death to do in her writing, take Freud beyond the point he was willing, or able, to go? The essay was first published in autumn 1998, in the New York-based literary journal, Raritan, whose policy is to publish without annotation so as to avoid the weight of the academy on the writing. To preserve that spirit, I have not restored the footnotes here.

> When grief ceases to be speculative, sleep sees her opportunity.
> Samuel Beckett: 'Yellow', *More Pricks than Kicks* (1934)

> by taking flight into the ego love escapes extinction.
> Sigmund Freud: 'Mourning and Melancholia' (1915)

> 'To enjoy your perfection—'
> 'I take your point. One must exclude.'
> 'The greater part of everything.'
> Virginia Woolf: 'The Evening Party' (1918)

There is a strange moment on the first page of 'Mourning and Melancholia' when Freud mentions, almost in passing, that mourning can be sparked, not only by the loss of a loved one, but equally by some abstraction: 'such as one's country, liberty, an ideal'. Since Freud is writing in 1915, it seems clear, as the papers on war from the same year will confirm, that what he is alluding to is the loss of belief in the redeeming power of Western civilisation precipitated by the carnage of the war. So when Freud goes on to insist that mourning is something to be worked at, completed, got over – already strange for a psychoanalysis which maintains that nothing ever goes away – I think it is fair to assume that a drive for political, or cultural, as much as psychic self-protection is at stake. Once the losses of the war have been mourned, Freud goes on to write, in his 1917 paper on 'Transience', 'it will be found that our high opinion of the riches of civilisation has lost nothing from the discovery of their fragility'. To put it simply, mourning must come to an end so that we can believe in ourselves once more. Seen in these terms, Freud's famous paper can be read as an attempt to drive mourning away (or at least to provide a narrative for mourning with a beginning, middle and an end). I want to use this lecture to suggest that this view of mourning bears all the signs of its genesis in a moment of cultural dismay; that if you are not seeking to preserve the abstraction of civilisation – or rather this particular abstraction of that civilisation – then mourning shifts her colours and her terms. No longer something to be dispatched, mourning becomes more amorphous and fluid, more interminable as one might say. Taking on the incalculable nature of mourning could then be seen as one of the defining features of modernism. And nowhere so intensely, I will also be suggesting here, than in the writing of Virginia Woolf.

The first publication of the Hogarth Press in 1917 was *Two Stories*, 'The Mark on the Wall' by Virginia Woolf, often reprinted, and 'Three Jews' by Leonard Woolf, more or less unheard of since – 'a signpost,' as Hermione Lee, Virginia Woolf's most recent biographer, puts it, 'pointing down a road he would not take' (in fact, the success of this first publication played a key part in allowing the press to expand). Two Jews meet on a park bench and discuss their loss of belief. They only go to synagogue ritually and out of 'pure habit' at Yom Kippur: 'I don't believe in it, of course; I believe in nothing – you believe in nothing – we're all sceptics.' The third Jew is a cemetery-keeper even more sceptical and disbelieving than the first two:

we can't believe everything in the Bible. There's the Almighty of course, well, who can say? He may exist, he may not – I say I don't know. But a life hereafter, I don't believe in it. One don't have to

believe everything now: it was different when I was young. You had to
believe everything then.

'I thought,' responds the first, who is telling the story of this graveside
encounter, 'of our race, its traditions, its faith, how they are vanishing
in the life that surrounds us . . . vanishing in the universal disbelief':
'Even he doesn't believe, the keeper of Jewish graves!'

If that was all there was to it, this would be a story of the modern
Jew stranded between two forms of non-belonging: no assimilation, no
faith; no fervour of ritual and spiritual belonging to set against the felt
repudiation of the English countryside: 'How it comes out! under the
apple-blossom and blue sky.' And yet, in this year of the Balfour
declaration, these Jews do belong; they 'belong to Palestine still'. And
this belonging is the sign not, as for so many, of nationalist or
religious commitment, but of a Jewishness reduced to nothing but the
external marks of itself: 'We're Jews only externally now' (which is
why these Jews so instantly recognise each other against the English
sky). It is not hard to imagine the likely response if these portraits,
clearly intended to clinch the point, had been penned or spoken by a
non-Jew:

> his dark fat face and the sensual mouth, the great curve of the upper lip
> and the hanging lower one. A clever face dark and inscrutable, with its
> large mysterious eyes and the heavy lids; and a nose, by Jove, Sir, one
> of the best, one of those noses, white and shiny, which, when you look
> at it full face, seems almost flat on the face, but immensely broad,
> curving down, like a broad high-road from between the bushy eye-
> brows down over the lips. And side-face it was colossal; it stood out like
> an elephant's trunk with its florid curves and scrolls.

I start with this story because it focuses so sharply on a drama of
lost belief which has nowhere, except Palestine, to run. It offers, if you
like, a modern Jewish version of the scepticism which Freud, at
almost exactly the same time, will give as one of the grounds to grieve
(the year of Balfour, one might say, is the year that the Jews had to
steel themselves to belief). It seems more than coincidental that the
story comes to centre on a cemetery, and that it finally transpires that
Jewishness is something which comes out, not only against the apple-
blossoms, but 'among the tombs'. By the end of the story, the

cemetery-keeper turns out to have the true spirit after all because of the ruthlessness with which he repudiates a son who marries out of the faith (Leonard had married Virginia in 1912). Belief never turns so ugly, you might say, than when it thinks it has done with itself.

What Leonard Woolf seems to me to be saying is that the lost spirit of the sceptic is in the custody of the keeper of tombs. That even if you lose all belief, the spirit of identity will pass through the generations almost despite itself. These Jews are in mourning, one might say, but there is something they cannot give up, even if they think they have, something which, even if they are sure they have lost it, will not go away. You may think you've stopped believing, but something – call it the unconscious – knows better than you think. To put it another way, for faith to continue despite one's best scepticism, it requires, even if only unconsciously, a form of involuntary, blind, identification with the dead.

Leonard Woolf writes this story in the same year as Freud's paper on 'Transience'. Given that the Standard Edition of the *Complete Psychological Works* of Freud gathered in the basement of the Woolfs' Hogarth House, it is not perhaps too much to suggest that these two different, somewhat disparate, Jewish cautionary tales of discontinuity shadowed Virginia Woolf's writing life (in fact, she did not start reading Freud until just before the Second World War). Today we know the historical outcome of that passing gesture – at once embraced and refused – towards Palestine (by 1928, when he writes *Imperialism and Civilisation*, Woolf will acknowledge the 'Arab national movement in Palestine'). We know, that is, how anxiety about continuity can transmute itself into demonic repetition. But Leonard Woolf's story is perhaps all the more remarkable for offering us a glimpse into one version of the kind of refuge that Palestine would become. Not externally (as would become more and more urgent in ways neither Leonard Woolf nor Freud could have predicted in 1917), but internally: Palestine as a place to run, or rather as something which almost slips out between the features of the Jewish disbeliever, to atone and redeem a threatened internal collapse. Loss of belief may represent a new freedom, but Woolf shares with Freud the conviction that it is also a danger and a threat. As a caution against pure scepticism, the cemetery-keeper warns his interlocutor that too much thinking can drive you mad: 'Now you may think for yourself. And *mind you*, it don't *do* to think too much; if you think too much about these things, you go mad, raving mad.'

Leonard Woolf's despairing sceptics bare a more than passing resemblance to the melancholic which, in 'Mourning and Melancholia', Freud sets against the one who successfully grieves (he offers us Hamlet who also thought too much). Famously in this paper, Freud opposes mourning as work to the pathology of melancholia which fails to detach itself from the lost object because it identifies with the object instead. 'The shadow of the object,' writes Freud, 'falls across the ego'; or to take the second epigraph of this article: 'by taking flight into the ego, love escapes extinction'. A number of questions immediately raise themselves (or rather they did when I reread this paper after a long gap in the course of the past year). Not just what was Freud trying to hang on to by way of cultural belief, but also – as the accompaniment and extension of that first anxiety – what psychic agenda is this? Just how much, in letting go of mourning, was he willing to let go? What does it mean, for example, to say that in mourning, in contradistinction to melancholia, 'there is nothing about the loss that was unconscious'? Couldn't one instead say, paraphrasing Freud on the hysteric, that the one who grieves knows and does not know at the same time? Or, we might ask, what is this love that, in mourning as opposed to melancholia, steadfastly, dedicatedly, works to extinguish itself? Again, we could turn back on to Freud his famous observation that no subject can envisage her or his own death. Love would not be love if it were able to contemplate, let alone work to bring about, its own end.

And what is Freud doing when he makes ambivalence a peculiarity of the melancholic: 'The conflict due to ambivalence,' he writes, 'must not be overlooked among the preconditions of melancholia' – a distinction which later in the same paper he has to retract. We might ask, then, not so much what distinguishes mourning from melancholia, but what is it about mourning that Freud is using melancholia to offload? It starts to look as if melancholia is being asked, among other things, to carry off the most violent part of identification. Mourning can be mollified, pacified, if melancholia bears the brunt of an ambivalence which Freud describes as nothing less than a struggle to the death: 'each struggle of ambivalence [loosens] the fixation of the libido to the object by disparaging it, denigrating it and even as it were killing it'.

We should remember, however, that Freud himself was the one who most convincingly argued that the object which has been murdered is precisely the one which is most mourned, that murdering an object is the start of identification and not the end (in 'Thoughts for the Time on War and Death', written in the same year as 'Mourning and Melancholia', he placed the ambivalence that arises through mourning at the foundation of our ethical life). What limits is Freud packing around the idea of mourning? What on earth does it mean, we might ask, to suggest that the living do not, should not, identify with the dead? Isn't it in fact Freud who teaches us – it is the opening premise of Diana Fuss's *Identification Papers* – that identification is by definition a ghostly affair? Something very strange is going on here. One by one or, to use Freud's own words, 'bit by bit, at great expense of time and cathectic energy', the cornerstones of psychoanalysis – the unconscious, identification, ambivalence and love – are purged from the mind. All this – in 1917 at least, as the relentless toll of the dead brings belief crashing to the ground – for sanity's sake. There is only so much, we might say, that even psychoanalysis can bear.

Recently reviewing Hermione Lee's new biography of Virginia Woolf, I found myself brought up short by this sentence, with which the chapter entitled 'Madness' begins: 'Virginia Woolf was a sane woman with an illness.' It struck me that for anyone working on Woolf's life and writing, there is an almost insoluble problem. To defend Woolf's sanity is to save her from one kind of dismissal; it is one way of giving her her due. But to side with her reason is to sidestep the thread of her writing which unwinds, unbearably and at the risk of what she herself more than once called her own 'madness', from the place of the dead. It is hard not to read the cemetery-keeper's warning as Leonard's coded warning to Virginia Woolf:

Now you may think for yourself. And *mind you*, it don't *do* to think too much; if you think too much about these things, you go mad, raving mad.

Hard, that is, not to see it as his way of acknowledging that loss of belief in a viable culture, Bloomsbury scepticism as we might call it, coupled with too much personal loss, might bring her, or her reason, to grief. Freud's comment in the paper on 'Transience' slides from one to the other, from the personal to the public, with strange and discomforting ease: 'Once the mourning is over, it will be found that our high opinion of the riches of our civilisation has lost nothing from the discovery of their fragility.' But Leonard, Virginia and their famous group, did not believe in 'civilisation' (any more indeed than in his better moments, many commentators would insist, did Freud). The patriotic fervour of the war was one of the things which drove Virginia Woolf, arms outstretched, over the edge:

> Honour, patriotism, chastity, wealth, success, importance, position, patronage, power – their cries rang and echoed from all quarters. 'Anywhere, anywhere, out of this world!' was the only exclamation with which one could stave off the brazen din . . .

This is how John Maynard Keynes, one of the first generation of Bloomsbury, opens *The Economic Consequence of the Peace*, which he wrote in 1919 after recovering from a nervous breakdown following the war:

> The power to become habituated to his surroundings is a marked characteristic of mankind. Very few of us realise with conviction the intensely unusual, unstable, complicated, unreliable nature of the economic organisation by which Western Europe has lived for the last half century. We assume some of the most peculiar and temporary advantages as natural, permanent, and to be depended on and we lay our plans accordingly. On this sandy and false foundation we scheme for social improvement and dress our political platforms, pursue our animosities and particular ambitions, and feel ourselves with enough margin in hand to foster, not assuage, civil conflict in Europe.

In March 1915, in the middle of the war, Virginia and Leonard Woolf had moved into Hogarth House. Ill, with four nurses in attendance, by her own later account she lay in her room: 'mad, and seeing the sunlight quivering like gold water, on the wall . . . listening to the voices of the dead'.

For the rest of this essay I want to suggest that Virginia Woolf's life and writing can be read as the creative response to Freud's anxious imperative – only in so far as there can be an end to it, only if the end is pre-given, let mourning begin. That she would have no truck with his fine psychic and face-saving discriminations. More simply, that she knew (although 'knew' isn't quite the right word here) better, or knew more. We know that grieving started very early in Woolf's life. Which might be one reason why her writing offers us such a forceful riposte to the idea that it should, or could, be brought to an end. Lee's biography graphically conveys the extent to which Woolf's life was shadowed by death. First private – the deaths of her mother, half-sister, father in the ten years between 1895 and 1904 (for Woolf death rings in the new century, as it were). Then public – the whole of her writing life passes across the two world wars. When, as Virginia Stephen, she moves with Vanessa and Thoby from Hyde Park Gate to Bloomsbury after her father's death in 1904, one of the most striking, and freeing things about the new residence was, as Lee puts it, that 'no one was dying in this house' (two years later her brother Thoby would die).

You can read Woolf's life as her attempt to move out of those early deaths (literally from Kensington to Bloomsbury), and then artistically transmute them into form. Or you can see her writing going back the other way and death as giving a unique form of authority to her fiction. In the words of Walter Benjamin, the storyteller used to 'borrow his authority from death' ('there used to be no house, hardly a room, in which someone had not once died'). But, in the course of modern times, dying has been pushed more and more out of the perceptual world of the living. 'Though almost all her novels are dominated by a death,' writes Lee, 'in almost all the death is not written in.' This makes death the absent-presence which stalks Virginia Woolf's writing, turning it Janus-like back as well as forwards through literary and historical time. Private and public trauma, death for Virginia Woolf is, one could say, more than elegy, more than mourning, more than a fear or pull to which she finally succumbs. Rather it is something through the eyes of which – literally in the case of her first novel, as I will go on to discuss – she *sees*. More than once, she herself places death at the source, as the life-pulse, of her own artistic vision: 'examine feelings with the intense microscope that sorrow lends, it is amazing how they stretch, like the finest goldbeater's skin, over immense tracks of substance'; 'my mother's death veiled and intensified, as if a burning glass had been laid over what was shaded and dormant . . . as if something were becoming visible without any effort'. We might then ask, contra Freud, not how mourning can be completed, but what is it that death, or remaining with death, might permit. As the narrator of *The Voyage Out* puts it: 'a barrier which usually stands fast had fallen, and it was possible to speak of motives which are generally only alluded to between men and women when doctors are present, or the shadow of death'. Seen in this context, Virginia Woolf's suicide, oddly, has detracted from death, acted as a screen. By acquiring something in the nature of a monopoly, it has crowded out the voices of all the rest.

Virginia Woolf's first novel, *The Voyage Out*, published in 1915, is normally considered as a piece of literary apprenticeship or literary-cum-sexual initiation. The heroine, Rachel Vinrace, travels on a ship to South America, a voyage of 'self-discovery' as the Penguin blurb puts it, except that the price of this discovery, which includes her own engagement, is that she contracts typhoid and dies. The novel is often read biographically, as a sign – it was written during her engagement to Leonard Woolf – of the lengths Virginia Woolf would go to to avoid intimacy. Since it includes moments of psychic devastation – one graphic passage of nightmare persecution by a blubbering and monstrous male presence – it is taken as a coded narrative: Woolf telling her readers of the early sexual invasions which would lead her body to part definitively from her mind. According to this reading, when Rachel Vinrace finally goes under, we are being given a premonitory version of Woolf in 1941 sinking beneath the waves.

I don't want to disparage this reading (although I know it sounds as if I have). It is true, for example, that the thoughts of the surviving fiancé, 'No two people have ever been as happy as we have been', bear an uncanny resemblance to the famous note that, more than a quarter of a century later, Virginia Woolf will leave for Leonard on the day she dies. But it does seem to me that to read the book in this way is to overlook what Virginia Woolf uses the death of her female character *for*. It overlooks, that is, the extent to which this inverse initiation – you go into, rather than emerge, from the depths – precisely because it is writing (this is not Virginia Woolf dying), is identification. In this first novel by Woolf, the first flickers of that fragmentary vision most famously associated with her writing weave their way – against Freud's warning one might say – into a dying mind.

This is the main passage:

> For six days indeed she had been oblivious of the world outside, because it needed all her attention to follow the hot, red, quick sights which passed incessantly before her eyes. She knew that it was of enormous importance that she should attend to these sights and grasp their meaning, but she was always being just too late to hear or see something which would explain it all. For this reason, the faces, – Helen's face, the nurse's, Terence's, the doctor's, – which occasionally forced themselves very close to her, were worrying because they distracted her attention and she might miss the clue. However, on the fourth afternoon she was suddenly unable to keep Helen's face distinct from the sights themselves; her lips widened as she bent down over the bed, and she began to gabble unintelligibly like the rest. The sights were all concerned in some plot, some adventure, some escape. The nature of what they were doing changed incessantly, although there was always a reason behind it which she must endeavour to grasp. Now they were among trees and savages, now they were on the sea, now they were on the tops of high towers; now they jumped; now they flew. But just as the crisis was about to happen, something invariably slipped in her brain, so that the whole effort had to begin over again. The heat was suffocating. At last the faces went further away; she fell into a deep pool of sticky water, which eventually closed over her head. She was nothing and heard nothing but a faint booming sound, which was the sound of the sea rolling over her head. While all her tormentors thought that she was dead, she was not, but curled up at the bottom of the sea. There she lay, sometimes seeing darkness, sometimes light, while every now and then someone turned her over at the bottom of the sea.

I suggest we read this passage as one of the inaugural moments of modernist fiction. It is because Rachel Vinrace is literally passing away that she receives her impressions in that peculiar mix of oversharp and disintegrating relief. Like a caricature of one of Woolf's own readers, she panics at her failed attempt – hopeless although never relinquished – to read the clues. The decoder of modernism determined to wrench meaning from the world will always be too soon or too late: 'She knew it was of enormous importance that she should attend to those sights and grasp their meaning, but she was always being just too late to hear or see something which would explain it all.' There is a narrative here: 'some plot, some adventure, some escape'; but it is narrative as false promise which slides into repetition and sends you back to the beginning again: 'just as the crisis was about to happen, something invariably slipped in her brain, so that the whole effort had to begin over again'. For a mind in fever ('hot, red, quick'), reason falls out of the world at exactly the same moment as the faces of others – held by more seemly forms of fiction at a comfortable distance – move in suffocatingly close.

It is perhaps almost too easy to recognise here the defining features of modernism. But we might ask, under what conditions, other than what goes by the term of madness, does reason so dramatically, so literally, so physically, slip away? Much has been written about the body in relation to Virginia Woolf – it is the defining trope of what has come to be defined as *écriture feminine*; although to call it a trope is already to settle a question, since it is the body as sheer physicality which is meant to rise to the surface of the text. But in what circumstances does a body so decisively usurp or dismantle the organising capacities of the mind? This is from a few pages on in the text:

> for long spaces of time she would merely lie conscious of her body floating on the top of the bed and her mind driven to some remote corner of her body, or escaped and gone flitting round the room.

In the endless debates about Virginia Woolf's sanity, madness might then be the unacknowledged codeword for death. The dying mind gropes for reason. The irony is perhaps that it should be death, more conventionally taken for the ultimate ending, which brings the possibility of narrative, closure, meaning and reason to an end. There is, we might say, no rhyme or reason to death. Why, as the surviving characters repeatedly ask in the penultimate chapter of *The Voyage Out*, did Rachel Vinrace have to die? ' "It seems so inexplicable," Evelyn continued. "Death, I mean. Why should she be dead, and not you or I." '

We might then go back and look again at the feminist argument which opposes femininity as body to the false telos of masculine logic, and consider recasting these terms. 'It seems clear,' writes Barthes in his essay on Poe's 'Valdemar', 'that what is taboo in death, what is essentially taboo, is the passage, the threshold, the dying.' In Woolf's novel at least, the body that forces itself to the surface of consciousness, the body most acutely a body, is the body about to die. What stands against reason is not femininity, but death. That penultimate chapter of *The Voyage Out* takes the form of a set of dialogues in most of which it feels as if the characters are talking to themselves. Reason/unreason – what it is reasonable to feel, to believe, or to expect – is all that the death of Rachel Vinrace leaves them with:

> 'You have heard, of course. My wife feels that she was in some way responsible. She urged poor Miss Vinrace to come on the expedition. I'm sure you will agree with me that it is most *unreasonable* to feel that.'
> ... There must be some *reason* why such things happen, she thought to herself, as she closed the door.

> Have I any *reason* to hope . . . ? I do not ask for a date . . . that would be most *unreasonable* [my emphasis].

It is like a refrain. But once you place death on the far side of reason, then the line that runs from mourning to scepticism (Freud's and Leonard Woolf's) becomes clear:

> 'It seems so inexplicable,' Evelyn continued. 'Death, I mean. Why should she be dead, and not you or I? It was only a fortnight ago that she was here with the rest of us. What d'you believe?' she demanded of Mr Perrot. 'D'you believe that things go on, that she's still somewhere – or d'you think it's simply a game – we crumble up to nothing when we die? I'm positive Rachel's not dead.'

Evelyn is the character who is left with the question. She carries forward into the rest of Virginia Woolf's fiction, as a matter of principle, the open-ended uncertainty we have come to associate with Woolf's later texts: 'she had a natural dislike of anything final and done with; she liked to go on and on – always on and on'. But running alongside that familiar refusal is a more radical uncertainty which turns the whole world into a blur. Modernism – we might say – as a way of refusing the appropriate relations of presence and absence which should hold between the living and the dead:

> Suddenly the keen feeling of someone's personality, which things that they have owned or handled sometimes preserves, overcame her; she felt Rachel in the room with her; it was as if she were on a ship at sea, and the life of the day were as unreal as the life in the distance.

To say that this first strain of Woolf's modernism – in a novel which is otherwise conventional and mainly realist in form – emerges from the place of death might seem far-fetched or at least peculiar to her own history. But Woolf is not alone in allowing death to determine the contours of her writing, even if hers is a particularly intense and proximate relation. We need, before passing back into Woolf's own vision, to stretch things out a little. Michael Levenson, in *A Genealogy of Modernism*, gives this reading of the first stanza of *The Waste Land*:

> Has there been sufficient emphasis (I think not) upon the peculiar angle of vision that governs the first line of *The Waste Land*? Spring comes not to men and women, nor to trees and birds, but to lilacs, which do not flower as one might expect, but are bred out of the earth. The view, that is, settled toward the ground. To be more precise, it looks at spring from beneath the ground, a fact that becomes more clear in the next few lines, which specify that there are 'roots' that are stirred and 'tubers' that nourish. The eye here sees from the point of view of someone (or something) that is buried. In what other circumstances would snow act as a cover? How else could tubers feed a 'little life'? Grover Smith has traced this latter image to James Thomson's 'To Our Ladies of Death,' in which there appears a line, 'Our Mother feedeth thus our little life,' and, more pertinent still, the line that follows: 'That we in turn may feed her with our death.' Thomson goes on to imagine his body after death, mingling with the soil: 'One part of me shall feed a little worm ... One thrill sweet grass, one pulse in bitter weed.' Given these considerations, may I be permitted my speculation that the opening of *The Waste Land* looks at spring from the point of view of a corpse?

As Levenson goes on to discuss, this is a corpse that sprouts. Life is breathed back into the body through a redemption which Eliot struggled towards and eventually reached, but which was not a viable option for most of the Bloomsbury group. But what links the two writers (apart from a literary life in common, the fact that Hogarth Press published Eliot's poem after it had first appeared in *The Dial* in 1922) is their shared genesis in the historic crisis of the war. It is public as much as private catastrophe that sends these two writers underground (death was at once her and her whole generation's 'special knowledge', to use the phrase of Gillian Beer). The carnage of the war robs death of contingency, turning it into an experience which, regardless of who is actually hit, regardless that is of whether you live or die, everyone has to share. This is Freud writing again in 1915: 'death is no longer a chance event. To be sure, it still seems a matter of chance whether a bullet hits this man or that; but a second bullet may well hit the survivor; and the accumulation of death puts an end to the impression of chance' ('Our Attitude Towards Death'). To say that Freud's remark precludes women, which at one level is obviously true, is precisely to limit what the power of identification can do. Claiming allegiance with the dead in fantasy, living death on the other's behalf, might be one way a woman writer could lay claim to a historically refused form of belonging. Behind Freud's remark lies what might be seen as a crushing banality (which his strictures on melancholia might be seen at least partly to defer). It just might – it could – it will, one day, be you.

Virginia Woolf had a very clear sense of the tragedy of her generation: 'It's life itself, I think sometimes, for us in our generation so tragic,' she wrote in 1921. Or more brutally: 'This generation must break its neck in order that the next may have smooth going.' In 1927, she would proclaim: 'can't you see that nationality is over? All divisions are rubbed out, or about to be.' 'They would all,' as Hermione Lee comments in parentheses after giving this quote, 'spend the next fourteen years seeing the flaws of this argument.' By the time she met the dying Freud in January 1939, she knew of course that both her optimistic convictions were a myth, that there was to be no smooth going for the next generation, that European civilisation would not so easily redeem itself. Perhaps, she suggested, if they had failed, Hitler would not have been (it was precisely to avert such triumphant catastrophe that Maynard Keynes had written *The*

Economic Consequences of the Peace). But Freud insisted 'with great emphasis' that, had they failed, Hitler would have been 'infinitely worse'. On this occasion the idea of a horror working itself out through one generation for the sake of the next has passed from Woolf, who doesn't believe it any more, to Freud. On Sunday 29 January 1939, she records in her diary: 'Dr Freud gave me a narcissus. On Hitler. Generation before the poison will be worked out.' As in 1915, writing in the middle of the First World War, Freud hung a great deal – against the psychic and historical odds one could say – on this idea of work. Compare Keynes: 'the spokesmen of the French and British peoples have run the risk of completing the ruin which Germany began'.

Freud, we could say, sends work back through the generations and forward through time. You work to grieve; you work to disperse the poison from the fabric of social, civilised, life. Things, as the saying has it, will work out. When he writes likes this, Freud is using work as a synonym for telos; the belief that, given the right type of effort and exertion, matters can be brought to a satisfactory or appropriate end (that the best end of the world was foretold in how the world began). Freud was, as has often been noted, attached to the language of economics: 'Transience value,' as he puts it – to give just one example of the economic saturation of his language, 'is scarcity value in time.' Although he was in fact aware that, on the subject of mourning, the economic metaphor upholding his concept of work was weak: 'we do not even know the economic means by which mourning overcomes its task'. He knew, that is, that there was something immeasurable involved: 'mourning is a great riddle, one of those phenomena which cannot be explained but to which other obscurities can be traced back'.

It has often been pointed out that Freud's economic theories, his belief in an organism driven towards its own stasis, carries the relics of a biologism which the rest of psychoanalysis went some, if not all the way, to discard. But today, given the resurgence of interest in Keynesian economics, it might seem something of an irony that Freud, despite moments such as those just cited, sought to invest the idea of work with the measure of the calculable, to make work economically viable at the very same time that Maynard Keynes was mounting his critique of classical *Homo economicus*, rational economic man. 'The first step in Keynes's thought,' writes Will Hutton in *The*

Revolution That Never Was, 'is to interpret *Homo economicus* as a creature who while driven by self-interests is not always certain how he should go about it and is subject to all kinds of hopes and fears.' Keynes's view of the economy is one of radical instability – 'a permanent process of uncertain experimentation' (against the idea of a market which naturally achieves its own stability, he proposed a market in constant tension: 'between the financial system's desire for liquidity – and the need for illiquidity in order for the real economy to finance the acquisition of physical capital assets'). True to his principles, one might say – or to what one commentator refers to as his 'combination of generosity and gambler's instincts' – in 1920 Keynes ruined 'not only himself but much of Bloomsbury, and even their distant relations by speculation in currencies'.

Above all, what classical economics ignores, according to Keynes, is the problem of time. In his 1937 article on 'The General Theory of Unemployment', he wrote:

> We have, as a rule, only the vaguest ideas of any but the most direct consequences of our acts . . . our knowledge of the future is fluctuating, vague and uncertain . . . the senses in which I am using the term (uncertain) is that in which the prospect of a European war is uncertain, or the price of copper and the rate of interest twenty years hence, or the obscelescence of a new invention, or the position of private wealth-owners in the social system in 1970. About these matters there is no scientific basis on which to form any calculable probability whatever. We simply do not know.

Knowledge with a foretaste of its own ignorance, or knowledge brushing at its limits, would be one way of defining the unconscious. But once you introduce the unconscious into the frame – or even Keynes's radical uncertainty – then it becomes impossible, even perhaps beyond Freud's own account, to regulate the forms of traffic between present, future and past, between the living and the dead. To be a subject, as Nicolas Abraham has best formulated it, is to be haunted. How could identity free itself – would it still be an identity? – of the traces of those who went before? Haunting, or being haunted, might indeed be another word for writing. This is Virginia Woolf:

> Is it not possible – I often wonder – that things we have felt with great

intensity have an existence independent of our minds; are in fact still in existence? and if so, will it not be possible, in time, that some device will be invented by which we can tap them? ... Instead of remembering here a scene and there a sound, I shall fit a plug into the wall; and listen in to the past. I shall turn up August 1890. I feel that strong emotion must leave its trace; and it is only a question of discovering how we can get ourselves attached to it, so that we shall be able to live our lives through from the start.

Mourning, in conclusion, no more comes to an end than history (the end of history contained more than a casual allusion to the triumph of free market economies against which Maynard Keynes's voice has had to be raised again today). But Freud's paper and Leonard Woolf's story, which is where I started, do indeed present us with a problem. And that is the problem of how best to think about the relationship of our psychic and political futures to our past. The idea that, 'bit by bit, at great expense of time and cathectic energy', we sever our links with the dead does not seem to me an idea on which any kind of viable psychic or political future can be built. Even if Leonard Woolf's story with its reference to Palestine is there to remind us that identity hanging on to its ancestry because it is frightened at the prospect of its own demise is capable of no end of historic injustice. Virginia Woolf played out her own particular version of this dilemma. In a way, the circumstances of her own personal life meant that she had no choice. But through the lines of her writing – and not only in the novel I have chosen to focus on here – can be glimpsed a way of negotiating these brutal alternatives. A way, that is, of refusing to let go of the dead while also refusing to identify with what Freud, still in 1915, was able to refer to without self-consciousness as the 'riches' of Western civilisation.

Bizarre Objects:
Hallucination and Modernism –
Mary Butts and Elizabeth Bowen

My two final women writers are Mary Butts and Elizabeth Bowen, more marginal than the others, both in the process of radical reappraisal as writers who seized, in dramatically different ways, the links between historical trauma and fiction. Delivered as a paper in Cambridge in 1999 at the third of a series of conferences on modernism, this one called 'Modernism in History, History in Modernism', published in Critical Quarterly, *Spring 2000, the essay suggests that there is something in these writers' relationship to history which, as with Woolf, pushes the boundaries of language beyond the point of reason. Do women writers have a special ability to seize the link between insanity and collective life?*

'Freud very useful in the case of irrational fear [. . .] [But] what had happened today was objective and odd.'

Mary Butts, *Armed with Madness* (1928)

'War worked at present as a thinning of the membrane between the this and the that . . .'

Elizabeth Bowen, *The Heat of the Day* (1949)

'Something had been coming out of him, certainly it had been coming out of him, certainly it was something. [. . .] This one was always having something that was coming out of him . . .'

Gertrude Stein on Picasso in 1912, cited in T. J. Clark, *Farewell to an Idea: Episodes from a History of Modernism* (1999)

This essay explores the relationship between history and perception in two texts – Mary Butts's *The Death of Felicity Taverner* of 1928, and Elizabeth Bowen's *The Heat of the Day* of 1949 – which seem to figure that relationship in a particularly acute way.[1] One of the common, familiar, charges against modernism is that history – call it 'real' history for a moment – is something which modernism blinds itself to; or, in an inverse accusation which could be seen as a version of the same thing, history is something which in its worst manifestations modernism is complicit with, either by directly embracing it, or more subtly, more insidiously, by failing to perceive key components of that history as the undercurrent – or in one recent and powerful argument, as the material precondition – of modernism's own operations.[2] Either way there is a historic shortfall, a failure of vision or something failing to be seen. It is, of course, a familiar trope of the institution called the literary academy to dress up one's arguments by claiming you are seeing something which no one has seen before.

So I want to talk about 'seeing' in relation to history as concretely as possible. By which I don't mean, or only mean, with as concrete a reference as possible to the histories which these two texts, in their different ways, both chart and respond to, but concrete in the sense of a world which, in its acute presence to the sensations – its physical quality – forces itself beyond what would normally be seen as endurable or at least sane. When I say that these two texts represent the relationship between history and perception in a peculiarly acute way, I am using, therefore, the term 'acute' advisedly. I am suggesting that one way of coming at modernism's relationship to history might be through the problem of perception, that is, by taking the issue of what can and can't be seen, not as the accidental vice or virtue of modernism's historical accountability, but as the central zone through which that connection moves or takes place.

We could in a sense start with the title of the conference where this essay was first presented, which beautifully hedged its bets by calling itself: 'History in Modernism, Modernism in History', wedging or boxing modernism in the middle with history on both sides, but in fact leaving open – presumably a point of the title – which of these should be seen as container, which contained. Either way, the effect of the ambiguity is to put at the centre of our concerns, not just whether or in what ways modernism is accountable to history, or engages and transforms our representation of history, but what kind of *objects* both modernism and history might be. It leaves the impression – one of my reasons for the opening epigraph from Gertrude Stein on Picasso: 'Something had been coming out of him, certainly it had been coming out of him, certainly it was something' – that something is being lifted, prised out of, or coming out of something else. Hence my title: 'Bizarre Objects', which I take from the psychoanalyst W. R. Bion, who shares with the two fiction writers I am going to discuss a particular form of attention (one of his books is called *Forms of Attention*), which arises, as he specifically states in his autobiographical writing, out of his experiences in the First World War.

But equally important – it is the second strand of this discussion – the hallucinatory quality which these texts force on the reader is backed or accompanied by what I think it would be fair to describe, in both cases although in different ways and for different reasons, as a failure of historical vision. Both texts track a moment of disturbing, and today without question largely unwelcome, historical affiliation with which they make it very hard for the reader not to identify (hence the critical trouble of these two texts). Or to put it more simply, both these texts come down, historically speaking, on the wrong side. *The Death of Felicity Taverner* has fairly been described by Ian Patterson, although the remark is then qualified, as a 'proto-fascist pastoral', more charitably as containing a 'probing exploration of anti-Semitism'.[3] The story turns on one family's desperate attempt to save their land, to save England, and the memory of their dead cousin from the mercantile ambitions of a Russian half-Jew; it entrenches anti-Semitism in the land, almost lulling you into a compliance with its terms. And the main problem with *The Heat of the Day* is that, so deep is the reader's sympathy with the romance of the central woman character, Stella, that she or he is in danger, like Stella herself, first of not believing and then frankly not caring that her lover, Robert, might be – as he indeed turns out to be – a Nazi spy. The problem is that the revulsion we may or may not feel for his position, when he finally gets to make his case for it, is more than matched by the revulsion which Bowen has so brilliantly crafted throughout the rest of the novel towards the middle-class English society out of which Nazism in his case is born. Like Virginia Woolf, Bowen believes that you can run a line between fascism in Europe and the comfortable self-deceptions, the relations of power and deceit which hold in the average English drawing room. But she goes further. She writes a novel in which she suggests that one effect for this for a woman who is rightly – it is wholly to her credit – disaffected with this class is that she just might, with a passion and intimacy in defiance of that class's sickening complacency, have taken a Nazi into her bed. Without knowing it. Just about as blind, we might say, as you can get.

Twenty years separates the two novels, but they have a number of key features that link them. They are both written by women writers who have, until fairly recently, been considered relatively marginal to the modernist canon. Both writers can be, and have been, described as war writers, Butts of the First World War and inter-war years, Elizabeth Bowen of the period leading up to and including the Second. This generational difference is at the heart of *Felicity Taverner*:

> Picus and Scylla were of the generation before the war; Felix of the half generation after it. And at the bottom of that dry gulf between half a generation there are corpses who did not notice the gulf was there.[4]

Both novels are grounded, narratively and ideologically, in property, specifically in a house – two in the case of Bowen – which, partly due to the economic conditions or aftermath of the war, is in the process of dramatically and painfully changing hands. And both choose to supplement the violence of the war, whether as memory and anticipation in the case of Butts or concrete, lived, backdrop in the case of Bowen whose novel takes place during the Blitz, with a death, or number of deaths, which remain at least partially and bafflingly contingent to the historic conflict whose emotional and psychic vicissitudes they also trace.

Above all, in so doing – and the question here is what might be the link between these two aspects of these novels – they push our sense of perceptual reality towards a type of vertigo or precipice. So to put this question at its simplest – what might be the link between hallucination and history? What might these two texts have to tell us about histories that throw into question not only our most cherished, sane, forms of political identity – liberal, rational, democratic – but our relationship to the perceivable world, our confidence that there is a world which, simply by looking at it, is there to be seen.

The hallucinatory nature of Butts's and Bowen's writing has received a great deal of commentary. In Butts's case it is most often identified with her mysticism, from which the most dubious aspects of her political imagination are then seen to follow. Or else it is attributed to an experimental vision which somehow counters or redeems them. In Bowen's case, it is with some form of aesthetic excess, or more simply with an intensity of feeling which gives the particular colour – the colour, say, of a woman writer – to her representation of the world. Or else, and this makes another link to Butts, the perceptual instability is also seen as partly redemptive, disintegrative of all knowing, a way of repudiating or undermining any problematic political undercurrents in her texts. But disintegration is not the same thing as hallucination. Words failing is not the same thing as objects too intensely felt or seen.

In both texts, something, to put it mildly, happens to the character's relationship to the phenomenal world, whether as dare, promise or threat. This description of Scylla, taken from *Armed with Madness*, of which *Felicity Taverner* is the sequel, gives the tone:

> Then to detach herself she played an old game, that she was lying out on the wood's roof: translating the stick and leaf that upheld her into herself: into sea, into sky. Sky back again into wood, flesh and sea.[5]

And here, from *The Heat of the Day*, is a description of the young woman, Louie, with whom the book opens and ends although – no less bizarrely – she appears minimally throughout the rest of the novel:

> Louie repeatedly stooped to touch petals, her raspy finger-tips being every time entered by their smoothness.[6]

Whether as a game, or in deadly earnest – and 'deadly', as we will see, is also used advisedly – the objects of the phenomenal world are granted the capacity to transfer their substance into humans and, in the first quote, the reverse. Things are in the wrong place. This is no metaphoric or figural migration, it is corporal, objective and above all – to refer back to another of the opening epigraphs – odd: 'what had happened today was objective and odd'. Just in case you miss the point, fail to grasp the perceptual quality, the narrator of *Felicity Taverner* spells it out:

> In this second silence the walls left them behind, preoccupied with

Felicity's passion and death; aware only that something was happening to the place where they sat, to describe which the comparisons of poets have been used to obscure reality. So that a literal description passes, even among poets, for metaphor, as when Wordsworth said: 'as if to make the strong wind visible'; 'as if' discounting what he had to say, who had seen the wind, and dare not say it.[7]

What Butts is describing moves backwards, therefore, from one influential strand in thinking about modernist representation. Instead of turning reference into figure, or exposing the already figural nature of our relationship to what we take to be the observable world, it turns figure into object. It concretises. Bodies, among other things, become too present to themselves: 'All that she could have explained was that she was aware of the backs of her ears; or the bones of her skull', 'something was trying to get out through his eyes'.[8] And the effects at moments are for me strikingly resonant of the kind of description which W. J. Bion offers of the world inside his consulting room. This is from his paper 'On Hallucination':

> When the patient glanced at me he was taking a part of me into him. It was taken into his eyes [. . .] as if his eyes could be sucking something out of me. This was then removed from me, before I sat down, and expelled again, through his eyes, so that it was deposited in the right hand corner of the room, where he could keep it under observation while he was lying on the couch.[9]

'This I put forward,' Bion comments, 'as the first step in the comprehension of hallucinatory phenomena: if the patient says he sees an object it may mean that an external object has been perceived by him or it may mean that he is ejecting an object through his eyes.' What seems relevant here is the descriptive account of the process, not any of the interpretations which follow – it is in fact crucial to this register that the question of meaning is suspended. As Donald Meltzer, one of Bion's best-known commentators puts it, what is really new about Bion's thinking here is his 'capacity for observation of hallucination as a phenomena of the consulting room', 'the opening up of new territories of phenomenology in the consulting room'.[10] What is 'burstingly original', to use another of Meltzer's expressions, or 'idiosyncratic' about Bion is a kind of doubling of analytic observation with its object, the ability of the analyst to observe the process of observation of his patient *as if it were* in itself phenomenal reality or object, even when or especially when that process has gone haywire.

The result, as Meltzer also points out, is hardly theoretical elucidation but 'poetry that is at once evocative and incomprehensible'.[11] In relation to modernism, 'evocative and incomprehensible' are of course complements. In any case, they seem to offer a fair description of the two novels I am talking about here. Bion, Butts and Bowen have, we could say, an aesthetic in common. Crucially this account – or this kind of experience – is uncontainable by the theoretical paradigms offered either by Freud or by Melanie Klein.

We could compare the Bion passage with these lines from Paul de Man on Baudelaire (T. J. Clark cites them in *Farewell to an Idea: Episodes from a History of Modernism*, from which I lifted my Stein quote, again in discussion of Picasso): 'Whether the light emanates from outside us before it is interiorised by the eye . . . or whether the light emanates from inside and projects the entity, as in hallucination or in certain dreams, makes little difference in this context'.[12] I would argue that it makes all the difference if something, as in the lines from 'Obsession', the Baudelaire poem being discussed, is coming out of your eyes:

But shadows themselves are pictures
In which there live, darting from my eyes by the thousand,
Vanished entities with familiar faces.

So a larger theoretical ambition also lies behind this essay. Which is to suggest that the turn to psychoanalysis in relation to modernist writing has been, if anything, a bit tame. Or to put it another way, the Freudian economy of repression is inadequate, by his own admission in the famous interchange with the poet and novelist H. D., for dealing with the quality of perception which these novels evoke. In her case, what she saw was writing on the wall. But even that seems to me today to hand itself over too readily, arms outstretched, to the idea of the unconscious, the unconscious writ large as it were. Let's forget about the writing for a moment – or rather writing as a metaphor for writing (one famous theoretical turn) – and think instead about what goes on between, or even what can happen to, walls:

> In this second silence the walls left them behind, preoccupied with Felicity's passion and death; aware only that something was happening to the place where they sat.[13]

At a key moment in *The Heat of the Day*, Stella returns to the house in Ireland in which long ago she conceived her only child. As she travels towards it, something physical, attributed ambiguously to memory and anticipation – she calls it a 'sensory train' – starts to come alight:

> Expectancy rather than memory from now on guided her – she could not tell at which moment of her return journey the sensory train had started itself alight. Now she seemed to perceive on all sides around her, with phantasmagoric clearness, everything that for the eye the darkness hid.[14]

And then, later in her room in the same house, in one of the hardest passages – syntactically, logically and perceptually – in the book:

> Ladies had gone not quite mad, not quite even that, from in vain listening for meaning in the loudening ticking of the clock. (She listened, looking back over her shoulder at the chimneypiece: in the marble centre, silence – the gilt nymphs' arms upheld only a faceless hollow.) Virtue with nothing more to spend, honour saying nothing but both present. Both, also, rising and following the listener when she left the drawing-room; she had been unaccompanied by them along no path she took. Therefore her kind made no choices, made no decisions – or, did they not? Everything spoke to them – the design in and out of which they drew their needles; the bird with its little claws drawn to its piteously smooth breast, dead; way in the woods the quickening strokes of the axes, then the fall of the tree; or the child upstairs crying out terrified in its sleep.[15]

In this passage, as in much of the novel, Bowen, you could say, hovers just this side of hallucination. Sensation comes alight, against the dark. Objects are first hollow and silent, refusing the comfort of meaning, but then, in so far as what follows can be understood, two glorious abstractions – virtue and honour – rise up as concrete present entities and follow her out of the drawing-room: 'Both, also, rising and following the listener when she left the drawing-room'. With the implication that they have always done so, if you can work your way through these double negatives of the next part of the sentence: 'she had been unaccompanied by them on no path that she took.' The point being that, since Stella has good reason to believe that her wartime lover is a Nazi spy, whether or not 'virtue' and 'honour' have accompanied her in the past – 'she had been unaccompanied by them on no path that she took' – they could well be deserting her now. That's why those double negatives seem so appropriate, they give her virtue and honour as her unfailing companions with one hand, and then take them back syntactically with the other. For the question is, and it is central to Bowen's critique of the English middle class, whether virtue and honour, taking them for granted in the past, are what have protected Stella or whether that very taking for granted is what has made her so hideously vulnerable: 'Therefore, her kind knew no choices, made no decisions – or, did they not?' Either way, it is the opening up of that fully political question, on which the whole drama of this novel turns, which allows the needlepoint on the tapestry, the dead bird, the axe strokes and the crying child, all to come crowding into the room. 'War', to cite the second epigraph to this essay, as 'the thinning of the membrane between the this and the that . . .'

If we want to talk about bizarre objects, Mary Butts is in a sense easier, because she goes, much more straightforwardly than Bowen – although straightforward isn't quite the right word – over to the other side. She isn't only terrified of this process, or rather doesn't only use this process as a way of representing terror, she also goes looking for it, and invests it with a kind of, indeed, mystic faith. She believes in objects, what she calls 'mana-objects' – the whole of *Armed with Madness* turns on one. So whenever perceptual reality tips over into this dimension, things may well be going more right than wrong. In this Butts was in quite deliberate and extensive dispute with Freud: 'Freud very useful in the case of irrational fear [. . .] [But] what had happened today was objective and odd.' Specifically she rejected his account of the supernatural as pure psychological projection. And in the process she mounts a wholly convincing critique of the limits, not to say, anthropocentrism of Freud's own views. In her biography of Butts, Nathalie Blondel via Jane Harrison spells this out:

> J. E. Harrison points out in *Themis* (1912) that in the subject of religion the 'cardinal question' revolves around 'what . . . we mean by the word "sacred". In bygone days', she agrees, 'the answer would have been prompt and simple, the thunderbolt is sacred because it belonged to a god. The god is presupposed and from him comes the sanctity.' This is indeed Freud's position. 'But', argues Harrison, 'we now know from a study of the customs and representations of primitive peoples, that, broadly speaking, the reverse is true, a thing is regarded as sacred and out of that sanctity, given certain conditions, emerges a *daimon* and ultimately a god. *Le sacré c'est le père de dieu.*'[16]

In other words, the sacred is not a psychological projection on to the external world, it is – in this world view at least – something which inheres in, and then arises, out of things. Blondel comments:

> This changes the whole equation. It is qualitatively different to maintain, as Freud did, that superstitious people *explained* the outer world by a range of deities based on a belief in anthropocentrism, and Harrison's conclusion that the gods were a *response* to, rather than an explanation of, natural phenomena and noumena. It is Freud's position, in fact, that is based on anthropocentrism in a 'man-fabricated' world.[17]

Investing objects with power in this sense is the opposite of investing them with meaning. What is disturbing here is not the source of the process but the consequence. After all, anything becomes possible, one might say, as soon as you believe that objects have a life of their own. Objects, which are normally the furniture or stuff of dreams, can get up and start walking around the room. You can of course call this process psychotic, but you could also take it as another way of seeing things. 'If I've got to have the universe in my head,' says Louie, in *The Heat of the Day*, in what is in fact a moment of light relief, 'I might as well look it in the eye.'[18] Writing on 'the extreme capacity for observation which is natural to some patients', Bion qualifies his own diagnostic confidence, 'I would like to consider the category "psychotic" and suggest that it is too gross [. . .] there may be *insane* psychotics and *sane* psychotics. It might be possible to help the insane psychotic to become efficient psychotic.'[19]

'We are helped in these difficult matters,' writes Winnicott in a famous comment, 'by remembering that hallucinations are dream phenomena that have come forward into the waking life and that hallucinating is no more an illness in itself than the corresponding fact that the day's events and the memories of real happenings are drawn across the barrier into sleep and dream formation.' A fact, he adds in a footnote, which although 'inherent in Freud's hypothesis of dream-formation [. . .] has often been overlooked'.[20] Bion's great capacity, writes Meltzer, was 'to observe the transactions of the consulting room as if they were all a dream and to listen to a patient's account of his life in the outside world as if it were the account of a dream'.[21]

If Butts invests this process with aura – she believes in it, one could say – she by no means simply romanticises it. At the end of *Armed with Madness*, in a moment of frenzy Clarence confuses Scylla with an icon, ties her to a tree, pierces her with arrows and nearly kills her. In order to convey the monstrosity of what he has done, Picus shouts at him: 'You actually *did* a dream.'[22]

'When and if I ever I do think of that, it's to be all the more certain I must have dreamed it!' Stella protests to Harrison, the man who is trying to blackmail her into becoming his lover in return for his not blowing the whistle on Robert. 'Still,' he retorts, 'there are dreams one checks up on, even so, don't you think? I mean, if I'd seemed to dream I saw a chap at the foot of my bed going through my pockets, I'd take a look through my pockets the next morning. Who wouldn't? You would.' 'I never,' she replies, 'have dreams like that.'[23] These are dreams that refuse to be *just* dreams. What do you do with a dream that won't lie down?

This essay began by suggesting that both these novels force the reader into a position of discomforting historical identification. The question then becomes: what does this perceptual register do to that history, and the reverse? One could of course argue that in the case of these two writers the hallucinatory intensity arises out of the trauma of war. Butts described herself as 'war-shocked': 'With an ache he did not know was for Versailles, Clarence had swung in'; and her generation as 'war-ruined': 'I belong to the war-ruined generation', she wrote in her diary the year *Felicity Taverner* was published.[24] For

Bowen, it arises out of what her narrator describes as 'the general rocking of London and one's own mind'.[25] You never come back, Robert explains to Stella in their final confrontation, from the 'extremity' of Dunkirk.[26] But while I would not want to downplay that factor, it seems to me that there is a risk of pathologising the perceptual peculiarity too quickly, as well as spreading, as often happens in recent theory, the category of trauma far too wide (indeed, to limit that spread in *Felicity Taverner*, there is one specifically war-traumatised character, the Russian exile from the civil war). It would make things easier if it could be claimed that the perceptual register I have been describing either upholds or sabotages what is most awkward about the political self-placing of these two texts. But I don't think you can. Part of the problem is of course that, while such moments are deeply unsettling (although to assume that such unsettling, the discomfort they cause the reader, sabotages the worst of the politics is still to move too fast), there is also a terrifying certainty about them. That's what makes them so vivid and powerful. They brook no argument, as you might say. They are stubbornly and unanswerably there. Like the mana-objects in which Mary Butts invests the destiny of England. Or rather one piece of English coastland, 'this bit of England . . . whose pattern was repeated in them, the stuff of a country made into man'.[27] And which – against the designs of Kralin, 'the man who would sell the body of our land to the Jews' – comes alive, with all the peculiar concreteness I have tried to describe, as its last dying gasp and protest. By the end of the novel, you can almost feel Butts taking what is most acute about her aesthetic vision and prising or squeezing it back into the earth.

Englishness is also what saves the day in Elizabeth Bowen's text. Faced with the enormity of her lover's political credo, his betrayal of a nation – with which Bowen, given her Irish legacy, of course only partly identifies – it is to England, in all its suddenly reassuring familiarity to which Stella turns: 'She had trodden every inch of a country with him [. . .] She could not believe they had not, in those two years, drawn on the virtue of what was around them, *the* virtue peculiar to where they were'.[28] It is, finally, for the saving of this English virtue that, against all the preceding confusions, Kralin the Jew is murdered at the end of *Felicity Taverner*, and at the end of *The Heat of the Day*, Stella's Nazi lover sweeps up all the delusions, 'the whole thing looked like a hallucination', before obligingly falling to his death from her roof.

Not since *Clarissa* (a deliberate exaggeration) have you had two people dispatched so blatantly for the ideological niceties of the text. In the case of Bowen, the demise of Stella's lover allows the novel to back off from a political identification whose logic, or rather attraction – sexual attraction – one assumes that, in writing her novel, she could not have predicted. Although Stella herself does predict it, or at least makes the explicit link between the horror of revelation and consummation: 'If actor, to her and for her so very good an actor, then why not actor also of love [. . .] No, no, no, she thought: better anything! Better what, then? Better to hear him say: "Since you *have* chosen to ask me – yes." That would be love; that would be the consummation.'[29] In the case of Butts, the final death serves to redeem a version of the world which, in the body of the writing, she has acknowledged to have no more, or rather as much, reality as a dream. At the end of both books, you can almost feel the world subsiding back, breathing out gratefully, into its proper place. For some good, some not so good historical reasons, both novels have raced away finally from the extremities of their own vision.

References

1 Mary Butts, *The Death of Felicity Taverner* (1928; New York: McPherson, 1991); Elizabeth Bowen, *The Heat of the Day* (1948; London: Penguin, 1962).
2 Lawrence Rainey, *Institutions of Modernism, Literary Elites and Public Culture* (London and New York: Yale University Press, 1998).
3 Patterson, ' "The Plan Behind the Plan": Russians, Jews and Mythologies of Change: The Case of Mary Butts', in Bryan Cheyette and Laura Marcus (eds), *Modernity, Culture and 'the Jew'* (Cambridge: Polity Press, 1997); Rainey, 'Good Things', *London Review of Books*, 16 July 1998.
4 Butts, *Felicity Taverner*, p. 174.
5 Mary Butts, *Armed with Madness* (1928; New York: McPherson, 1991), pp. 67–8.
6 Bowen, p. 17.
7 Butts, *Felicity Taverner*, p. 181.
8 Ibid., pp. 193, 148.
9 W. J. Bion, *Second Thoughts* (1967; London: Karnac Books, 1984), p. 67.

10 Donald Meltzer, *The Kleinian Development*, Part 3: *The Clinical Significance of the work of Bion* (Perth: Clunie, 1978), pp. 28, 29.

11 Meltzer, p. 25.

12 Cited in T. J. Clark, *Farewell to an Idea: Episodes from a History of Modernism* (London and New York: Yale University Press, 1999), p. 219.

13 Butts, *Felicity Taverner*, p. 181.

14 Bowen, p. 166.

15 Ibid., p. 174.

16 Nathalie Blondel, *Mary Butts: Scenes from the Life* (New York: McPherson, 1998), p. 83.

17 Ibid., pp. 83–4.

18 Bowen, p. 249.

19 Cited in Eric Rhode, *On Hallucination, Intuition and the Becoming of 'O'* (Binghampton: esf Publications, 1998), p. 25.

20 D. W. Winnicott, 'Creativity and its Origins', *Playing and Reality* (London: Tavistock, 1971), p. 67.

21 Meltzer, p. 18.

22 Butts, *Armed With Madness*, p. 155.

23 Bowen, p. 130.

24 Butts, *Felicity Taverner*, p. 126; cited Blondel, p. 474n.

25 Ibid., p. 90.

26 Ibid., p. 272.

27 Butts, *Felicity Taverner*, p. 259.

28 Bowen, pp. 274–5.

29 Ibid., p. 173.

II: BORDER CROSSINGS

'On Not Being Able to Sleep': Rereading *The Interpretation of Dreams*

This essay was first delivered as a paper at a special event organised by the Sigmund Freud-Gesellschaft in Vienna to mark the centenary of The Interpretation of Dreams *held on 6 May 2000, the date of Freud's birthday. It was subsequently published in the newsletter of the Society and in the* Zeitschrift für psychoanalytische Theorie und Praxis *of autumn 2001. Rereading Freud's monumental text in a discussion group with PhD students, I had been struck by the bizarre nature of the final chapter on sleep, the psychic boundaries – even beyond those most often associated with Freud – which it appeared to cross. Famously ignorant of, or blind to, each other's writing, Freud and Marcel Proust seem to share a capacity to push the mind beyond its own limits, into a terrain almost inconceivable by the mind itself. Does psychoanalysis share with modernism – Woolf, Butts, Proust – the temptation, or need, psychically to overreach itself?*

'It is essential to assume that there is such a thing as a state of sleep for the inner life.'

Freud, The Interpretation of Dreams (1900)

'We are building out into the dark.'

Ibid.

'A man who falls like a stone into his bed night after night, and ceases to live until the moment when he wakes and rises, will surely never dream of making, not even great discoveries, but the merest observations about sleep.'

Proust, Sodome et Gomorrhe (1921)

It is not easy to think about sleep. Probably because we assume that when we sleep, we relinquish our thinking selves. 'The dream-work,' as Freud put it in a famous comment at the end of Chapter 6 of *The Interpretation of Dreams*, 'does not think.' Although the whole task of the book was to restore the dignity of the psyche to the dreamer ('the *dignity* – die *Würde* – of being a process of the psyche',[1] and although Freud insisted that dream-thoughts are 'entirely reasonable' and 'formed with all the expense of psychical energy we are capable of', he none the less shared with his predecessors the belief that there is something about the dreaming mind that differs radically from the mind awake: 'It is not that [the dream-work] is more negligent, more unreasonable, more forgetful, more incomplete, say, than waking thought; it is qualitatively different from it, and so at first not comparable to it. It does not think, calculate, judge in any way at all.'[2] That difference is attributable in significant measure to sleep. 'At bottom,' Freud adds in a footnote in 1925, 'dreams are nothing other than a peculiar form of thinking made possible by the conditions of the state of sleep'.[3]

Although Freud will crucially identify all the features of the dream-work, not only in symptom formation, but also in jokes and slips, the dream – through sleep – at least partly escapes the mantle of these forms. It breaks the line which Freud – in a gesture which might be seen as the founding gesture of psychoanalysis – runs from the neurotic to the everyday (the 'approximately normal person' as he famously describes himself in the preamble to the specimen dream). Sleep changes everything. It is a special case; or, to put it another way, it is the state of sleep which makes a special case of the dream: 'a mental disorder occurring during sleep';[4] 'a "hallucinatory wishful psychosis"' to use the more explicit, stronger, formula of 'A Metapsychological Supplement to the Theory of Dreams'.[5] In sleep, our unconscious thoughts take on a hallucinogenic form. It is sleep therefore which brings dreams closer to psychosis than neurosis, closer to the madness with which the first chapter of *The Interpretation of Dreams* comes to an end. For Kant, Freud observes, 'The lunatic is one who dreams while awake' ('the madman is a waking dreamer'), for Schopenhauer, 'the dream a brief madness and madness a long dream'.[6]

The central question of this essay, then, is: what was sleep for Freud? What kind of problems did it present him with, where did it lead? 'I have had little occasion,' Freud asserts on the first pages of his book, 'to occupy myself with the problem of sleep, for this is essentially a problem of physiology.' 'So,' he continues, "in my account I have disregarded the literature on sleep'[7] the only literature in the magisterial overview of the first chapter which he pays the compliment of leaving alone). Predictably enough, perhaps, given the boldness of that dismissal, sleep returns and, in the final chapter of the work, it more or less occupies centre stage. 'I am,' Freud asserts, 'an excellent sleeper'.[8] But in the course of this work it seems as if, against the normal order of things, sleep is the one thing that will not let him rest. 'The dream,' he states in Chapter 1, 'appears as a reaction to everything that is simultaneously present and currently active in the sleeping psyche'.[9] The psyche, one could say, never sleeps. For the interpreter of dreams, there is no sleep for sleep. Then, as if exhausted by his own labours, by what he has himself asked of the psyche to redeem it into meaningfulness, he affirms in the final chapter: 'It is essential to assume there is such a thing as a state of sleep for the inner life' (less a statement than a plea).[10] Because it is so peculiar and challenging to Freud, so agitating as one might say, sleep – I will be suggesting here – can tell us about far more than the dream.

Of all the chapters in *The Interpretation of Dreams*, Chapter 7, the most psychological, at first glance therefore the most un-psychoanalytic, seems to have received the least attention. Ernest Jones describes it as the 'most difficult and abstract of Freud's writings', something which belonged for Freud halfway between an obstruction and a whim: 'Freud gets *held up* by the *impulse* to sketch out the essay on general psychology' (my emphasis); 'Evidently the final chapter is giving a great deal of trouble'.[11] On 27 June 1899, Freud wrote to Fliess: 'The chapter is becoming more drawn out,' and 'will be neither nice nor fruitful'.[12] But although Freud describes the chapter as drudgery in this letter ('a duty'), almost exactly a year before (20 June 1898) he describes it to Fliess as something he had composed 'as if in a dream'.[13] According to Jones, Freud's daughter Mathilde confirmed that, while he was writing it, he would arrive at family meals 'as if sleep-walking'.[14] In the last chapter of *The Interpretation of Dreams*, it seems that far from making his exit from the work, Freud cannot get out of his dream.

In fact, Chapter 7 was one of two blocks – or gaps – impeding completion of the book: 'the gap in the psychology as well as the gap left by the [removal of the] thoroughly analysed sample [dream]'.[15] By association, therefore, the block in the psychology and the omission of the hidden details of Freud's life are linked. From the wording, it sounds as if, at one stage of composition, the whole chapter on the dream of Irma's injection, not just selective details, had been removed as too revealing from the text. Something more intimate or private than abstraction ('the most difficult and abstract of Freud's writings'), something more like a dream ('composed as if in a dream') seems therefore to have been at stake. In Freud's mind at least, theory and intimacy join hands. Certainly the correspondence suggests that, in the course of writing Chapter 7, Freud shifted uneasily between dream and reason, from inside to outside his topic. Perhaps then, it is not the abstract nature of the chapter which is the problem, but the opposite – the effort it took Freud to wrest himself clear from the processes he was trying to describe (the heave into abstraction, abstraction as a 'duty' and impossible goal). Instead of psychology acting as aberration for psychoanalysis, a kind of scientist relic, in this case things appear to have worked the other way around. If Chapter 7 of *The Interpretation of Dreams* is difficult, it is because it shows us Freud forced back inside the very realm or space which he was attempting to master for the future of his science – the space which the psychoanalyst, unlike the sleeper, could talk about.

At the start of Chapter 7, Freud writes: 'We must be clear in our minds: the stretch of our way that makes for easy going lies behind us.' Remarkably proceeding as if everything up to this point has been crystal clear – a world of light, enlightenment and full understanding – he continues:

> Until now, if I am not much mistaken, all the paths we have trodden have led us into the light, to enlightenment and to full understanding ('ins Lichte, zur Aufklärung und zum vollen Verständnis'), from the moment we propose to go more deeply into the psyche's inner processes of dreaming, all our ways lead into the dark.[16]

Nothing will be explained here; the realm he is entering into now is unknown: 'It is impossible for us to get as far as *explaining* the dream as psychical process, for explaining means tracing back to what is already known.' He can only proceed 'speculatively', taking care 'not to spin [the new assumptions] too far beyond their first logical links, for if we do, their worth will vanish into uncertainty'.[17]

And yet there is something strange about these disclaimers. It is not as if this is the first (or indeed the last) time in the book that uncertainty appears in Freud's thought. Returning, only a few pages on, to the dream of the burning child with which the chapter opens – the one of which he famously comments that it requires no interpretation – Freud writes: 'Indeed, the dream-thoughts we come upon as we interpret cannot in general but remain without closure, spinning out on all sides into the web-like fabric of our thoughts' (this is the dream's 'navel', the place where it plumbs into the 'Unknown').[18] Not knowing, as he also observes in this part of the chapter, is of course the condition of analytic work: 'As long as anyone has not decided to let go of the question of certainty when tracing an element from the dream, the analysis will come to a standstill'.[19]

Why, then, does Freud present the enquiry of this chapter as especially vulnerable to uncertainty (the 'gravest uncertainties', as he will repeat in the 'Metapsychological Supplement to The Theory of Dreams';[20] or as if uncertainty, instead of being an indispensable part of the investigation, were an obstacle? There seems to be more going on here than the often observed tension between the enlightenment and speculative impulses in Freud's thought – less hesitation than dread. Uncertainty appears here like a night-terror, something a child goes to sleep afraid of confronting in the dark: 'all our ways lead into the dark'. As soon as we take sleep as our focus, then fear of the dark, instead of a metaphor for the limits of knowledge, a salutary caution against psychoanalytic knowingness, turns real, becomes – precisely – fear. It traces itself on the mind – like the 'luminous particles and lines of the retina's own light', which, in one of the early accounts of dreaming to which Freud alludes in Chapter 1, sketch out the shape of the dream.[21] When asked by her mother why she had not spoken to the doctor of her fear of the dark, the little girl in Winnicott's famous case, *The Piggle*, replies that she had ' "packed all the dark away" '.[22] Freud, we could say, is up to something similar. What he seems to be trying to do in Chapter 7, although he also knows the task to be impossible, is to build bridges into the dark: 'We are building out into the dark' ('ins Dunkle hinaus zu bauen' – the Standard Edition translates this 'we are building our way out into the dark', which renders the phrase somehow safer, as if we could be sure the way was ours and that it had – or at least would – be found.[23]

Could it be then that the greatest fear for the analyst is not the fear of not knowing, one loss of omnipotence, but another, more tangible, more physical, the fear of slipping backwards (regression is of course also central to this chapter), of turning – with awesome, hallucinogenic vividness – into a frightened child? This might have implications for the way Freud tends to be read in the humanities departments of universities, but also for certain schools of analytic thought. On the one hand, it makes it harder to take the crisis of knowledge, divested of physical, childlike actuality, as the key to Freud's thinking; but then nor would it be possible to raise that same child, its lived experience, to the status of true analytic object to be redeemed by insight, since the analyst herself would have to recognise the very movements of interpretative theory as potentially struck dumb and blind – like the sleeper – with her own fear: 'we are paralysed in dreams'.[24] 'It is,' Proust writes, 'the image of sleep which sleep itself had projected' – 'My eyes blinded, my lips sealed, my limbs fettered, my body naked' – which then, like Giotto's portrait of envy with a serpent in her mouth, takes on monstrous shapes.[25] '*Unrestrained, exaggerated, monstrous*' are the words Freud also uses to describe the activity – the '*productive*' nature – of the dream.[26]

Once you start thinking of it like this, then sleep appears, less as metaphor for, more a pathway *into*, something else. When we go to sleep, we close our eyes. 'The task which [sleep] assigns to us,' Proust writes, 'we accomplish with our eyes closed.'[27] This is of course at least partly misleading. As Fritz Perls, psychoanalyst turned founder of gestalt therapy, remarked on the subject of insomnia, closing your eyes is no help, since your eyes close as a consequence of – rather than as a means to – falling asleep. Sleep, as all insomniacs know, cannot be willed. It only comes inadvertently. The best way to fall asleep is to think of anything but sleep. As if sleep were, in Proust's words, 'our other master', and falling asleep is one of the ways we pay tribute to the unconscious, to the idea of something vital and uncontrollable in our minds (ibid.). If sleep cannot be willed, crucially we never know what will happen – or where exactly we are going – when we go to sleep.

At the time of writing *The Interpretation of Dreams*, Freud still instructed his patients to close their eyes: 'In order for [the patient] to give all his attention to self-observation,' he writes in Chapter 2, 'it is

helpful for him to lie down and close his eyes'.[28] Not quite sending the
patient to sleep, analysis aimed to freeze or suspend the patient,
impossibly one might say, at sleep's threshold: 'it is a matter of
producing in the psyche a condition sharing a certain similarity in
distribution of psychical energy (mobile attention) with the condition
present just before falling asleep'.[29] Four years later, as a footnote in
the Standard Edition points out, this requirement has been dropped:
'he does not even ask them to close their eyes'.[30] Along with all the
other things which psychoanalysis will relinquish – hypnosis: 'a
condition sharing a certain similarity . . . with the condition present
just before falling asleep (and certainly with the hypnotic state too)',
male hysteria according to the recent argument of Juliet Mitchell[31] –
psychoanalysis, one could say, lets go, or will ask its patients to let go,
of sleep.

In the famous letter to Fliess of 2 November 1896 about the death
of his father, which inaugurates *The Interpretation of Dreams*, Freud
writes:

> I must tell you about a nice dream I had the night after the funeral [. . .]
> I was in a place where I read a sign:
>   You are requested
>   to close the eyes.
> The sentence on the sign has a double meaning: one should do one's
> duty to the dead (an apology as though I had not done it and were in
> need of leniency), and the actual duty itself [Masson, p. 202].[32]

What happens, we might ask, when someone closes their eyes? Or to
what else might someone be alluding, even if unconsciously, when
they are talking about sleep? If we run a line from this letter to the last
chapter of Freud's text, then one of the things we are joining, one
could say, is father to child. 'In my inner self,' he writes in the same
letter to Fliess, 'the whole past has been reawakened by this event'.[33]
The father dies; the child, inside the son, reawakes. Almost too
symmetrically, the last chapter begins with the dream of the burning
child – lying dead in reality in the adjacent room and whose shroud
and arm has caught fire – who awakes, to reproach his father, from
death.

Child or father, something awakes, against the odds, in each case.

What are the conditions from which one does, and does not, awaken? 'There has indeed been death,' Proust writes, 'as when the heart has ceased to beat and a rhythmical traction of the tongue revives us'.[34] In a move which blurs the image of psychoanalysis as a one-way passage from darkness into light, Freud holds himself and the dreamer, Janus-faced, at the point where they divide; or where light, instead of illuminating, fulgurates (the dream 'blazes up in a moment [. . .] like a firework'.[35] What is an awakening? 'According to Delboeuf,' Freud writes in the first chapter, 'there is no valid criterion whether something is a dream or waking reality except [. . .] the sheer fact of awakening' ('der Tatsache des Erwachens').[36] Freud is once again being more of a philosopher than he thinks (and more of a philosopher than the subsequent evolution of psychoanalysis has allowed). For 'the literature of philosophy' since Freud, writes Donald Meltzer in *Dream-Life*, one of the crucial questions has remained: 'Can we know that we are dreaming?'[37] There is a world of difference, one could say, between a psychoanalysis which sees its task as waking the soul into reason, and a psychoanalysis which does not know, cannot be sure, whether it is itself awake.

How far are we awake when we sleep? 'I am bound to draw the conclusion,' Freud writes on our ability to tell ourselves that we are dreaming, '*that, through the entire state of sleep, we know just as certainly that we are dreaming as we know that we are asleep*'[38] (Freud's emphasis). And yet, it is one task of the dream-work, that of secondary revision 'to lull to sleep a certain agency/instance' (einer gewissen Instanz) so as to 'reduce the significance of what has just been experienced and help to make what follows bearable' (to allow the dream to continue so that the dreamer can sleep; (p. 318). The ego, in Freud's later formulation, both sleeps and does not sleep: 'The ego is the mental agency [. . .] which goes to sleep at night, though even then it exercises its censorship on dreams' (works in its sleep, we could say; *The Ego and the Id*, p. 17). Freud's attempt to distribute these features between different mental agencies and functions is only partially successful (the second topography repeats the problem in new guise). Like an insomniac, he never stops counting off the parts of the mind. Sleep remains obdurate and indivisible. And ungraspable. 'Our actual awakenings,' Proust writes, 'produce an interruption of memory [. . .] we describe these states of sleep because we no longer remember them.' When we wake, sleep 'races' against us 'to obliterate' its own traces: 'After all these centuries we still know very little about the matter'.[39]

So, does the dreamer sleep? In one of Freud's most celebrated formulas, he asserts: 'The dream is *the guardian of sleep, not its disturber*' ('*Der Traum is der Wächter des Schlafes, nicht sein Störer*'); '*Every successful dream is a fulfilment of this wish*' (the one 'universal, invariably present, and constant wish', 'allgemeine, regelmässig vorhandene und sich gleichbleibende', Freud's emphasis).[40] And yet, 'the dream never wastes its time on trifles. We do not allow a mere nothing/trifle to disturb our sleep' ('um Geringes lassen wir uns im Schlaf nicht stören').[41] Sleep is only ever partial: 'What is repressed in the system *Ucs* does not obey the wish to sleep.'[42] 'None of the evidence that Freud brought to bear in this respect,' argues Meltzer on the first page of *Dream-Life*, 'argues any more strongly for the thesis that dreams are the guardians of sleep than that they are its destroyers.'[43] In his correspondence with Fliess (9 June 1899), Freud self-disparagingly dismisses his conviction that the dream is the guardian of sleep as a 'platitude' or 'commonplace': '*tant de bruit*' (as if his own concept were the unwelcome noise getting in the way of his sleep) (Masson, p. 354).[44] By the time of *An Outline of Psycho-Analysis*, he has qualified it: 'a dream is invariably an *attempt* to get rid of a disturbance of sleep [. . .] The attempt may succeed more or less completely; it may also fail'.[45] Although sleep is in the service of the ego ('a narcissistic withdrawal of the positions of the libido onto the subject's own self'),[46] it can in extreme cases renounce its own nature, let go of sleep, 'because of its fear of its dreams': 'They did not dare to sleep because they were afraid of their dreams.'[47]

The dream of the burning child is famous, but there is another moment, less commented on, which seems to me to be as important in this context, and which also turns on a child, on waking or not waking, and on what that transition in itself – the passage between the two states ('the condition present just before falling asleep') – might provoke by way of fear. No dream this time, but a vision which summons up therefore even more boldly the hallucinogenic colour of sleep, which is at the heart of Chapter 7: a mother wakes in a room to the presence of her uncle, whom she knows to be in a lunatic asylum, and rushing to her child to protect him from the sight, covers him over with a sheet. Behind the vision is a childhood memory of being told by a nursemaid that her mother had suffered convulsions ever since the time her brother had appeared to her disguised as a ghost. Covering her child to protect him from a vision (which is in fact her hallucination), the mother wards off the dreaded identification with the insane uncle, whom her son uncannily resembles, but of course what she has done is shroud her child (repeat the vision and turn him into a ghost). To what lengths will a parent go to protect a child – to protect herself – from fear?

From the father's dream to the mother's vision, an impossible boundary is crossed. Each time, it is the child who is called on to make the journey. Commentaries, such as that of Lacan, which emphasise death as unspeakable in relation to the father's dream,[48] or which more simply draw attention to the death of Freud's father as the instigator of the work, seem to me therefore to miss a dimension which is more or less staring us in the face. They miss, that is, the passage, the state of transition – the psychic no man's land of waking and not waking – where Freud situates the dream. We might be getting closer to understanding why sleep returns in the final chapter of *The Interpretation of Dreams*. Not because of some scientific-cum-psychological digression (or 'impulse'), but because sleep brings with it some of the most important questions Freud has to ask about the limits, the outermost boundaries, of the mind.

A further question then arises which gathers up all the rest. Does the child sleep? If we read back through *The Interpretation of Dreams*, you could then argue that this is, if not the founding, at the very least one of the central questions of the whole work. Father of six children as well as founding father, Freud could not help but be preoccupied, at the most mundane level, by the problem of sleep (even if we may have difficulty imagining him getting up in the middle of the night). On 12 June 1900, *The Interpretation of Dreams* finally completed, he writes to Fliess:

> Do you suppose that someday one will read on a marble tablet on this house:
>   Here, on July 24, 1895,
>   the secret of the dream
>   revealed itself to Dr Sigm. Freud.

In the same letter, he reports on his eight-year-old son: 'Ernst has been ill again with a sore throat and fever for four days. His energy is inexhaustible. Even when he has a temperature of 38.5, he still shouts: "One could not possibly feel better, I want to get up." [. . .] This manic vivacity and wildness sometimes strike me as uncanny, like that of a consumptive.' That children are inexhaustible is of course the commonest parental complaint (the 'uncanny' is Freud's own note, heralding the 1919 paper of the same title in which the traces of the child in the mind of the adult will once again be linked to fear). Freud's letter simply inflates both halves – both perversions – of parenting, pushes them to an extreme. Monumentalising himself for posterity (the plaque is of course in Vienna today), hovering anxiously over his son's vitality as something to boast of and to fear. Parents may try to control, but what parent, one might ask, can *read* the energy of a child?

Even before Chapter 7, the question of whether the child sleeps is present in Freud's text. 'We find,' he writes with reference to one set of dreams, '*the child, with its impulses, living on in the dream*' (Freud's emphasis).[49] No wish will make itself felt in the dream, he argues, unless an unconscious infantile wish has attached itself to it. And yet it is not always clear whether Freud means a childhood wish (a wish *of* childhood), or – as seems far more to be the case – the wish *to be* a child. When Freud speaks of infantile wishes, it seems to be above all the wish *for* infancy of which he speaks. Long before he formulates his account of topographical regression, the theory starts, as it were, to regress: 'Paradise is nothing other but the mass fantasy of the childhood of the individual [. . .] dreams can take us back to this Paradise every night.'[50]

If we dream of nakedness it is because children are not ashamed (in the 'Metapsychological Supplement', Freud describes sleep as an 'undressing of the mind', 'eine ganz analoge Entkleidung'.[51] If we dream of the death of loved ones, it is because children are uninhibited in their murderousness towards rivals. We are not ashamed of our repudiated wishes; more than anything we wish to be uninhibited and unashamed: 'these processes which I have called irrational are not falsifications of normal processes, not intellectual errors, but modes of activity of the psychical apparatus that are free of inhibition'.[52] There are, one could almost say, no contents to these wishes (another reason why trying to pin them down to a content feels like something of a wild goose chase), nothing to be achieved, other than the desire to fulfil – as in propel – oneself; to be gloriously unfettered, ruthless, unabashed: 'Children aim quite ruthlessly at [. . .] satisfaction.' In this the dreamer is like the hysteric who wants nothing so much as to be a naughty child: 'the similarity of what we call the hysterical character with that of a naughty child is really quite striking'.[53]

Pitch the child adrift on a sea of plenty, of multitudinous wishes jostling and clamouring for satisfaction, you are already on the wrong track (sentimental or punitive, or both). The image is a decoy, even if the wishes are real, and for the child overwhelming, enough. They all need to be swept up under the adult wish which, when we think of the child in this way, they are being used to conceal. The overwhelming wish of the dreamer is – no more or less than – to wish: 'the first psy. system is utterly incapable of taking anything unpleasant into the context of its thoughts. All the system can do is wish.'[54] By the time Freud gets to his account of regression in Chapter 7, the ground has therefore been prepared well in advance. Perceptual identity repre- sents the wish as fulfilled. But it is also a way that the system has of remembering itself. Repetition is a wish: 'The repeating of what had been experienced in that period is in itself a fulfilment of a wish' (10 March 1898).[55] Above all, the wish seeks representation, to be actualised, to come to life in the mind. 'Dreaming is a part of the – surmounted – childhood life of the psyche' (p. 370). The Standard Edition translates: 'a piece of infantile mental life that has been superseded'; in the German: 'child-soul/psyche-life' is one word: '*des überwundenen Kinderseelenlebens*' (Freud's emphasis).[56] It is the living psyche, the soul, of the child that awakens in the dream.

The image of the child at work in *The Interpretation of Dreams* will of course be subject to dramatic modifications; the whole edifice of infantile sexuality is yet to come. But this might be one of those moments in Freud's work where, precisely because something has not yet been uncovered, because the child is not yet abrim with a sexuality which draws all the attention, something else is able to slip through the net. Freud is working with a literal idea of remembered scene: 'a renewal of a visual stimulus that once actually happened, brought alert by the memory of it'[57] (in the letter of 10 March 1898, he distributes dreams, fantasies and psychoneuroses according to what was, in the 'prehistoric' period of one to three years old, '*seen, heard, experienced sexually*'; Freud's emphasis).[58] But those who use this moment to discredit Freud's later views, most famously Jeffrey Masson, can only do so by stressing the scene itself at the expense of the metapsychological questions which accompanied it at this stage of his work. To make it a real scene, or only a real scene, they have to divest it of its hallucinatory quality; lift it quite clear out of the visualising mind. In fact, they do not give the scene *too much* reality, but *not enough* (Masson, not that this perhaps needs to be stated, has missed the point).

The problem, then, is not the arrival of fantasy in Freud's thought, not the loss of a reality no less banal for being cruel (the famous seduction theory of neurosis), but the opposite. It is the loss of the journey which, in Chapter 7 of *The Interpretation of Dreams*, Freud sets us on into the darkest, but also most vivid, hallucinatory recesses of the mind. Subsequent psychoanalytic theory will distinguish between hallucinogenic wish-fulfilment and hallucination, will insist on the distinction between inside and outside the mind (Meltzer: 'the differentiation between internal world phenomena and external ones is a *sine qua non* of sanity, just as the differentiation between good and bad is central to mental health', p. 115) – clearer on these matters than Freud, tidying up the dark even more than Freud, one could say. Every night, Freud writes, the adult relives a 'prehistoric' way of being with compelling sensory vividness. This comment could almost (apart from the style, which is of course everything) have been lifted out of Proust: 'even in people who do not normally have a visual memory, their earliest childhood recollections are characterised by a sensory vividness that is retained and persists into later years'.[59]

Remember, too, that one of the other things to which the body of the sleeper is most fully awake, more finely attuned than the waker, is the innermost vitality – the sights and sounds – of the body itself: 'those agile vegetative powers whose activity is doubled while we sleep';[60] 'in dreams, all the current bodily sensations assume gigantic proportions'.[61] When we dream we are all hypochondriacs, a condition to which Proust was also more than attuned. 'World of sleep – in which our inner consciousness, subordinated to the disturbances of our organs, accelerates the rhythm of the heart or the respiration [. . .] as soon as we have embarked on the dark current of our own blood.'[62]

'I find it distressing to think,' Freud writes on the subject of absurd dreams, 'that many of the premises at the basis of my psychological solution will produce incredulity and laughter once I have published them.' When he tells his patients that impressions from the first or second year of life leave 'lasting traces' in their emotional life, they are, he says, in the habit of 'parodying this newly acquired insight' by declaring they are 'ready to look for memories from the time when they were *not yet in the land of the living*' (Freud's emphasis).[63] As if going along with the absurdity, Freud himself at this stage of his writing referred to the period of infancy re-evoked by the dreamer as 'prehistoric': 'Biologically, dream life seems to me to derive entirely from the residues of the prehistoric period of life (between ages one and three); (10 March 1898, p. 302). But, in his own words from the same section of his work: 'dreams are often at their most profound when they appear at their craziest' ('So ist der Traum oft am tiefsinnigsten, wo er am tollsten erscheint').[64] In their ridicule, Freud's patients may be on to more than they think. For if the part of our mind which travels back ('regressively back transformed', 'regredienter Gedankenverwandlung',)[65] is unconscious to us, how can we possibly be sure, when we sleep, where it might take us, just how far back in fact we go?

A passage from Proust, which is I think worth quoting in full, makes the point:

> We possess all our memories but not the faculty of recalling them [. . .] What then is a memory which we do not recall? Or indeed let us go further. We do not recall our memories of the last thirty years; but we are wholly steeped in them; why then stop short at thirty years, why not extend this previous life back to before our birth? If I do not know a whole section of the memories that are behind me, if they are invisible to me, if I do not have the faculty of calling them to me, how do I know whether in that mass which is unknown to me there may not be some that extend back much further than my human existence? If I can have in me and round me so many memories which I do not remember, this oblivion (a *de facto* oblivion, at least, since I have not the faculty of seeing anything) may extend over a life which I have lived in the body of another man, even on another planet.[66]

Not for the first time outstripping Freud on the same ground, Proust could be said here to be taking him beyond the point he is willing to travel. While giving the mind infinite extension, he also shatters its continuity even more radically than Freud, concluding the passage: 'The being that I shall be after death has no more reason to remember the man I have been since my birth than the latter to remember what I was before it.'[67] Compare this sentence which Freud added to the last page of *The Interpretation of Dreams* in 1909 on unconscious wishes in their 'most fundamental and truest shape': 'we shall have to remember, no doubt, that psychical reality too has more than one form of existence'.[68] This curious, ghostly addition – which allows us to envisage a psyche more like that of Proust's, extending, multiplying, dividing itself – is then replaced in 1919 with the following: 'we shall have to conclude, no doubt, that *psychical* reality is a particular form of existence not to be confused with *material* reality'.[69] The beauty of the first formula was that the question of the nature of the psyche's reality – concrete, material, infinitely plastic – was left completely in suspense; as indeed was the question of with what it should, or could, be confused. 'Perhaps,' Proust suggests, 'there are other worlds more real than the waking world.'[70]

In *On Not Being Able to Paint*, Marion Milner's autobiographical account of teaching herself to paint, she describes the anxieties aroused by space – space, that is, lifted to the surface of consciousness, actualised and brought to life: 'I remembered a kind of half-waking spatial nightmare of being surrounded by an infinitude of space rushing away in every direction for ever and ever. In the same way, the term "vanishing point" aroused vistas of desolation.' As soon as she tried to think about space, 'the whole sensory foundation of the common sense world seemed to be threatened'.[71] Milner is creating an analogy between painting and a waking dream (or nightmare since it involves the fear of being mad). In fact, it is less analogy than a recovery, a way of bringing up 'dream imaginings up above (inside)'.[72] Not a retreat from the adult world, more 'like a search [. . .] a going back to look for something', a kind of 'uncommon sense', a 'primary madness' which all of us 'have lived through and to which at times we can return'.[73] 'The dream,' Milner writes, 'comes first', because 'we are not born knowing the difference between thoughts and things.'[74]

Milner's account of painting, or rather of what has to be confronted in order for anyone to paint, bears at moments uncanny similarities to everything I have been describing here in relation to *The Interpretation of Dreams*. Her book reads like an artistic or poetic, above all a waking, transfiguration of the same space, something which she has decided to summon, or grasp in her hands. Painting, like the dream, draws on the part of the mind that feels like a body. It threatens the same loss of the waking self. A picture, Cézanne wrote, 'is an abyss in which the eye is lost'. 'All these tones,' he asks, 'circulate in the blood, don't they?'[75] (Compare Proust: 'as soon as we have embarked on the dark current of our own blood'.) By closing her eyes, Milner generates a 'meeting which destroyed neither the dark possibilities of colour nor dimmed the light of consciousness' (the possibility of colour on the inner eye is 'dark', only consciousness lays claim, without hesitation or scruple, to the light). In her Postscript, Milner describes the experience as ecstatic, a 'blissful surrender', a harking back to the 'all-out body giving of infancy'. But in the main text what she describes is more like a journey through her own fears: 'of embracing, becoming one with, something infinitely suffering, fears of plunging into a sea of pain'.[76] Compare, again, Proust on sleep:

> As soon as I succeeded in falling asleep, at that more truthful hour when my eyes closed on the things of the outer world, the world of sleep [. . .] reflected, refracted the painful synthesis of survival and annihilation, in the organic and now translucent depths of the mysteriously lighted viscera.[77]

'Sleep,' writes Proust, 'is 'the only source of invention.'[78] Freud was famously reticent about artistic invention, but on the earliest pages of his work, citing Egger, he allows that we all become artists in the very process of retrieving, retranscribing and transforming our remembered dreams: 'on devient artiste à son insu'.[79] On the very last pages of *The Interpretation of Dreams*, he asks:

> Do not the unconscious impulses revealed in dreams possess the value of real forces in our inner life? Is the ethical significance of our suppressed wishes to be treated as an unconsidered trifle (*gering anzuschlagen*), for just as they create dreams, they may one day create other things?[80]

(Remember: 'We do not allow a mere trifle to disturb our sleep', 'um Geringes lassen wir uns im Schlaf nicht stören'.) Freud is attempting to absolve the dreamer of their moral anxieties; attempting too, no doubt, to dissuade his readers from retreating appalled from the unconscious desires he claims to have uncovered in the dream. But he is also, it seems to me, saying something else. That although dreams are not prophetic, they are generative, forward-looking, not in the predictable but unpredictable sense. Precisely because they lead us back into the deepest recesses of the psyche – to the point where for Proust the psyche goes beyond the psyche – they lead forward into something else.

The only quote on the back of the new English translation of Freud's work (not that Freud needs a publicity blurb) are these lines from a letter of 1899, which wonderfully convey how little is elucidated or settled – all paths are open – even if you think you have left the dark behind:

> The whole thing is planned on the model of an imaginary walk. First comes the dark wood of the authorities (who cannot see the trees). Then there is a cavernous defile through which I lead my readers [. . .] and then, all at once, the high ground and the open prospect and the question: 'Which way do you want to go?'

Things can gain from being unclear. In his last introductory lecture on dreams, Freud cites the Chinese proverb: 'Little what see much what wonderful' to make the point.[81] Much of Milner's book is a critique of present-day educational methods, which she believes are stultifying the creative energies of the child. Likewise Freud seems to be saying, in a rare comment on creativity in that last plea of *The Interpretation of Dreams*, that ethical piety in recoil from the night is killing. It pulls us away from the world of the dream, keeps us awake, and stops us from being able to paint.

Special thanks to the discussion group at Queen Mary College, London University, with whom I read the new translation of *The Interpretation of Dreams* and whose ideas and insights have contributed much to this paper: Amanda Dackombe, Matt Ffytche, the late Sandra Lahire, Lisa O'Sullivan, Maeve Pearson, Aimee Shalan and Drew Shaw.

References

1 Sigmund Freud, *The Interpretation of Dreams* (1900; Oxford: Oxford University Press, 1999; *Die Traumdeutung*, *Studienausgabe*, Frankfurt: Fischer, 1972), p. 65; p. 100; page reference to German follows reference to translation.

2 Ibid., p. 329; p. 486.

3 Freud, *The Interpretation of Dreams, The Standard Edition of the Complete Psychological Works* (London: Hogarth Press, 1953) 5, p. 506n; p. 486.

4 Freud, 'An Outline of Psychoanalysis', 1938, *Standard Edition*, 23, p. 195, *Gesammelte Werke* (Frankfurt: Fischer) 17, p. 126.

5 *SE*, 14, p. 229; *GW*, 10, p. 420.

6 *The Interpretation of Dreams*, p. 75; p. 111.

7 Ibid., p. 9; p. 53.

8 Ibid., p. 177; p. 236.

9 Ibid., p. 176; p. 235.

10 Ibid., p. 387; p. 561.

11 Ernest Jones, *Sigmund Freud: Life and Work*, 2 vols (London: Hogarth Press, 1954–7), 2, p. 292

12 Jeffrey Moussaieff Masson (trans., ed.), *The Complete Letters of Sigmund Freud to Wilhelm Fliess 1887–1904* (Cambridge, MA: Harvard University Press, 1985), p. 357.

13 Ibid., p. 318.

14 Jones, 2, p. 394n

15 Letter of 23 October 1898, Masson, p. 332.

16 *The Interpretation of Dreams*, p. 331; p. 490.

17 Ibid.

18 Ibid., p. 341; p. 503.

19 Ibid., p. 336; p. 495.

20 Freud, *SE*, p. 228; *GW*, p. 420.

21 *Interpretation of Dreams*, pp. 29–30; p. 58.

22 D. W. Winnicott, *The Piggle: An Account of the Psychoanalytic Treatment of a Little Girl* (London: Hogarth Press, 1977), p. 49.

23 *The Interpretation of Dreams*, p. 359; p. 524; *SE*, p. 549.

24 *Project for a Scientific Psychology* (1895; *Standard Edition*, 1), p. 338.

25 Marcel Proust, *A la recherche du temps perdu*, 1913–27, Pléiade edition, 3 vols (Paris: Gallimard, 1954) 2, *Le côté de Guermantes*, 1920, p. 146, p. 163; *In Search of Lost Time*, translation by C. K. Scott Moncrieff and Terence Kilmartin, revised by D. J. Enright, 6 vols (London: Chatto & Windus, 1992); page references to the French follow reference to the translation.

26 *The Interpretation of Dreams*, p. 70; p. 105.

27 Proust, 3, p. 717; 6, p. 32.

28 *The Interpretation of Dreams*, p. 81; p. 121.

29 Ibid., p. 82; p. 122.

30 Freud, *SE*, 7, p. 250; *GW*, 5, p. 5. Also *Interpretation of Dreams*, ibid., p. 121n.

31 Juliet Mitchell, *Mad Men and Medusas: Reclaiming Hysteria and the Effects of Sibling Relations on the Human Condition* (London: Allen Lane, 2000).

32 Masson, p. 202.

33 Ibid., p. 202.

34 Proust, 3, p. 94; 2, p. 88.

35 *Interpretation of Dreams*, p. 377; p. 549.

36 Ibid., p. 45; p. 77.

37 Donald Meltzer, *Dream-Life: A Reexamination of the Psychoanalytical Theory and Technique* (Perth: Clunie, 1984), p. 24.

38 *Interpretation of Dreams*, p. 374; p. 544.

39 Proust, 6, p. 32; 2, p. 335.

40 *Interpretation of Dreams*, pp. 180, 181; p. 240.

41 Ibid., p. 140; p. 195.

42 *SE*, p. 225; *GW*, p. 415.

43 Meltzer, p. 11.

44 Masson, p. 354.

45 *SE*, 23, p. 171; *GW*, 17, p. 93.

46 *SE*, 14, p. 83; *GW*, 10, p. 149.

47 *SE*, 16, p. 218; *GW*, 11, p. 224.

48 Jacques Lacan, *Les quatre concepts fondamentaux de la psychanalyse, Le séminaire XI* (Paris: Seuil, 1973; London: Hogarth Press, 1977), pp. 53–62; pp. 53–64.

49 *Interpretation of Dreams*, p. 147; p. 203.

50 Ibid., p. 188; p. 250.

51 *SE*, p. 222; *GW*, p. 412.

52 *Interpretation of Dreams*, p. 400; p. 574.

53 Ibid., p. 193; p. 256.

54 Ibid., p. 396; p. 570.

55 Ibid., p. 302.

56 *SE*, p. 567; *GW* p. 540.

57 *Interpretation of Dreams*, p. 358; p. 522.

58 Ibid., p. 302.

59 Ibid., pp. 357–8; p. 521.

60 Proust, 3, p. 93; 2, p. 88.

61 *SE*, p. 223; *GW*, p. 413.
62 Proust, 4, p. 185; 2, p. 760.
63 *Interpretation of Dreams*, pp. 291–2; p. 436.
64 Ibid., p. 285; p. 429.
65 Ibid., p. 357; p. 521.
66 Proust, 4, p. 444; 2, p. 985.
67 Ibid.
68 *Interpretation of Dreams*, p. 620; p. 587.
69 Ibid.
70 Proust, 5, p. 132; 3, p. 123.
71 Marion Milner, *On Not Being Able to Paint* (London: Heinemann, 1950), p. 12.
72 Ibid., p. 21.
73 Ibid., pp. 11, 28.
74 Ibid., p. 27.
75 Ibid., p. 25.
76 Ibid., p. 76.
77 Proust, 4, pp. 184–5; 2, p. 760.
78 Ibid., 5, p. 133; 3, p. 124.
79 *Interpretation of Dreams* (citing Egger), p. 41; p. 71.
80 Ibid., p. 411; p. 587.
81 *SE*, 15, p. 231; *GW*, p. 238.

Freud in the Tropics

Another boundary is explored here, between psychoanalysis and Australia, a boundary not exactly crossed, since, despite Freud's intellectual and at moments personal preoccupation with this part of the world, his encounter with it can only be described as failed. Like, indeed, the relationship with Carl Gustav Jung, in which Australia also played its part. In this historic encounter between Freud and Jung, the furthest reaches of the psyche are disturbingly figured in terms of the Aboriginal mind.

Today their dispute can be detached neither from the spreading shadow of anti-Semitism in mid-century Europe, nor from the conflict over Aboriginal rights in Australia which has come to a head in the past decade. The essay was written as a paper to be delivered at the tenth anniversary Congress of the Brisbane Centre for Psychoanalytic Studies which in the end – with a strange symmetry to the forms of disconnection described in the essay – I was unable to attend. It was published in History Workshop Journal, *47, 1999.*

> Whoever wishes not to ignore a truth will do well to distrust his antipathies.
> Sigmund Freud, 'On Psycho-Analysis', paper sent by Freud to be read before the Australasian Medical Congress, Sydney, September 1911.

> 'I wonder if I shall fall right *through* the earth! How funny it'll seem to come out among the people that walk with their heads downwards! The Antipathies, I think— . . . But I shall have to ask them what the name of the country is, you know. Please, Ma'am, is this New Zealand or Australia?'
>> Lewis Carroll, *Alice's Adventures in Wonderland* (1865)

I had not realised until recently how important Australia was to Freud, a fact which may not seem obvious.[1] He never visited Australia, but in 1911 when approached by the secretary of the neuropsychiatric section of the Australasian Medical Congress, 'a Dr

Davidson' who introduces himself as 'a subscriber to the *Jahrbuch* and supporter of psychoanalysis', he wrote the article from which my opening epigraph is taken ('My teachings are still completely unknown in Australia'). 'At least,' he writes to Jung in a letter on sightings of psychoanalysis in distant parts, 'the name [Davidson] sounds familiar.' This, he states with no apparent irony, was 'the first sign of life from Australia', as if – and I think we can be sure that this is more or less what he thought – Australia only comes into being, as a viable psychic entity, when it first discovers Freud.[2]

If this was all there were to it, if this were the long and the short of Freud's engagement with Australia (or rather the short and the short since the piece runs to barely three pages), there would be little to say. But it is far more complex and strange than this. Freud and Jung's correspondence on this topic (they were both, together with Havelock Ellis, asked to submit papers) is hesitant, panicked almost, and fraught. 'I too have received the Australian invitation,' Jung replies. 'What will you write? I really don't know what to do.'[3] Days later Freud replies: 'What to do about Australia? I have been wondering if we couldn't write a short programmatic article for their programme; a few pages extracted from our Worcester lectures – and if we mightn't do it together. I could write something and send it to you to complete or modify; then we could sign it together.'[4] This vision of benign collaboration is, however, not to be. Jung replies, in what it is hard not to read as a combination of insight and wilful mishearing, by assuring Freud that he will not 'be poaching on his preserves'[5] (as if collaboration could only be theft). 'For Australia I had in mind a closer co-operation,' Freud replies, 'but have it your way. I will send you my extract in any case.'[6] In fact, in the end they do not even send each other their papers, which seem to become a source of embarrassment to them both: 'a stupid thing you had better not see' (Jung); 'My business prospectus is going off to Australia tomorrow and is evading your inspection for the same reasons of shame and delicacy that have led your article to evade mine' (Freud).[7]

What, I want to ask in this essay, was the cause of the shame? What can we read in this bizarre and trebly missed encounter with Australia (they do not go, they fail to collaborate, they do not send each other what they write)? What was Australia being used at once to evade and to traffic between them? To say that Australia is a phantom of psychoanalysis may seem overstated, but this is a crucial not to say definitive moment of psychoanalytic history: the rupture between Freud and Jung, already figured in this uneasy exchange, will be more or less clinched in the following year (Freud starts work on *Totem and Taboo* in 1911 and Jung publishes *Symbols of Transformations* in 1912). Australia is also at the heart of this famous and infamous text by Freud. This is from the first page:

> For external as well as for internal reasons, I shall select as the basis for this comparison the tribes which have been described by anthropologists as the most backward and miserable of savages, the aborigines of Australia . . .[8]

The 1998 election in Australia, commonly referred to as the 'race election', could be seen as the election which brought to crisis point, although by no means for the first time, the forms of prejudice which Freud so unapologetically expresses here. It was triggered by the attempt by John Howard, leader of the conservative Liberal–National Coalition, to restrict Aboriginal claims to traditional lands (his Amendment to the Native Title Act proposed to extinguish native title, first granted in the historic Wik decision in 1993, on land already leased to pastoralists). Pauline Hanson, leader of the racist One Nation Party, made huge gains in the Queensland state elections in June although these were not maintained in the federal election in the autumn, when Howard was returned to power. For many, the issue of Aboriginal rights, alongside the uncovering of some of the worst aspects of this history – the systematic confiscation of indigenous children by the state in the 1930s and 40s – made this Australia's election of 'shame' (protestors outside Parliament House in July opposing Howard's Amendment spelt out the word 'shame' with a sea of hands).[9]

I thought it might be interesting, therefore, to return to this early moment of psychoanalysis to see what it might teach us about prejudice in the modern world. But it should be said straight away that there are two things which I will deliberately not be doing. I will not be using psychoanalysis as the analyst of racism, as the discourse which allows us to get some kind of grip on its historic persistence and returns. Nor – despite that quote from *Totem and Taboo* (he had every reason to be ashamed, one might say) – will I be doing the reverse, which is to take psychoanalysis as the cardinal text of prejudice, to accuse it of ethnocentrism; even though this is a charge against which, I should say, I consider it to be defenceless (or at least defenceless as soon as you put it in those terms).

Instead I want to use this occasion to explore the place of Australia in the psychoanalytic imagination. What did Australia force Freud to do with his thought? It seems to me that this historic clash between Freud and Jung stages with startling clarity the forms of blindness and insight likely to beset the Westerner, no less today, in trying to understand, or enter into some dialogue with, another world – although to call it 'another' already begs and settles the question. If you try to confront another system of thinking or way of being in the world, what does it do to – what does it expose, unsettle – about your own? By putting it like this, I am hoping to avoid one kind of psychoanalytic *hubris*. Rather than ask what psychoanalysis might be able to tell us about Australia and its specific crisis of prejudice, my question is: what can Australia, in this weirdly staged encounter from the beginnings of the century, tell psychoanalysis, and the forms of Western thinking which it both embodies and queries, about itself?

For reasons which have, I think, something to do with the anxieties we have already seen passing between Freud and Jung, *Totem and Taboo* proved to be a difficult and worrying text for Freud to write. According to Ernest Jones, 1912 was a particularly anxious and unhappy year for Freud ('early in the year he heard from Jung that there had been a stormy agitation in the Zurich newspapers; psycho-analysis was being angrily attacked'); although he also considered it one of his most productive – 'one of the septennial years with which Freud associated his highest periods of creative activity'.[10] The completion of the work ended the fear, expressed in a letter to Jones early in January 1911, that his 'originality was vanishing'; 'he himself at one moment ranked the work as the best he had ever written'.[11] But in a 1911 letter to Sandor Ferenczi, he described the work as a 'beastly business', forcing him to 'slither' through material which was useless to him: 'With all that I feel as if I had intended only to start a little liaison and then discovered that at my time of life I have to marry a new wife.'[12]

As he approaches the end of the work, Freud is, however, clear

about one thing, that the publication of *Totem and Taboo* will put the
final stamp on the rupture with Jung, deepening the 'gap by fathoms'
and making a 'sharp division between us and all Aryan religiosity'.
'That,' he concludes in a letter to Karl Abraham, 'will be the result of
it.'[13] In a symmetrical judgement, Jung states in the chapter on Freud
of his memoirs that he knew that the chapter on sacrifice with which
he ends *Symbols of Transformation*, published in the same year, 'meant
my own sacrifice'.[14] Clearly then, the conflict over non-Western belief
systems was a struggle over other forms of religious belonging and
faith. Behind Freud and Jung's engagement with sacrifice and ritual,
in which they were equally – and equally passionately – involved at
the same moment, we already discover the barely concealed conflict
between Aryan and Jew.

When *Totem and Taboo* was republished as part of Freud's
Gesammelte Werke in 1934, he chose to include the Preface to the not
yet published Hebrew translation (it appeared in Jerusalem in 1939),
which includes this – perhaps Freud's most famous – statement about
his Jewish identity:

> No reader of [the Hebrew version of] this book will find it easy to put
> himself in the emotional position of an author who is ignorant of the
> language of holy writ, who is completely estranged from the religion of
> his fathers – as well as from every other religion – and who cannot take
> a share in nationalist ideals, but who has yet never repudiated his
> people, who feels that he is in his essential nature a Jew and who has no
> desire to alter that nature. If the question were put to him: 'Since you
> have abandoned all these common characteristics of your countrymen,
> what is there left to you that is Jewish?' he would reply: 'A very great
> deal and probably its very essence.'[15]

In the final break with Jung, Freud will accuse him of hiding
behind a 'religious-libidinal cloud'.[16] 'I own,' he writes on Jung's
rejection of the centrality of incest, 'to a strong antipathy to your
innovation.' (Jung's belief, which would be central to their rupture,
was that the desire for incest was a cover for more adult anxieties and
that the patient who circulates around this dilemma is in flight from
the real challenges of her or his world.)[17] The letter of the previous
year, announcing the dispatch of his 'business prospectus' to
Australia, had warned him more gently that his investigation into the

occult would earn him the tag of mystic, but it concludes with this admonition: 'Don't stay in the tropical colonies too long.'[18] We could say then, that one of the things Freud's going (or rather not going) to Australia forces him to do is to confront his own antipathies.

The bare bones of Freud's argument in *Totem and Taboo*, or rather the version which has been discredited since, have become notorious: Freud's claim to have uncovered the origins of society in the Oedipal struggles of primitive man. Freud found it tedious to write, but it is also one of his texts which for long stretches is inordinately tedious to read, until you get to the juicy bit – I use all these terms advisedly – which is the account of the origins of the incest taboo in the myth of the primal horde (the brothers, rivals for the mother's possession, who unite in the murder of the father and then ritually re-enact his murder in the sacrificial meal as their deferred obedience to his law). 'Society,' as Freud writes in a famous comment, 'was now based on complicity in the common crime.' If kinship 'implies participation in a common substance', it is not just that the shared substance is blood, but that the deed itself was bloody.[19] You can, as commentators have pointed out, drop the myth of origins while retaining Freud's conviction that there is something ineradicably violent about the social tie.

Already I would suggest we can see sketched out here, if not a critique of liberalism, certainly what could be read as a form of advance impatience with any politics seeking, through a shared discourse of shame, to wipe the worst violences of its own history from the collective, national, mind. For Freud, collective identity is unavoidably violent (you unite by placing the enemy on the outside, but the violence will always also be yours). Any attempt to use a purely redemptive language to heal a nation is not only likely to be self-deceptive, but in the long run is almost inevitably bound to fail.

This is from a recent article by anthropologist, Elizabeth A. Povinelli, who acted at the request of the Northern Land Council for the Belyuen in the Kenbi Land Claim, which she describes as the longest-running land claim in Australia. Her article is called 'The State of Shame: Australian Multiculturalism and the Crisis of Indigenous Citizenship':

> the state and its normative publics imagine that their experience of
> radically other cultures and practices can be unhinged from horror and

abjection ... not by refusing to accept the shame, but by embracing, foregrounding, and using it as a source of identification for their political projects. They did not simply trumpet the good of state law, but lamented its villainy, as if the state were not a part of its own institutionality. And in doing so they showed how institutions are claimed to have feelings and how these feeling institutions translate liberation struggles against them into their own legitimation.[20]

Shame, or rather what Povinelli calls the 'legal traffic in shame' can be a front (the question is not whether it is genuine but what does it conceal). It is never more suspect than when it goes public and too boldly declares – Povinelli's word is 'trumpets' – itself. Shame may represent a stage of recognition but it can also serve, through the very intensity of emotion released, to avoid the more difficult material decisions of redistribution which it should logically and historically entail (to whom does the land belong?).

Shame is also something that can be manipulated. Janette Turner Hospital's *Oyster* tells the story of an apocalyptic figure who appears as if from nowhere in an isolated outback community which survives only by believing, or struggling to believe, that it has cut itself adrift from history. Swayed by his false inspirational promise, those who become Oyster's followers then proceed as a group to blow themselves to pieces. The messianic figure of Oyster takes a community to its grave by closing 'everyone in on their shameful secrets': 'How did he make everyone *believe* that he had access to their secret shames?'[21] In this novel, shame is the psychic underbelly of violent, apocalyptic, self-defence. Underneath that final and earth-shattering violence is another one, more corrosive: the violence of a history – of land theft and the forms of violence needed to maintain it – no longer confident that it can justify itself. This is Susannah Rover, one of those who protested and then went missing, who has also taken to reading from *Alice* to signal the insanity of this world (the second epigraph to this essay). Here she is mocking Oyster's language, revealing, one might say, the secret – and shame – of his power.

Blessed are the graziers, she would mock, who live on vast cattle properties and who believe the government is out to get them, for they shall be protected from state and federal interference.[22]

Or in the words of one of Oyster's followers: ' "It's our land they're after, the buggers. World heritage, national parks, the bloody Abos, one damned excuse after another." '[23]

If *Totem and Taboo* has been criticised, it has been first and foremost for the image of the primitive Aborigine on which it is based (the work is subtitled 'Some Points of Agreement between the Mental Life of Savages and Neurotics'). More specifically, it is for its apparent equation between Aborigine and infant, for suggesting that non-Western cultures contain the raw, undeveloped, relics of a former stage of civilisation otherwise only discernible to us in the omnipotent, animistic world view of a child's mind. From the outset, this project is, however, highly ambiguous. Is Freud assuming, as has often been argued, that primitives are childlike? Is it that primitive man represents the childhood, the pre-history, of the race? Or is it that we have something to learn from the rituals of primitive society that we can uncover, get closer to, by observing what we have had to repress (have to go on repressing), at great internal cost, in the psychic life of the child?

'An attempt is made in this volume,' Freud writes in his Preface, which he wrote in Rome in 1913, 'to deduce the original meaning of totemism from vestiges remaining of it in childhood.'[24] This suggests that the child is there to teach us the original meaning of primitive ritual, a meaning recalcitrant to our observations and which study of the so-called primitive cannot in some easy and obvious way be relied on to disclose. When Freud was in Rome completing this Preface, he visited Michelangelo's Moses every day, later describing his feelings for his subsequent essay on this topic, as a 'love-child': 'Only much later did I legitimatise this non-analytic child.'[25] One of the things Freud seems to be struggling with during this time, therefore, is what, exactly, is a child? (If pride is the associated affect of cultural privilege, one of the things a love-child can clearly be is a source of shame.)

In relation to *Totem and Taboo*, the problem is not helped in this instance by translation. The most famous chapter, whose title is translated by Strachey as 'The Return of Totemism in Childhood' is in German 'Die infantile Wiederkehr des Totemismus', which can equally be translated (as it was in the Brill edition of 1919) as 'The Infantile Recurrence of Totemism'. Is it totemism that returns in

childhood, or childhood that recurs in totemism? At the very least, it
is unclear who, in this childhood=primitive equation, is assumed to be
living the most fulfilled of lives, or in the best of all possible worlds:

> I am under no illusion that in putting forward these attempted
> explanations I am laying myself open to the charge of endowing
> modern savages with a subtlety in their mental activities which exceeds
> all probability. It seems to me quite possible, however, that the same
> may be true of our attitude towards the psychology of those races that
> have remained at the animistic level as is true of our attitude towards
> the mental life of children, which we adults no longer understand and
> whose fullness and delicacy of feeling we have in consequence so
> greatly underestimated.[26]

As Ernest Jones put it in his 1924 essay on psychoanalysis and
anthropology, critics of the equation have missed the emphasis on the
unconscious. The primitive is not being accused of acting like a child;
what is at issue is 'not so much a difference between adult and child as
between two modes of thinking which are present in both. Stated in
terms of value, this results in a greater respect for the mind of the
child and a less respect for that of the adult.'[27]

Today we can read *Totem and Taboo* in terms of such diminishing
adult returns (even if Freud's idealisation of primitive and child in
that last quote can of course also be read as merely the other side of
prejudice). But it seems to me that *Totem and Taboo* is one of Freud's
uneasiest texts for good reason. Feminists have noted that his famous
1931 paper on 'Female Sexuality', ostensibly an account of the little
girl's advance into sexual normality, moves rhetorically further and
further back into the intractability of the pre-Oedipal relationship
between the mother and girl child. Likewise, Freud's 1913 narrative
repeatedly undermines the progression on which it putatively relies. It
appears to be giving an account of the advance from 'primitive' to
'civilised', but just as often all the evidence seems to point the other
way. I do not think, for example, that it is only the modern reader
who will be brought short, embarrassed even, by this account of the
adult primitive man's advance from the hallucinatory wish fulfilment
of the infant to a capacity to bend the world to his will: 'His wishes are
accompanied by a motor impulse, the will, which is later destined to
alter the whole face of the earth to satisfy his wishes.'[28] Who, exactly,

is Freud describing here? It is not, that is, only today's reader who will read this as self-diagnosis, a perfect image for the chronic, imperious and colonising advance of the European nation states carving up the modern world. (Between the so-called 'primitive's omnipotence of thoughts and modern, technologically backed, omnipotence of the will, which is the lesser evil?)

Nor are we likely to be so confident now that the ambivalence which Freud characterises as typical of primitive emotion is something to be mastered or surpassed (something about which indeed Freud himself was already in 1913 not so sure). More than Freud, it is Jones – summarising *Totem and Taboo* in his biography – who turns this into a progress narrative: 'What emerges is that primitive peoples have a more intense capacity for ambivalent feelings than civilised ones, or, put otherwise, that the latter have progressed further towards reconciling opposing feelings.'[29] But even this formula is revealing; the two halves of his statement do not add up. Do we know that reconciling ambivalent feelings is an advance on our capacity to sustain them? 'Where, in earlier times,' Freud writes, 'satisfied hatred and pained affection fought each other, we now find that *a kind of scar has been formed in the shape of piety*' (or to put it another way, we are better at duping ourselves).[30] Later he concludes: 'It is possible that psychological conditions in general are unfavourable to getting rid of these antithetical emotions.'[31] Perhaps the Aborigine is better at sustaining what civilised man only thinks he has lost.

Although it will not be until his writings on the Great War that Freud will derive the origins of ethical life from the ambivalence of mourning, he already allows in *Totem and Taboo* that to respect and grieve for the enemy you have slain, like the Aborigine, might be one way – the good enough way – of honouring the dead. Nor, he insists, can denial of paternity among the Arunta be attributed to primitive ignorance (he has been misrepresented on this perhaps more than on anything else), but is instead a form of 'speculation designed to honour the souls of their ancestors'.[32] Maybe biological paternity is an obstacle to forms of belonging not bound or confined to the here and now. Can we envisage a way of being and belonging as 'abiding', our connection to our ancestors as a tribute to place, rather than as lineage, appropriation, possessive familial continuity over time? (this is not of course Freud's question but that of the anthropologist and writer on

Australia, Tony Swain).[33] The epigraph to Book One of *Oyster*, citing Aboriginal voices from *Noonkanhah: Whose Land? Whose Law?*, ends: 'We are walking on top of our old people's bodies.'[34]

When Tony Swain puts his question in *A Place for Strangers: Towards a History of Australian Aboriginal Being*, he runs it back into the history of exile. There is something refusing to be ordered in the Aboriginal mind (hence, we might say, the troubled dynamic of Freud's text). Only a driven people has to mark time. Linear time, Swain speculatively suggests, comes into being with the expulsion of the Jews:

> I would suggest linear time was a 'fall' from place. History, associated quintessentially with the Hebrews, was something which intervened when the Israelites had lost their place. The covenant, God's promise, was to reinstate place but this was only feasible by the Godhead entering a world given over to time. From the moment God said to Abraham 'Leave your country', instead of their place, the Hebrews had history and a promise of land – and *Zakhor*, remembrance [. . .] For Aborigines, as indeed it may have been true for the ancient Hebrews, cosmic time emerged with the breaking of the connection between a land and its people.[35]

What, we can therefore ask again, did Freud want from the Australian Aborigines? What was this Jewish exile, in exile from his people, looking for in *Totem and Taboo*?

'It might be said,' he writes in an extraordinary passage on projection, 'that in the last analysis the "spirit" of persons or things comes down to their capacity to be remembered and imagined after perception of them has ceased.'[36] It is not, after all, only the primitive who 'projects'. Could it be rather that the latter possesses an ability, a mobile capacity to move back and forth across the different strata of the mind:

> It is not, of course, to be expected that either the primitive or the present day concept of a 'soul' will be separated from that of the other portion of the personality by the same line of demarcation which our modern science draws between conscious and unconscious mental activity. The animistic soul unites properties from both sides. Its volatile and mobile quality, its power of leaving the body and of taking

possession, temporarily or permanently, of another body – these are characteristics which remind us unmistakably of the nature of consciousness. But the way in which it remains concealed behind the manifest personality is reminiscent of the unconscious; immutability and indestructibility are qualities which we no longer attribute to conscious but rather to unconscious processes, and we regard the latter as the true vehicle of mental activity.[37]

I want to suggest then that the most productive way to read *Totem and Taboo* is as Freud's dissection – albeit tentative and anxious – of authority, one of the texts in which, for all the drive in the opposite direction, he knows the precariousness of his own reason. This would make the journey of the book not from primitive to civilised, from Australia to Europe, but into the heart of a civilisation that is aware, if only unconsciously, just how shaky it is on the ground. When, in 1931, Freud followed the little girl back into her trouble with mother, he lighted on the question: 'What does she want?' to which feminists have been quick to point out he never provided the reply. But that femininity should vanish into an unanswerable question has also been seen as a perversely satisfactory outcome for those of us who think it is the merit of Freud's 'failure' that something about sexuality remains unknown. Likewise in *Totem and Taboo*, the law is a mystery – to its adherents, to its enforcers and to itself. Taboo, we should not forget, is one half of the story. That a law should operate without reason might tell us something about the unreasonable nature of law. On this topic too the distinction between primitive and civilised man, from the opening page of the book, immediately breaks down. This again from the Preface:

> taboos still exist among us. Though expressed in negative form and directed towards another subject-matter, they do not differ in their psychological nature from Kant's 'categorical imperative', which operates in a compulsive factor and rejects any conscious motives.[38]

The myth of primal murder will be Freud's way of trying to give back substance to this distinction. Instead of the law's origins being unknowable, which implicates all cultures equally, they become unconscious – it is modern man's legacy to bear the repressed history of a more primitive world (guilt is our reluctantly inherited memory of the original crime). At the very least this narrative serves to redraw the lines. But Freud knows that his thesis is 'monstrous' (his word), like the law – punitive, ungraspable, relentless – which it is meant to ground.[39] He knows, that is, that you cannot ask the 'primitive' to carry the weight of what is most inscrutable and paradoxical about the law. Authority is something protective and terrifying in and of itself: the Nubas of East Africa believe they can evade the death which follows entry into the house of a priestly king by having him lay his hand on their shoulder: 'Here we are met by the remarkable fact that contact with the king is a remedy and protection against contact with the king.'[40] A ruler, Freud comments citing Frazer, 'must not only be guarded, he must also be guarded against': 'Some of the taboos laid upon barbarian kings remind one vividly of the restrictions imposed upon murderers.'[41]

If a king needs protection, it is also of course because death marks the limit to his power. How best should a king, or a leader – Freud for example – react to the prospect of his own demise? to the first stirrings of dissent? In March 1912, Jung ends a letter to Freud with this quotation from Nietzsche ('Let Zarathustra speak for me'):

One repays a teacher badly if one remains only a pupil.
And why, then, should you not pluck at my laurels?
You respect me; but how if one day your respect should tumble?
Take care that a falling statue does not strike you dead![42]

In November 1912, Freud and Jung, together with a group of analysts, met in Munich to discuss Freud's plan of leaving the *Zentralblatt* to Stekel and of founding a new international journal. At this famous encounter, which consolidated the differences between them (Freud to Putnam: 'I shall hardly be able to accept his modification of the libido theory since all my experience contradicts his position'),[43] Freud fainted in the same room in which he had a similar experience four and six years before. On his return, Jung writes to Freud: 'I am glad we were able to meet in Munich, as this was the first time I have really understood you. I realised how different I am from you.' 'This realisation,' he insists, 'will be enough to effect a radical change in my whole attitude. Now you can rest assured that I shall not give up on our personal relationship. Please forgive the mistakes I will not try to excuse or extenuate.'[44]

Freud responds by describing his Munich attack as a repetition, 'a bit of neurosis that I ought really to look into' (in a letter to Jones in December he attributes the syndrome more revealingly to his early relationship to Fliess: 'some unruly homosexual feeling at the root of the matter').[45] But Jung will not let matters rest. As far as he is concerned, this 'bit of neurosis' 'should be taken very seriously indeed because, as experience shows, it leads "usque ad instar voluntariae mortis" ["to the semblance of voluntary death"]'. According to Jones, Freud's first words when he came to after Jung carried him to a couch, were: 'How sweet it must be to die.'[46] As Jung sees it, there are no lengths to which Freud will not go to avoid a challenge to his authority:

> As for this bit of neurosis, may I draw your attention to the fact that you open *The Interpretation of Dreams* with the mournful [*sic*] admission of your own neurosis – the dream of Irma's injection – identification with the neurotic in need of treatment. Very significant.

He continues:

> Our analysis, you may remember, came to a stop with your remark that 'you could not submit to analysis *without losing your authority*'. These words are engraved on my memory as a symbol of everything to come.[47]

For Freud, however, no analyst should apologise for identifying with the patient: 'It is a convention among us analysts,' he writes in the letter in which he breaks off their personal relationship, 'that none of us need feel ashamed of his own bit of neurosis.'[48]

So what is the (mournful) tie linking authority to identification? Why does it bring their relationship to grief? Jung's reproach to Freud could be rephrased as a question. Does psychoanalysis – does the psychoanalyst – gain or lose from entering into the distress and disorder it aims to analyse? Or to put it another way, is proximity to the unconscious a good or bad thing? Several years ago, Hannah Segal responded to my suggestion that some of her remarks during the course of an interview might be construed as homophobic, by amending the text to include the statement, axiomatic for analysts as she saw it, that 'there but for the grace of God go I'. This seemed to me to make matters considerably worse: thanking God for not being a homosexual is not my idea of how to get close. It all depends – the problem we have seen Freud struggling with in *Totem and Taboo* – on whether you think psychoanalysis is a myth of progress, of civilised advance and advantage, a way of leaving something distasteful (primitive?) behind. One man's privilege is another man's shame. Or to put it another way, is losing your authority – your distance, your normality, your belief in the logic of your own thought – something to be ashamed of? To whom does the neurosis, and the shame, properly belong?

In response to Jung's challenge, Freud replies: 'Let each of us pay more attention to his own than to his neighbour's neurosis'[49] – the words on which almost *verbatim* he had ended the paper he had sent to Australia the previous year: 'Whoever wishes not to ignore a truth will do well to distrust his antipathies, and, if he wishes to submit the theory of psycho-analysis to a critical examination, let him first analyse himself.'[50] Antipathies might, however, be the hardest thing to relinquish (as he himself had put it to Jung: 'I own to a strong antipathy to your innovation').[51] Jung's reply is enraged:

> May I say a few words to you in earnest? I admit the ambivalence of my feelings towards you, but am inclined to take an honest and absolutely straightforward view of the situation. If you doubt my word so much the worse for you. I would, however, point out that your technique of treating your pupils like patients is a *blunder*. In that way you produce either slavish sons or impudent puppies [. . .] I am objective enough to see through your little trick. You go around sniffing out all the symptomatic acts in your vicinity, thus reducing everyone to the level of sons and daughters who blushingly admit the existence of their faults. [. . .]
>
> You see, my dear Professor, as long as you hand out this stuff I don't give a damn for my symptomatic actions; they shrink to nothing in comparison with the formidable beam in my brother Freud's eye. I am not in the least neurotic – touch wood![52]

'[What would] you say,' he concludes, 'to a patient with a tendency to analyse the analyst instead of himself. You would certainly ask him:

"*Who's* got the neurosis?"' 'I wanted to know,' Jung states in his memoirs, 'how one could escape having a neurosis.'[53]

Jung accuses Freud of refusing any challenge to his authority. But on what, we might ask, does psychoanalytic authority rely? On the uprooting of ambivalence? (Remember this was at the heart of *Totem and Taboo*.) In March of this same year Freud had written to Jung that he had uncovered the secret of totemism which 'has long been known to me': 'The source of all taboo and hence of all conscience is ambivalence'; in the same letter he accuses Sabina Spielrein of being 'abnormally ambivalent': 'her destructive drive is not much to my liking because I believe it is personally conditioned' (it is hard not to read this as a forewarning to Jung).[54] Freud, that is, is also on a type of fault-finding mission. Something has to be got rid of, or at the very least be seen – destructively but unambiguously – to belong to somebody else (in the case of Spielrein, Jung's former patient, colleague and lover). Jung promises that if Freud should ever rid himself entirely (*sic*) of his complexes – 'as though,' as he puts it on another occasion, 'that explained anything. A wretched theory'[55] – 'I will mend my ways and at one stroke uproot the vice of being in two minds about you' (is ambivalence a vice?). He then challenges him: 'Do you *love neurotics* enough to be always at one with yourself? But perhaps you *hate* neurotics. In that case how can you expect your efforts to treat your patiently leniently and lovingly *not* to be accompanied by somewhat mixed feelings.'[56] The Freud/Jung letters beautifully demonstrate that ambivalence – which at the very same moment Freud is attempting, and failing, to hand back to aboriginal man – will not go away.

Once you look at it in these terms, it seems to me that what Freud and Jung are engaged in is a refined – or rather not so refined – form of mudslinging (an expression Freud himself did use: 'Morton Prince is just a mudslinger').[57] In *Memories, Dreams, Reflections*, Jung describes the decisive – and alarming – moment when Freud asked him to promise never to abandon the sexual theory, but to make of it a 'dogma', an 'unshakeable bulwark against the black tide of mud of occultism':

'You see, we must make a dogma of it, an unshakeable bulwark.' . . . In some astonishment I asked him, 'A bulwark – against what?' To which he replied, 'Against the black tide of mud' – and here he hesitated for a moment, then added – 'of occultism.'[58]

But Jung, of course, is no less concerned than Freud to pull psychoanalysis out of the slime. 'It was,' he writes in *Memories, Dreams, Reflections*, 'a profound disappointment that all the efforts of the probing mind had apparently succeeded in finding nothing more in the depths of the psyche than the all too familiar and "all-too-human" limitations':

> Incest and perversion were no remarkable novelties to me, and did not call for any special explanation. Along with criminality, they formed part of *the black lees* that spoiled the taste of life by showing me only too clearly the ugliness and meaningless of human existence. *That cabbages thrive in dung* was something I had always taken for granted . . . enlightenment will [not] cure neurotics; they can only regain their health *if they climb out of the mud* of the commonplace.[59] [My emphasis.]

'The problem still remains,' Jung writes, 'how to overcome or escape our anxiety, bad conscience, guilt, compulsion, unconscious, and instinctuality.' (What, we might ask, for a psychoanalyst is left?)[60]

Symbols of Transformation, Jung's *magnum opus*, makes it clear just how high are the stakes. More than a text *about* sacrifice – Jung knew that the chapter on Freud would mean the sacrifice of his relationship with Freud – this is writing as sacrifice, the ritual re-enactment of the genesis, the purified rebirth, of the world which would otherwise 'wither or end catastrophically in a welter of perversity':[61] 'To the extent that the world and everything in it is a product of thought, the sacrifice of the libido that strives back to the past necessarily results in the creation of the world'; 'The world comes into being when man discovers it. But he only discovers it when he sacrifices his containment in the primal mother, the original state of unconsciousness.'[62]

If Freud and Jung are engaged in mudslinging, they are also playing at mothers and fathers. How much, or who, are they willing to give up in the process of sacrificing each other? It all depends, you might say, on which parent you want, or are willing, to sacrifice. Jessica Benjamin once made a suggestion to me, which I found wholly convincing, that different theoretical preferences among feminists could be partly understood in terms of which parent one was trying to protect. Jung, we might say, is trying to protect the mother from (his) desire. If not apocalyptically, certainly with striking rhetorical violence, he is trying to purify the world and himself. The taboo against incest, he argues in a letter to Freud, is a front: 'Like you I am absorbed in the incest problem and have come to conclusions which show incest primarily as a fantasy problem.' No adult, he continues, really experiences incestuous desires towards the mother: 'what was valuable for the child – the mother – and is so worthless for the adult that it is kicked into the bush'; the problem with the primitive is that, such is the extent of his 'free-floating anxiety' that he regresses, reactivates infantile material and then turns it into a 'ceremony of atonement (as though incest had been, or might have been desired)'.[63] There is, we might say, no real incest, no real desire for the mother, behind the incest taboo. Lust does cover for atonement (rather than the other way round). There is no real shame in shame.

There was a time, Jung suggests, when the father did not count. In fact, he exclaims in parentheses: '(there was no such thing as a father's son!).'[64] Under matriarchy, the father was so fortuitous, promiscuity so general, that he would have had no interest in enacting laws against the son. Freud replies: 'It seems likely that there have been father's sons at all time.'[65] The entry into social being passes inexorably for Freud through the father's law. This would make both theories a type of family romance: one parent has to go. But more profoundly perhaps than this quarrel over which parent, it is for both of them the pull of the mother, the nature of our connection to her – degrading or ennobling, repeated or transcended – which is at stake (after all, if the desire for the mother were not deemed so uncontrollable in Freud's version, the father would not have had to be slain). When Jung reproaches Freud for forcing his patients into a libidinal regression, mimicking the flight of their illness, it seems to be this journey back to the mother to which he most intensely objects. Freud's theory, Jung writes in *Symbols of Transformation*, is 'hysterical'. Like the neurotics he purports to treat, it drags the patient back through worlds and time: 'Freud makes his theory of neurosis – so admirably suited to the nature of neurotics [it is hard not to notice the contempt] – much too dependent on the neurotic ideas from which precisely the patients suffer . . . the theory matches the hysterical attitude that causes the patient to be neurotic.'[66] Today, ironically, this might be seen as a virtue of Freud's theory. That he identifies with his hysterical patients because he knows (if only unconsciously), that he too is a woman, because he knows, even if this identification is no less complex, difficult and at moments demeaning, that he is a Jew.

So, who – to repeat Jung's earlier question to Freud – has got the neurosis? ('I wanted to know how one could escape having a neurosis.')[67] Or to rephrase the question once more: how far can theory detach itself from its object, exempt itself from suffering, climb out of the mire? Should it try? And when it does so, what kind of power or omnipotence of thoughts is it claiming for itself: 'Sacrifice brings with it a plenitude of power that is equal to the power of the gods.'[68] Is it the aim of psychoanalysis to help subjects 'purify' themselves of their past? Or to put it another way, must psychoanalysis unavoidably write its version of beginnings – cultural and psychic – in the image of its worst fears?

In this endlessly renewed struggle, the Australian Aborigine continues to be the reference point: 'Even on the primitive level,' Jung writes, 'among the Australian blackfellows, we meet with the idea that the life-force wears out, turns "bad" or gets lost, and must therefore be renewed at regular intervals. Whenever such an *abaissement* [lowering/degradation] occurs the rites of renewal must be performed.'[69] For a writer like Tony Swain, this is to read the world upside down. For Aboriginal culture, staying close to earth, matter, is the only true state in which to be. Only when the earth had been impoverished by the violence of colonial contact did power come to reside in the sky. It is the particular, admiral quality of their response to that violence, that the Aboriginals refuse apocalyptic solutions to their dilemma (unlike Jung and unlike Turner Hospital's Oyster, we might say):

> [they adopt] the possibility that the reestablishment of moral equilibrium might only be attainable by purging the world of intrinsically bad (evil) elements. I argue, however, that Aboriginal people resisted allowing that possibility to become a means of salvation.[70]

It may seem too obvious to conclude that – although there is much to learn from their conversation – it is not the Australian Aborigine that either Jung or Freud are, or were ever, talking about.

Finally, I think it is important to remember that this quarrel between Freud and Jung on the nature of Aboriginal culture, or rather on the place of the Aborigine in the history and mind of mankind, took place on the eve of the First World War. That a kind of apocalypse was about to descend on the land of Europe (the Great War was seen by many as the end of European civilisation). This was also the war which allowed Claude Lévi-Strauss to open his famous 1962 book on *Totemism* with a description of the totemic behaviour of the 42nd or 'Rainbow' Division ('a name chosen because it was composed of units from so many states that their regimental colours were as varied as those of the rainbow').[71] The men started by believing that the appearance of a rainbow was a happy omen, then that a rainbow could be seen every time they went into action ('in spite of incompatible meteorogical conditions'), then took to wearing a badge in the form of a rainbow ('in spite of the belief that the wearing of distinctive insignia had its origin in a punishment inflicted on a defeated unit'), until by the end of the war the American Expeditionary Force was organised into 'a series of well-defined and often mutually jealous groups each of which had its individual complex of ideas and observances'.[72] The emergence of this behaviour did much, Lévi-Strauss comments, to contribute to recent indifference to the problem of totemism after the 1920s (Lévi-Strauss presents his book as a return to the theme). What can it tell us about non-Western cultures if man at the height of modern military endeavour behaves in exactly the same way?

I want to end, however, with the war that came after, the one that broke out a few weeks before Freud's death when there was no longer any contact between Freud and Jung. I have a second-hand copy of Edward Glover's 1950 *Freud or Jung*.[73] Loose inside I discovered a copy of two undated letters to a newspaper, which I have not managed to identify, on the subject of 'Jung and Nazism', one of which includes these lines by Jung from *Zentralblatt für Psychotherapie*, Volume 7, 1934:

In my opinion it has been a grave mistake on the part of psychological medicine to apply Jewish categories uncritically to German Christians, for in doing so it has declared that precious secret of Germanic man, the creative-visionary foundation of his soul, to be a childish-banal swamp. He did not know the Germanic soul – as little as all his successors knew it. Has the powerful phenomenon of National Socialism, at which the whole world looks with astonishment, made them realise their error?[74]

Notes and References

1   I would like to thank Mary O'Brien of the Brisbane Center for Psychoanalytic Studies for all the information and documents which she sent me about contemporary Australian politics, and Robyn Davidson for her much appreciated suggestions and the material she shared with me.

2   Freud to Jung, 14 March 1911, *The Freud/Jung Letters*, edited by William McGuire, translated Ralph Manheim and R. F. C. Hull (London: Hogarth Press and Routledge & Kegan Paul, 1974), pp. 404–5.

3   Jung to Freud, 19 March 1911, ibid., p. 407.

4   Freud to Jung, 25 March 1911, ibid., p. 409.

5   Jung to Freud, 28 March 1911, ibid., p. 410.

6   Freud to Jung, 30 March 1911, ibid., p. 411.

7   Jung to Freud, 8 May 1911; Freud to Jung, 18 May 1911, ibid., pp. 420, 422.

8   Freud, *Totem and Taboo: Some Points of Agreement between the Mental Life of Savages and Neurotics* (1913; *Standard Edition*, 13, London: Hogarth Press), p. 1.

9   Christopher Zinn, 'Aboriginals win title to the sea', *Guardian*, 7 July 1998. Howard's aim was to reverse the Wik Decision of 1993 which granted native title to the Wik and Thayorre people claiming rights over land where two pastoral leases had been granted by the Queensland government. Much of my information comes from *The Ten Point Plan on Wik and Native Title: Issues for Indigenous Peoples*, Wik Team, Aboriginal and Torres Strait Island Commission, June 1997, and *Coexistence: Negotiation and Certainty. Indigenous Position in Response to the Wik Decision and the Government's Proposed Amendments to the Native Title Act*, prepared by the National Indigenous Working Group on Native Title, April 1997. For a discussion of the dispute over evidence in these cases, especially with reference to the place of Aborigine women, see Beatrix Campbell, 'The autumn of the matriarch', *Guardian Weekend*, 15 March 1997.

10 Ernest Jones, *Sigmund Freud: Life and Work*, 2 (London: Hogarth Press, 1955), pp. 103, 392.

11 Ibid., pp. 392, 103.

12 Ibid., p. 394.

13 Ibid., 2, p. 396.

14 Carl Gustav Jung, *Memories, Dreams, Reflections* (London: Collins and Routledge & Kegan Paul, 1964), p. 163.

15 Freud, *Totem and Taboo*, Preface to the Hebrew translation, p. xv.

16 Freud to Jung, 18 February 1912, *Freud/Jung Letters*, p. 485.

17 Freud to Jung, 23 May 1912, ibid., p. 316.

18 Freud to Jung, 12 May 1911, ibid., p. 422.

19 Freud, *Totem and Taboo*, pp. 146, 135.

20 Elizabeth A. Povinelli, 'The State of Shame: Australian Multiculturalism and the Crisis of Indigenous Citizenship', *Critical Inquiry*, 24:2 (special issue on *Intimacy*), (Winter 1998), pp. 581–2.

21 Janette Turner Hospital, *Oyster* (London: Virago edition, 1996), pp. 166, 266.

22 Ibid., p. 263.

23 Ibid., p. 282.

24 Freud, *Totem and Taboo*, Preface, p. xiv.

25 Ernest Jones, *Sigmund Freud*, 2, p. 411.

26 Freud, *Totem and Taboo*, p. 99.

27 Ernest Jones, 'Psycho-Analysis and Anthropology', 1924, *Essays in Applied Psycho-Analysis*, Vol. 2: *Essays in Religion and Folklore* (London: Hogarth Press, 1951), p. 128.

28 Freud, *Totem and Taboo*, p. 84.

29 Jones, *Sigmund Freud*, 2, p. 400.

30 Freud, *Totem and Taboo*, p. 66 (my emphasis).

31 Ibid., p. 145.

32 Ibid., p. 118.

33 Tony Swain, *A Place For Strangers: Towards a History of Australian Aboriginal Being* (Cambridge: Cambridge University Press, 1993).

34 Hospital, *Oyster*, p. 15.

35 Swain, *A Place For Strangers*, pp. 27, 287.

36 Freud, *Totem and Taboo*, p. 94.

37 Ibid.

38 Ibid., Preface, p. xiv.

39 Ibid., p. 142. For an extensive discussion of this question in relation to *Totem and Taboo*, see Mikkel Borch-Jacobsen, 'The Law of Psychoanalysis', *diacritics* (Summer 1985).

40 Freud, *Totem and Taboo*, p. 42.

41 Freud, citing Frazer, ibid., pp. 41, 35.

42 Jung to Freud, 3 March 1912, *Freud/Jung Letters*, p. 491.

43 Freud to Putnam, 28 November 1912, cited ibid., p. 522.

44 Jung to Freud, 26 November 1912, ibid., p. 522.

45 Jones, *Sigmund Freud*, 1, p. 348.

46 Ibid. In his memoirs, Jung describes a dream presaging his break with Freud in which he encounters the stooped figure of a customs official who had died some years ago: ' "He is one of those who could not die properly." ' *Memories, Dreams, Reflections*, p. 158.

47 Jung to Freud, 3 December 1912, *Freud/Jung Letters*, p. 527.

48 Freud to Jung, 3 January 1913, ibid., p. 539.

49 Freud to Jung, 5 December 1912, ibid., p. 529.

50 Freud, 'On Psycho-Analysis', (1913; *Standard Edition*, 12) pp. 210–11.

51 Freud to Jung, 23 May 1912, *Freud/Jung Letters*, p. 507.

52 Jung to Freud, 18 December 1912, ibid., pp. 534–45.

53 Jung, *Memories, Dreams, Reflections*, p. 162.

54 Freud to Jung, 21 March 1912, *Freud/Jung Letters*, pp. 494–5.

55 Jung to Freud, 3 December 1912, ibid., p. 526.

56 Jung to Freud, 18 December 1912, ibid., p. 535.

57 Freud to Jung, 27 April 1912, ibid., p. 501.

58 Jung, *Memories, Dreams, Reflections*, pp. 147–8.

59 Ibid., p. 161.

60 Ibid., p. 149.

61 Jung, *Symbols of Transformation: An Analysis of a Prelude to a Case of Schizophrenia* (1912; revised edition, 1952; London: Routledge & Kegan Paul, 1956), Chapter 7, 'The Sacrifice', p. 432.

62 Ibid., p. 415.

63 Jung to Freud, 27 April, 8 May, 17 May 1912, *Freud/Jung Letters*, pp. 502–6. In his reply to Jung's letter of May 17, Freud compares Jung's theory to Adler's who also claims the neurotic has 'no desire at all for his mother, but wants to provide himself with a motive for scaring himself away from his libido; he therefore pretends to himself that his libido is so enormous that it does not even spare his mother'; and then comments, 'This still strikes me as fanciful, based on utter incomprehension of the unconscious.' Freud to Jung, 23 May 1912, ibid., p. 507.

64 Jung to Freud, 8 May 1912, ibid., p. 503.

65 Freud to Jung, 14 May 1912; Jung to Freud, 8 May 1912, ibid., pp. 503–4.

66 Jung, *Symbols of Transformation*, pp. 419–20.

67 Jung, *Memories, Dreams, Reflections*, p. 162.

68 Jung, *Symbols of Transformation*, p. 420.

69 Ibid., p. 432.

70 Swain, *A Place for Strangers*, p. 118.

71 Claude Lévi-Strauss, *Totemism* (1962; Boston: Beacon Press, 1963), p. 7.

72 Citing R. Linton, ibid., p. 7.

73 Edward Glover, *Freud or Jung* (London: Allen & Unwin, 1950). Glover was at the heart of the controversies about the future of psychoanalysis after Freud. Originally a supporter of Melanie Klein in the dispute with Anna Freud, he went on to become one of her strongest critics.

74 Part of this quotation appears in Andrew Samuels's discussion of Jung and anti-Semitism, *The Political Psyche*, Chapter 12: 'Jung, Anti-Semitism and the Nazis' (London: Routledge, 1993).

Of Knowledge and Mothers:
On the Work of Christopher Bollas

No English-speaking psychoanalyst captures as vividly as Christopher Bollas the dilemma of psychoanalysis in relation to unconscious processes which cannot be known. In his sometimes hallucinatory evocation of mental states beyond our grasp, he therefore takes up his place in the company of other writers in this collection, literary and psychoanalytic, for whom the project of writing is to seize something too evanescent or painful for the conscious mind. Freud famously could not talk about mothers, but the mother is central to Bollas's thought. The question here, which links back to the essay on Sylvia Plath, is: does the woman, do mothers, only enter the frame as culpable; or does the mother, when she makes her appearance, usher in something unspeakable, exposing the limits of what any language can know about itself? The essay was first delivered as a paper at a conference to celebrate Christopher Bollas's work, organised by the Independent Group of Psychoanalysts and held at the Institute of Psychoanalysis in June 1995. It was subsequently published in the new US psychoanalytic journal, Gender and Psychoanalysis, *in 1996.*

About ten years ago a student who had been taking a course on Freud and feminism with me at the University of Sussex, came to me in a state of some anxiety. It seemed to her, from her reading of the late papers on femininity, that psychically speaking there were only mothers in the world. If the boy desires the mother, and if the girl's main psychological task is to detach herself from a maternal presence whose traces are never fully dispersed, then all love objects are in a sense mothers. (In first marriages, Freud argues, it is the relationship to the mother that surfaces and most often as not wrecks the home.) Or to put it more crudely, there is no getting away from mothers. They are there where you least expect them, most troublingly when you thought you had left them behind.

I must admit that I did not have a way of alleviating this student's anxiety, since it seemed to me she had touched on something important. No amount of trying to stress the infinite plasticity of the unconscious, the fluidity, transferability, mobility of its objects quite worked – which should suggest the opposite, that there is no stopping point, that whoever you think you are dealing with, it is always also somebody else. It was as if everything we had discussed, with equal emphasis, about unconscious process was in a sense powerless in the face of this mother, her capacity to draw back everything to herself. Freud famously ignored the mother, but as many commentators have pointed out, her figure haunts the work.[1] The somewhat triumphant, absolute, nature of her arrival on the scene of those late papers bears all the marks, one might say, of the return of the repressed.

I start with this anecdote because what the student experienced is, I think, not wholly dissimilar to the feeling I find myself experiencing whenever I read the work of Christopher Bollas. There is, I think, no psychoanalytic writer in English – and this becomes more and more the case in the most recent writing – who conveys such a strong sense of the ungraspable unconsciousness of the unconscious, and the endless, unstoppable, play of its work. But equally, there is no psychoanalytic writer who gives me such a strong, and at moments sinking, sense of the utter unmovability of the mother. This essay will address what I see as the dynamic tension between these two components of the writing: between on the one hand the unconscious as a limit to knowledge, as a break on what it is possible for any subject of the unconscious to know of either the other or herself; and on the other hand, the mother as a figure there to be uncovered, the one you always somehow knew would be there.

Freud himself provides a precedent for the relationship between mothers and the question of knowledge in his (1925) paper on 'Negation'. At the start of the essay, in what might appear as an exemplary moment of self-analysis, he uses the example of denial of the mother to usher in the discussion of the origins of thought: ' "You ask who this person in the dream can be. It's *not* my mother." We emend this to: "So it *is* his mother." '[2] (In Freud's paper, the mother stands twice over in the place of knowledge. First in this example, for analytic certainty, the moment when the analyst can be most unswervingly sure. But as the paper unfolds, she appears again, this time as the founding condition of judgement since it is in relation to her body that the function of acceptance and rejection of what constitutes a world comes to be. 'To affirm or negate the content of thoughts is the task of the function of intellectual judgement [. . .] Expressed in the language of the oldest – the oral – instinctual impulses, the judgement is "I should like to eat this", or "I should like to spit this out." '[3] In this famously dense paper, Freud manages, not for the first time, to set the mother up as blindness and insight. No one is so inept, so embarrassingly giveaway as the mother-denying patient, but without a capacity for denial, grounded in that primordial connection to her body, there would be no such thing as thought.

It is customary to read the development of object-relations theory in Britain, with its focus on the mother, as remedying a glaring deficiency in Freud. My question, however, is not whether we should be talking about mothers – I assume that on the whole to be a very good thing – but what happens to our relationship to knowledge when mothers are around. When the traces of the mother are uncovered in analysis, is it the end of the line? Can we think about mothers and keep an open mind? Can we think ironically about mothers? (This is not the same as Winnicott's question as to whether a mother can relate playfully, ironically, tongue-in-cheek or, in Christopher Bollas's most recent work, comically with her child.) What does thinking about mothers do to thinking? If you make the mother *the* unconscious object, what hermeneutic arrest have you stumbled into, what violence have you committed to the unconscious as process, or to use one of Bollas's most famous formulas, to the category of the 'unthought'?

In fact that's only half his formula, only half the story, since his concept is more exactly the 'unthought known'. To put the question in terms closer to the language or spirit of his work: is the 'unthought known' the place where knowledge unravels from its own self-possession, from its pretension *as* knowledge; or is it the place where the mother, the imprint of her care on the being of the subject, is once and for all to be found? Are we dealing, to use his own words from an essay in *Being A Character*, with 'a force of dissemination that moves us to places beyond thinking';[4] or, by analogy with the mother in one of her most famous incarnations of stereotypes, with a type of first and last resting place? And if the second, does the mother acquire the status of only truth or rather the only place – given that psychoanalysis could be said to have made the idea of one truth its first casualty –

where truth is still allowed to be? It is probably already clear what I would like the answer to that question to be, but of course nothing is ever that simple.

It has often been pointed out that the mother has a lot to answer for in the writings of the Independent School. These quotes are almost all taken from *The Shadow of the Object*, Bollas's first collection of essays; 'his mother's absence'; 'his disappearing and dismissive mother'; 'the refusing mother'; 'the contagious confusion of the mad mother'; 'strange and absent mother'; 'cumulatively dis-incarnated by maternal failure'; and perhaps most devastating of all, 'she hired a nanny'.[5] It is, one could fairly say, and especially in the early work, something of a refrain. But it seems to me to be a trap, too easy – although that is exactly what I have just done – to just list these instances, to see them only as marking a blindspot in the writing, where one feminism, the feminism that sees psychoanalysis as a pure emanation of patriarchy, would read the ideological prejudice of a whole tradition, and one form of psychoanalysis (the Lacanian) would see a failure to acknowledge the absence at the heart of being, a way of laying at the door of the mother what is irredeemable about human desire.

One of the problems of those kinds of objection, even though they may each have a crucial point, is that they blind themselves to the institutional histories out of which theories are made and unmade. It therefore seems important to recognise the argument to which this appeal to the mother belongs. What worse fates is this dreadfully failing mother being called on to save us from? Paradoxically, it seems as if this hopeless mother, in relation to whom no doubts are entertained, is intended to ward off another form of certainty, knowledge, omniscience. In a strange twist, which I see as central to Bollas's project, the dulling sameness of her invocation is designed to protect the patient from the potential tyranny of psychoanalysis itself. Better her neglect than its coercion. Better to have been overlooked in the beginning than to find yourself bound, in the analytic setting, to an interpretive presence that won't let go. More explicitly, this emphasis on the mother's powers, in the reality of a patient's past, to move and stall a life – a power I would not wish to dispute – has two targets. On the one hand it is aimed at Kleinian hermeneutic confidence about deep phantasy, on the other at the version of object-relations interpretation which reads everything in the analytic setting in terms of that setting alone, as having as its sole referent, with a no less oppressive sameness, the analytic here-and-now. As Bollas puts it, not without a trace of irony, in the final paper of *Forces of Destiny*, his second collection of essays: 'the British analysts of the 1940s freed the boring patient from the analyst's narcoleptic countertransference [. . .] by understanding the patient's narrative as a metaphor of the patient's ego experience of the analytic object, the clinician was suddenly alive in a field of meaningful plenty'.[6] Ignoring the mother, the analyst makes himself significant.

Bollas's constant reference to the mother is, if I have understood correctly, part of an appeal to history. Hence his repeated stress on her actuality. Again, despite my own caveat, I found myself listing the number of times, also in the early work, that the insistence on a concrete retrievable reality appeared, a reality almost invariably given the status of single determinant or cause: 'This is *objective fact*'; 'a belief that was *a fact* in his infantile life'; not meaning, as it might appear, that his phantasy was a psychic reality to the child, but that his belief accurately reflected his world: 'It *was a fact* that neither parent, for different reasons, could identify with their child's needs' (this is both parents, but it is the mother's disappearance early in the child's life that precipitates the problem); 'an *actual family setting* with which [the ego] cannot cope'[7]. 'It is a source of puzzlement,' writes Bollas in disagreement with Bion who, as he sees it, attributes the source of the child's attacks on alpha functioning to the child alone:

> why madness within the mother or the father, or between the parents, or in that atmosphere that is created by all participants in the child–parent interaction, should be eliminated as one of the potential sources of disturbance in the child's development of alpha function.[8]

If we place the work in this tradition, it seems clear that, after Winnicott, Bollas wants to reassert early environment against fantasy, what is done to the infant against what the infant or patient projects on to her world. But in Bollas's case, the argument about reality avoids the obvious critique – that this move is a positivist reduction, that psychoanalysis must be about phantasy before anything else – because of the way it is constantly run into the question of knowledge. (How much can we ever know? How sure can or should the analyst ever be?) It is almost as if the irreducible nature of phantasy, partially or momentarily lost to the objective facts of the case, resurfaces in the form of a radical uncertainty which gives back to the unconscious its greatest unsettling force. And in so far as it was in relation to the mother that Bollas seemed originally so sure, it is appropriately her figure who stands to lose (or rather gain) most from such any such loss of conviction. By linking the Winnicottian stress on environment to the question of knowledge, Bollas therefore opens up a rift in his own work which allows us fruitfully to track the implications of this centring of the mother for the category of the unconscious. For the rest of this essay, I want to trace the ways in which his writing incrementally unravels that early hermeneutic certainty about the mother and in the process provides some dramatic and at moments disturbing insights into what a mother can carry, for theory, for analysis, for being a subject in the world.

There is a moment in H. D.'s *Tribute to Freud*, the poet's account of her analysis with Freud in Vienna, when she describes the symptom – writing on the wall – which of all her symptoms, he confessed to finding most disturbing: 'of a series of strange experiences, the Professor picked out only one as being dangerous, or hinting of a danger or a dangerous tendency or symptom'.[9] Freud analyses this hallucinated writing as desire for union with the mother, but later he comments: 'I must tell you (you were frank with me and I will be frank with you), I do *not* like to be the mother in the transference – it always surprises and shocks me a little. I feel so very masculine.'[10] On the wall, or off the wall ('Off the Wall' is the title of one of Bollas's papers from his second book), what flashes up as a moment of danger in H. D.'s symptom, and the moment of analytic frankness it precipitates, is the point where the boundaries of consciousness are transgressed, where the limits between inside and outside, between a subject and the world of objects that surround her, breaks down. As with the 'oceanic feeling', which in his famous exchange with Romain Rolland he declared himself immune to, Freud responds by an intimate confession which in fact involves a rigid redemarcation of lines.[11]

If object-relations theory, in its Winnicottian form, has taken upon itself to enter the space where Freud did not dare to tread, this particular form of danger – that there might be a world without boundaries where all founding distinctions are lost – seems, for the most part, to have been ignored (rerepressed one might say). Indeed, you could argue that the emphasis on the adequacy and inadequacy of the mother – what she can and should do – has served to make safe or occlude this space: not the space of a necessary lack-in-being in Lacanian terms, but the opposite, a space too full, a space that will become our dream of the mother, but which is in fact a space with no single origin, and for which no one is accountable, where the divisions inside my own mind, and between me and the other, are unclear. One of Bollas's strongest early points – and a great deal follows from here – is that if Freud refused the mother as referent, he more than embraced her into the setting of analysis (Freud's blindness as the insight of analytic work). It would then be possible to read Bollas's writing as going back over this ground, unearthing its latent implications, shadowing forth its hidden shape.

More and more in the essays, analysis is a dream setting, 'a kind of *countertransference dreaming*', a meeting of one unconscious with another, the analyst as 'medium', processing in his body the unintegrated instincts and affects of a hysteric with nowhere else to go.[12] If at first this feels like an extraordinary maternal idealisation of the analytic encounter, in which feminism would see simply the inverse image of the mother who fails, it is only for a moment. And that is because the very movement which makes of this analyst all-receiver, reparative mnemic trace for what failed before, also dissolves all identity, wrests from us any certainty of being, turns us into shadows, spirits, ghosts.

'I seem to be saying,' writes Bollas in 'Off the Wall', 'that analysts are mediums for the psycho–somatic processing of the patient's psyche-soma'; or again, from *Cracking Up*, the analyst bears 'the analysand's psychic state in his own body'.[13] This quote from the title article of *Being a Character* could, I think, be taken as a type of manifesto of the later work, certainly for the last two books:

> Being a character means that one is a spirit, that one conveys something in one's being which is barely identifiable as it moves through objects to create personal effects, but which is more deeply graspable when one's spirit moves through the mental life of the other, to leave its trace.[14]

The opening essay of *Cracking Up*, 'Communications of the Unconscious', draws out even further the extent to which, if you go down this path, what you begin to lose is the possibility of any conviction that there are, conventionally speaking, two separate consciousnesses in a room. 'Unconscious Communication' takes off from this remark from Freud's paper on 'The Unconscious': 'It is a very remarkable thing that the *Ucs* of one human being can react upon that of another, without passing through the *Cs*.'[15] We are close here to telepathy which, as other recent commentators have pointed out, is, no less than femininity, an undercurrent to Freud's work (not in either case its wild fringe, but something whose links with the discoveries of psychoanalysis are unavoidable but difficult because in each case they push it over its own theoretical edge).[16] First dismissed by Freud, telepathy then *returns* in the 1932 essay 'Dreams and Occultism', rather like mothers we might say (everything clearly returns to the 1930s). 'The phenomenon of thought-transference,' Freud writes, 'which is so close to telepathy and can indeed without much violence be regarded as the same thing'; 'by inserting the unconscious between what is physical and what was previously called "psychical" [psychoanalysis], has paved the way for the assumption of such processes as telepathy'.[17]

It seems to me therefore that there are two very different mothers, or fantasies of the mother, at work in Christopher Bollas's writing. Mother as fact, the one safe haven of interpretation; but then mother, or her space, as the vanishing point of all identities, where no form of knowing could ever reach. For if it is the case that in this second space subjects pass through each other like spirits in the night, more intimate, closer than any other form of contact could hope to be, the one thing that Bollas insists on is that this insight spells the end of the fantasy that subjects could ever know each other, or be known. 'It is interesting,' he continues in 'Communications of the Unconscious', 'that psycho-analysis, which would have us look truth in the eye, also makes use of the most powerful illusion we generate: that we convey ourselves to other people'.[18]

Compare that comment with this one from 'The Analyst's Multiple Function': 'Is not one pleasure of loving and being loved the realisation that one is truly known . . . In other words, to love and to be loved is an act of deep appreciative knowing.'[19]

And here is the mother: 'Maternal care, then, is a knowing that is an act of love, and whether we have our right to a destiny or whether we are to have a fate will, in my view, depend on whether a mother can love her infant in a knowing way.'[20] Which I would simply wish to qualify, to save the child from such maternal omniscience, with this remark by Bollas from 'Off the Wall': 'Each analyst who comes to know his patient [. . .] must unknow him.'[21]

Paradoxically, then, it is by invoking the maternal space as powerfully as he does, pushing the metaphor as one might say to its furthest limits, that Bollas himself 'unknows' the mother, undoes her as referent, placing the whole scenario – what it is to be an analyst, a patient, a human subject – beyond knowing's reach. Hence my sense that the most immediate feminist response to this tradition, crucial as it is, is too limiting. For if you simply demand that the Winnicottian image of the mother be modified – saved from her total accountability, recognised even more fully than he did in its radical ambivalence – or more simply demand that she be given her own voice (when does a mother get to speak, where are the case studies of women as mothers in the work?), you none the less remain essentially in the same referential frame.[22] As long as the question remains: what would be a truer representation of the mother, the limits of knowledge as knowledge remain untouched. Which is not to dismiss that question but to suggest that things become even more complex when we throw the unconscious back into the frame. Speaking on behalf of unconscious ambivalence is not the same thing as trying to address what the unconscious does to any position from which we might speak. These quotations are from 'The Psychoanalyst's Use of Free Association':

> Regardless of how well analysed we may be, we shall always be a subject who only ever partly knows. Partly knows the other. Partly knows the self. Partly knows life. Most of our life is lived unconsciously, in dialogue with the other's unconscious, within the field of unconscious social processes.

> I do not agree [that it is possible to comprehend our patients]. I think we fail to 'grasp' them, because anyone – including oneself – is substantially beyond knowing. [. . .] the unconscious never ceases its

work and the psychic material in which it plies its trade is profoundly beyond our knowing.[23]

It is, as Bollas states in his Introduction to *Cracking Up*, the founding paradox of analytic work that the analyst aims to 'understand unconscious communication in terms of a theory of the unconscious which *theoretically* makes such communication impossible'.[24] I would suggest that one of the roles of the mother, in theory, has been to carry the burden of that paradox.

I will now therefore turn things around a little and make my question not what the mother does to the category of knowledge, but, as a way of extending that question, what she is being asked to bear. In what has become one of her most famous essays, 'Stabat Mater' (1983), written shortly after the birth of her son, psychoanalyst and writer Julia Kristeva comments:

> Belief in the mother is rooted in our fascinated fear with the impoverishment of language. If language is powerless to situate me for, or speak me to, the other, then I presume – I yearn to believe – that someone somewhere will make up for that impoverishment. Someone, or rather someone female, *before* there was speech, *before* it – before the unconscious – spoke, before language pummelled me, via frontiers, separations, vertigos, into being.[25]

'Let us call "maternal",' she says near the start of her essay, 'that ambivalent principle that is bound to the species on the one hand, and on the other stems from an identity catastrophe that causes the proper Name to topple over into the unnameable. It is that catastrophe which we imagine as femininity, non-language or the body.'[26] I read Kristeva as saying that language fails us, both because of what it cannot speak and because the entry into language is a type of forced passage in itself. To recognise that, or to be in touch with the points where language brushes against its limits, is a type of catastrophe for those subjects (pre-Freudian we might say) who have vested their all in the accomplishment of identities and their poise. This felt catastrophe is simply the fact that there is an unconscious, that we cannot fully know, as Bollas puts it in those quotations, either the other or ourselves. We try to limit the damage, we protect ourselves from the felt danger, by fleshing out our anxiety, giving that zone of anguish a name: femininity, non-language, body. But the name we give it before all others, the one we really hold answerable for it, is the mother.

One could then say that, if mothers know anything – to give them back their subjectivity in the matter for a moment – it is the travesty of that projection. Maternal love, Kristeva writes, is 'a surge of anguish at the very point where the identity of thought and the living body falls apart'.[27] Do not idealise the early union of mother and child. Not just because things are more complex than that, but because that vision of union has so often served in Western thought to veil over the disunity of being to which motherhood, if anything, owes its most fundamental allegiance. 'I am breaking apart like the world' (I take that line from Sylvia Plath's extraordinary voice poem, 'Three Women', in which three women's voices speak across and through each other in a maternity ward).[28] Once again this goes beyond the question of the complexity, agency of the mother. It is more what this figure of the mother forces us to confront about the limits of our being. What passes through the mother, writes Kristeva, 'gnaws away at the all-mightiness of the Symbolic'.[29]

Even more perhaps, that vision or fantasy of primary union hides the extent to which the mother and child, in their negotiations with each other, however playful and loving, are, among other things, up against a radical confusion of tongues. This is Jean Laplanche, in his book *New Foundations for Psychoanalysis*, glossing Ferenczi's famous formula.[30] He is discussing what he sees as the incommensurable dialogue between the mother and her infant: the mother a sexual being, the infant thrown into a world of words and desires to which it is quite impossible that she or he could be equal:

> [We are dealing with] an encounter between an individual whose psychosomatic structures are situated predominantly at the level of need, and signifiers emanating from an adult. Those signifiers pertain to the satisfaction of those needs, but they also convey the purely interrogative potential of other messages – and those other messages are sexual. These enigmatic messages set the child a difficult, or even impossible, task of mastery and symbolisation and the attempt to perform it inevitably leaves behind unconscious residues. . . . We are not, then, dealing with some vague confusion of tongues, as Ferenczi would have it, but with a highly specific inadequacy of languages.[31]

And again:

> The primal relationship is therefore established on a twofold register:
> we have both a vital, open and reciprocal relationship, which can truly
> be said to be interactive, and a relationship which is implicitly sexual,
> where there is no interaction because the partners are not equal . . .
> Someone is moving from the straight and narrow; we have here a
> 'Traviata', someone who has been led astray and seduced.[32]

Or, to use terms that will be more familiar – the last but not least of
the eighteen reasons Winnicott offers as to why the mother hates her
child: 'He excites her but frustrates – she mustn't eat him or trade in
sex with him.'[33] If the mother feels hate for her infant, it is because she
loves the infant – the form her love takes at moments *is* – too much.

If, as I have been describing so far, I read a progress or move in
Bollas's writing towards the vanishing point of all knowing, I equally
read an increasing and symmetrical stress on what is excessive or
unmanageably baffling about the nature of the world for the child.
Though in relation to sexuality, would it be fair to say that, although
there is an erotics of the patient's idiom and frequent discussions of
object choice, there is not much sex in the good, or bad, old perverse
Freudian sense, in this writing? (There are the essays on the trisexual
in *The Shadow of the Object* and on homosexual cruising in *Being a
Character*, but these are, I think, cases apart.)[34] I also remember that
when Laplanche, in a talk to the Institute of Psychoanalysis ten years
ago, said something similar to what I have quoted here, his suggestion
that the mother's message to the child might be bafflingly sexual,
might indeed be sexual at all, caused something of an outrage (in the
discussion Juliet Mitchell suggested that what was going on was in
itself a 'confusion of tongues').

But it does seem to be the case that in the later writing, notably in
the wonderful essay, 'Why Oedipus?' there is a new emphasis on the
madness, not of the mother, but of the options open to the child as he
negotiates his way through a set of essentially unresolvable predica-
ments – that madness as Bollas puts it in one of my favourite of his
formulas, 'that ego psychology terms reality'.[35] We are dealing, as he
puts it in the later essay, 'Cracking Up', with 'a world of the real that
is deeply thoughtless'.[36] 'For this is the age, is it not,' he asks in 'Why

Oedipus?', 'when the child comes to understand something about the oddity of possessing one's own mind?'.[37] The Oedipal child's 'moment of truth', he continues, is a discovery 'that in some ways matches the search that Oedipus inaugurates when he aims to get to the origin of a curse that dooms his civilisation':

> That curse is the bittersweet fact one suffers in having a mind, one that
> is only ever partly known and therefore forever getting one into trouble,
> and one that in the extreme can be rather lost (as in the losing of a
> mind) and one whose discovery by the child is a most arresting
> moment.[38]

It is not possible to get justice in relation to the conflicts of the family scene, and the realm where we are meant to seek it, that of the group, is, as Freud himself pointed out, the bearer of its own insanity. 'We are,' Bollas states, 'amidst two quite profound unconscious orders – our own mind and that of the group – which break the symbiotic and Oedipal cohesions.'[39] Crucially, none of this can be laid at the door of the mother. These dilemmas, which will check our dreams of safe haven for ever after, no one is accountable for: 'Our own subjectivity,' he exclaims, 'will abuse us all!'[40]

So why do we lay so much on the mother? What is it, finally, ultimately, that we are asking her to protect us from? In 'What Is This Thing Called Self?', one of the essays from the latest collection, Bollas writes: 'The mother who gives birth to us also brings us in touch with death.'[41] (Likewise Kristeva describes motherhood as a 'veiling over of death in death's very place'.)[42] In Freud's essay on 'The Theme of the Three Caskets', silent Cordelia, dumb in the face of her father's demand for love, bearing a love in excess of speech, is also, going back over an old mythological equivalence, the representative of a death to which she finally brings him (cradled in Lear's arms in the last scene, her latent identity as mother surfaces inside out at the end of the play). Again, a line from Plath's poem 'Three Women', this time the second voice: 'the world conceives / Its end and runs towards it, arms held out in love'.

I don't think it would be going too far to suggest that this is also a strand which runs through Bollas's writing. In this, as with everything else I have described, he could be seen as bringing to the surface of a whole tradition in relation to the mother what she is being asked to carry. He could be showing us what psychoanalysis – writing of her and returning to her in what so often feels like a punishing scrutiny – no less than any other discourse, repeats. (Why do we expect psychoanalysis to be free of all this?)

In the first essay in *The Shadow of the Object*, in a sense the flagpiece for what's to come, there is an extraordinary line: 'the search for the perfect crime or the perfect woman is not only a quest for an idealised object'.[43] That sentence, with its brazen equation, brought me up short and sent me looking for other signs in the writing of this link between woman and crime. For that early paper, these fantasised figures are seen as making good a deficiency of early experience, which at this stage of the writing can lead only to the mother. But, as I have been arguing, Bollas also has, to my thinking, some far better ideas. Perfection (I reread his sentence) is criminal, women must be perfect, because it is the woman who, by wresting us from a world of certainty, committed the first crime.

Mother as criminal may seem an odd note with which to conclude, but it is in a sense where Bollas's own writing leads. The last collection, *Cracking Up*, ends with two papers – 'The Structure of Evil' and 'Cracking Up' which read like alternative versions, back to back, of each other. In the first, evil is described as the compulsive repetition of a death-in-being in which the infant was once the victim of a crime, the 'murder' of the true self.[44] Only this can explain, Bollas convincingly argues, the extraordinary balance struck by those we consider evil between benign and inhuman authority, the way that the serial killer, for example, lulls his victim into a false dependency which he is then so hideously able to turn inside out and exploit: 'Shocking harm erupting in the midst of a benign texture of the real ... the grandmother turns into a hungry wolf.'[45] Unknowable, unpredictable – 'we cannot see where he is coming from and ... whatever we know about him does not help us find him'[46] – the one we consider evil presents us with a grotesque, inflated, parody of our inability to control our own ends and the ends of the world.

In the next and final essay, 'Cracking Up', mother once again rushes in, only this time with a difference. This mother is a clown. Death-defying, she goes back in the opposite direction from the serial killer, turns 'disaster into pleasure', taking into herself, 'right before the baby's eyes', the baby's own 'internal madness': 'Does she do,' he asks, 'what comic and humorists have been doing all these centuries, taking up into their bodies and souls these disturbing aspects of life?'[47] 'Is [the comic moment] death defying? . . . For a brief moment, then, the funny man defies the forces of life and death. He does deliberately what most of us do by chance.'[48]

And if death is in the frame, then so, exceptionally I would say, is sexuality. The instincts, explicitly sidelined in the rest of the work, return when it is a question of really cracking up – control of the world, of bodies, of thought all falling apart: 'The force that the humorist grasps when he crosses the boundary is the constant unconscious movement of instinctuality . . . The comic moment may be a descent into the underworld, where it dips into the force of instincts and returns with enough energy to split sides.'[49]

I like this mother as clown. I think it's the best version we've had so far. Not least of all, because the excessive, unmanageable nature of what she is being asked to carry has become the explicit theme. As if that tension, dialectic, balancing act between knowing the mother and the flight of knowledge, has finally toppled over, as if it had to come back to the mother where she is rediscovered as negotiating boundaries whose nature is to be unnegotiable. (As the *I Ching*, in fact one of the most patriarchal texts ever written, would put it: 'No blame'.) Once we are in a world of instincts and unconscious, there are some things, rather a lot in fact, that not even a mother can do.

I want to end by trying to convey a sense of how maddeningly hard I have found it to write about the work of Christopher Bollas. I decided in the end that it was not just that I was being difficult, but even more because of the type of demand that he places on his reader, a demand connected, I think and in the best sense, to what I have been trying to describe. It is not just the extraordinarily powerful way that Bollas evokes the analytic scene, the extent to which, because he is so often writing about the limits of its own capacities, he mimics in his writing the form of a theory which *should* be ungraspable if it is to remain faithful to its object – the unconscious as an ever-receding form of truth. It is more or as much, since the two are not unrelated, that he issues a very particular challenge to the reader. I would say that Bollas asks his reader to treat him like his ideal version of how a mother would treat her child. He thereby undoes, by passing the position back to the reader and out into the world, the extent to which, if there is an ideal mother anywhere to be found, it is the analyst – or rather this analyst – himself (the strongest desire of this writing seeming to be at moments the desire to be one's own mother). Read me, hold me, but don't crush me, don't get too close. Above all, don't think you know, and I would want to add, don't expect to get it right.

Literary critics who have turned to Freud in the last decade have spent a lot of their time concentrating on footnotes and asides. It started with the case of 'Dora', the argument being that if you wanted to find an answer to everything that went wrong with that case, it was in the footnotes – indeed by Freud's own acknowledgement – that it could be found.[50] So I end with one aside and one footnote. First the aside, from the Introduction to *The Shadow of the Object*: 'I do not discuss how one might analyse the presence of the actual mother's mothering. I look forward to doing so in another work.'[51] Second, the footnote, from the essay 'Violent Innocence' in *Being a Character*.

> As reconstructions decrease, and as the patient's character is increasingly understood within the transference, the question of what the mother actually did, or who she actually was, fades into its proper place: into the areas of speculation and hypothesis, profoundly tempered by a forgiveness intrinsic to the more important realisation of one's own generated disturbances. I intend to discuss this important question, of the invocation of the name of the mother in psychoanalytic reconstruction, in a future essay.[52]

In response to which, I would simply want to say (it is the message of this entire essay): I can't wait.

Notes

1 Melanie Klein was, of course, the first analyst to concentrate on the mother. For more recent analysis of the mother–child bond, see Jessica Benjamin, *The Bonds of Love* (New York: Pantheon, 1988); and for an analysis of the absence–presence of the mother in Freud's work, see Madeleine Sprengnether, *The Spectral Mother: Freud, Feminism, and Psychoanalysis* (Ithaca, NY: Cornell University Press, 1990).
2 Sigmund Freud, 'Negation', *Standard Edition*, 19 (1925; London:

Hogarth Press, 1961), p. 235.

3 Ibid., pp. 236–7.

4 Christopher Bollas, *Being a Character: Psychoanalysis and Self-Experience* (New York: Hill & Wang, 1992), p. 17.

5 Christopher Bollas, *The Shadow of the Object: Psychoanalysis of the Unknown Thought* (London: Free Association Books, 1987).

6 Christopher Bollas, *Forces of Destiny: Psychoanalysis and Human Idiom* (London: Free Association Books, 1989), p. 194.

7 Bollas, *The Shadow of the Object*, p. 77.

8 Ibid., p. 142.

9 H. D., *Tribute to Freud* (1956; Boston: David R. Godine, 1974), p. 41.

10 Ibid., pp. 146–7.

11 Sigmund Freud, 'To Romain Rolland', *Standard Edition*, 20 (1926; London: Hogarth Press, 1959), p. 279.

12 Some of these ideas were already present in the earlier work, such as 'The Psychoanalyst and the Hysteric', in *The Shadow of the Object*, but the later paper goes further. Christopher Bollas, *Cracking Up: The Work of Unconscious Experience* (New York: Hill & Wang, 1995), p. 12.

13 Bollas, *Forces of Destiny*, p. 59; *Cracking Up*, p. 12.

14 Bollas, *Being a Character*, p. 63.

15 Sigmund Freud, 'The Unconscious', *Standard Edition*, 14 (1915; London: Hogarth Press, 1957), p. 194.

16 Jacques Derrida, 'Telepathy', trans. N. Royle, *Oxford Literary Review*, 10 (1988), pp. 3–41.

17 Sigmund Freud, 'New Introductory Lectures on Psycho-Analysis', *Standard Edition*, 22 (1932; London: Hogarth Press, 1974).

18 Bollas, *Cracking Up*, p. 19.

19 Bollas, *Forces of Destiny*, pp. 112–13.

20 Ibid., p. 113.

21 Ibid., p. 63.

22 Rozika Parker explores most fully the issue of maternal ambivalence, addressing Winnicott's work, notably his 1949 paper 'Hate in the Counter-Transference', in *Torn in Two: The Experience of Maternal Ambivalence* (London: Virago, 1995).

23 Bollas, *Being a Character*, pp. 116–17, 131.

24 Bollas, *Cracking Up*, p. 6.

25 Julia Kristeva, 'Stabat Mater', in T. Moi, ed., *The Kristeva Reader* (1983; Oxford: Blackwell, 1986), pp. 175–6.

26 Ibid., pp. 161–2.

27 Ibid., pp. 175–6.

28 Sylvia Plath, 'Three Women', in *Winter Trees* (London: Faber & Faber, 1971).

29 Kristeva, p. 185.

30 Sandor Ferenczi, 'Confusion of tongues between adult and child', in *Final Contributions to the Problems and Methods of Psycho-Analysis* (London: Hogarth Press, 1933).

31 Jean Laplanche, *New Foundations for Psychoanalysis*, trans. D. Macey (Oxford: Blackwell, 1989), p. 130.

32 Ibid., pp. 103–4.

33 D. W. Winnicott, 'Hate in the Counter-Transference', in *The Maturational Processes and the Facilitating Environment* (1949; London: Hogarth Books, 1979), p. 201.

34 Bollas: 'The Trisexual', in *The Shadow of the Object*; 'Cruising in the Homosexual Arena', in *Being a Character*.

35 Bollas, *Being a Character*, p. 243.

36 Bollas, *Cracking Up*, p. 243.

37 Bollas, *Being a Character*, p. 239.

38 Ibid., p. 240.

39 Ibid., p. 244.

40 Ibid., pp. 240–1.

41 Bollas, *Cracking Up*, p. 174.

42 Kristeva, p. 177.

43 Bollas, *The Shadow of the Object*, p. 18.

44 Bollas, *Cracking Up*, p. 195.

45 Ibid., pp. 191–2.

46 Ibid., p. 190.

47 Ibid., p. 242.

48 Ibid., p. 253.

49 Ibid., p. 252–3.

50 This point is made by a number of the essays in Charles Bernheimer and Claire Kahane, eds, *In Dora's Case: Freud–Hysteria–Feminism* (New York: Columbia University Press, 1985).

51 Bollas, *The Shadow of the Object*, p. 7.

52 Bollas, *Being a Character*, p. 178.

What Makes an Analyst?

It is little known how Freud's perhaps most far-reaching border crossing resided in his vision of a psychoanalytic institution which would be open to the people and which, in its training procedures, would engage with other disciplines in the humanities – the history of civilisation, mythology, religion and literature – so as to stop psychoanalysis from entrenching itself either as official knowledge or as esoteric lore. In this essay, I describe the failure of that vision and the attempts, also unsuccessful, of the French psychoanalyst, Jacques Lacan, to restore it, and ask what price psychoanalysis, as institution and practice, has paid as a result. We do not need the endless wrangles about the character of Freud (the famous 'Freud Wars'). If it is indeed time for psychoanalysis to critique its own history and performance, it should look to how it reproduces itself as an institution, at its most basic, to how analysts are trained. My exploration of this question, which returned me to an earlier engagement, from the 1980s with the writings of Lacan on feminine sexuality, was stimulated by the work of the Egyptian-born, Paris-based psychoanalyst, Moustapha Safouan, translator in the 1950s of The Interpretation of Dreams *and Hegel's* Phenomenology *into Arabic, and one of the few analysts to situate psychoanalysis – both in its history and in its radical potential – at the interface between social institutions and the unconscious. A longer version of this essay formed the introduction to my translation of his 1986 book on the topic:* Jacques Lacan and the Question of Psychoanalytic Training *(Macmillan, 2000).*

'Institutional training is probably antithetical to analysis.'
> Adam Limentani, 'The Training Analyst and the Difficulties in the Training Psychoanalytic Situation', *International Journal of Psychoanalysis* (1974)

'I have never spoken of the formation of analysts; what I have spoken of are the formations of the unconscious. There is no analytic formation [training]. Out of analysis an experience evolves which it is a complete

mistake to classify as didactic. Experience is not didactic.'
Jacques Lacan, 'A propos de l'expérience de la passe et de sa
transmission', proposition of November 1973, *Ornicar?* special issue,
Sur la passe, 12–13, December 1977, p. 121

A recent conversation with a South African psychologist at the
University of Natal in Durban, keen on psychoanalysis in a largely
unsympathetic academic context, led to what for me was a surprising
conclusion. At the same time as he was very eager for psychoanalysis
to spread in post-apartheid South Africa, he was deeply suspicious of
the first stirrings of psychoanalytically inspired activity in Johannesburg, and suggested instead that if psychoanalysis was to become a
positive presence in South Africa it should be through its dissemination in the general culture and not through its institutionalisation.
Which must mean that nearly fifty years after the collapse of the first
attempts at creating a community of practising analysts in South
Africa, for this promoter of psychoanalytic ideas – he is the founder
and editor of a journal, *Psychology in Society*, which devotes much of
its space to their consideration – the best way to ensure the future of
psychoanalysis was through its *not being practised*.

I am not taking this as a representative view, nor as indicative of the
prospects for psychoanalysis in post-apartheid South Africa – it is its
oddity, or rather the oddity of the question it provokes, which
interests me. How has it come about that psychoanalytic institutions
can be seen as an obstacle to the influence of psychoanalysis in the
world? This is a very different question from the more obvious one of
how to make psychoanalysis politically responsive, if not accountable,
to the worlds in which it may, or may not, play a part. (What has
psychoanalysis to say about apartheid? Is it irrevocably contaminated,
in confronting racial questions, by its origins in the West?) In his
critique of the 1977 Constitution of the International Pyschoanalytic
Association, 'Géopsychanalyse et le reste du monde...', Jacques
Derrida confronted the neutrality of the Constitutional Statement on
the abuse of human rights, its failure to name countries where
psychoanalysis might be implicated even if only indirectly with such
abuse, placing the statement against what is meant to be the specificity
of the psychoanalytic process.[1] My starting anecdote about South
Africa is meant to suggest that one place to look for an explanation of
that failing might be in the history of psychoanalytic training. If
psychoanalysis cannot turn the light of its founding discoveries on

politics, it might have something to do with the history of its own institutionalisation. It might then be the failure of psychoanalysis to deal adequately with these problems – as much as the specific historical traumas of South Africa since 1949 (the year when the National Party, instigator of apartheid, first comes to power which was also the year when Wulf Sachs, the first practising analyst in South Africa, died) – which has made the idea of a fully institutionalised psychoanalysis in South Africa seem, at least to one keen supporter of its theories, like a bad idea.

So is there something about psychoanalytic institutions which are radically at odds with the purpose of psychoanalysis? It is not widely known just how deeply questions of training were at the heart of Lacan's rupture with the International Psychoanalytic Association in 1963, and then again in the founding and subsequent dissolution of his own school. By a strange irony, in the English-speaking world, Lacan's notoriety has run alongside and even, it might be argued, served to marginalise the institutional questions which were so central to his own polemic. Critics of Lacan are able to allude to the 'scandal' of his short sessions, make reference to the famous difficulty of his thought, without realising that in the process they are severing Lacan from his history, from his own protracted engagement with the official psychoanalytic institutions on which his writing can be read as one continuous commentary. As if psychoanalysis were its practice and its theorisation alone. As if there were not something in a sense more fundamental or prior to both of these – the process through which someone becomes an analyst, that is, the question of analytic training.

The relative silence on the issue of training has made Lacan easier to dismiss because it makes his institutional critique invisible. No less ironically, it also completes the work of the International Psychoanalytic Association itself by keeping that institution's training procedures and Lacan so effectively apart (the 1963 IPA ruling made membership of the Société psychanalytique de France, of which Lacan was a member, conditional on the exclusion of Lacan from its training programme). And by the same token, the humanities, and especially literary, university departments which have famously been so much more hospitable to Lacan's thought, have inadvertently furthered the task. As they have so effectively demonstrated, and as Freud himself insisted on more than one occasion, the fertility of psychoanalytic thought does not rely on its therapeutic role or official institutional belonging alone. In 1953 the Société psychanalytique de France split from the first French psychoanalytic organisation, the Sociéte psychanalytique de Paris, which had been founded by Marie Bonaparte (it was the application of this secessionist society for membership of the International Psychoanalytic Association which led to its ruling on Lacan). When in 1953 Lacan put forward his proposals for the new society, he prefaced his document with this famous statement of Freud's:

> If – which may sound fantastic today – one had to found a college of psychoanalysis, much would have to be taught in it which is also taught by the medical faculty: alongside of depth-psychology, which would always remain the principal subject, there would be an introduction to biology, as much as possible of the science of sexual life, and familiarity with the symptomatology of psychiatry. On the other hand, analytic instruction would include branches of knowledge which are remote from medicine and which the doctor does not come across in his practice: the history of civilisation, mythology, the psychology of religion and the science of literature.[2]

So is there something about psychoanalytic institutes which is radically at odds with the purpose of psychoanalysis? After all, psychoanalysis has the merit of combining in one the three professions – education, therapy and government – whose impossibility was stressed by Freud: in the words of an analyst at the 1993 Fifth IPA Conference of Training Analysts, 'a *government* for *education* in *psychoanalysis*'.[3] Translating Moustapha Safouan's *Jacques Lacan and the Question of Psychoanalytic Training* has provided me with an opportunity to think about this question.[4]

In a paper first delivered in 1938, 'The Problem of Training Analysis', although not published in English for nearly thirty years, Anna Freud wrote:

> We do not hesitate to brand it as technically wrong if for the purposes of therapy an analyst selects his patients from his circle of acquaintances; if he shares his interests with them or discusses his opinions either with them or in their presence; if he forgets himself far enough to judge their behaviour, to disclose his criticism to other people, and to permit

it to affect decisions; if he actively manipulates the patient, offers himself as a pattern, and ends analysis by permitting the patient to identify with him personally and professionally. Nevertheless, we commit every single one of these deviations from the classical technique when we analyse candidates. Further we do not inquire frequently enough how far these deviations complicate the transference and obscure its interpretation.[5]

What does it mean, then, to think that psychoanalysis can be taught? More, that it can be taught through (during the course of? alongside? in conjunction with?) a procedure – the personal analysis – which Freud situated in radical tension with, if not opposition to, teaching: 'that one should be analysed for the purpose of learning the method had occurred to none of us'?[6] What is the analysand meant to be learning about? And if the answer is – as Freud would insist – her or himself, what cost the process of professional identification alluded to by Anna Freud? At a recent conference on the role of women in the history of psychoanalysis, Juliet Mitchell, returning to Dora, argued that the training process fostered a hysterical identification with the analyst/physician. Thus deftly did she run the question of Dora's hysteria, which has been so central to feminist discussion of Freud, into the heart of training. Dora lost her own way as a woman, one could say, because of the too powerful identifications that surrounded her (identification as the most ruinous seduction of them all).[7] At the very least there is a creative and technical tautology at stake. What exactly is the trainee identifying with, or indeed learning, given that if the analyst is proceeding correctly, the method of any one analysis will be generated by the patient *her or himself*:

> Some of the more gifted students accept *en bloc* the technique of their own analyst, which they have carefully observed, but they follow him too slavishly, and do not realise that the particular line taken by their own individual analysis, and its concrete features, *have been largely determined by the peculiarities of the object, that is, of themselves.*[8] [My emphasis]

In many ways Lacan's history can be read as an attempt to build an institution which would inscribe this complex, awkward, insight at its base. The only thing that makes an analyst is her or his experience of analysis. Or to put it in the words of Lacan's most controversial formula on training: 'The analyst's authorisation derives from her or himself alone.'

The official psychoanalytic institution has not, however, been alone in sidestepping some of the more difficult implications of this insight. Humanities departments have made their acceptance of psychoanalysis, and especially Lacan, conditional on leaving the institutional question to one side. When Shoshana Felman wrote her discussion of Freud, Lacan and teaching, 'Psychoanalysis and Education', she barely touched on the issue of the institution (it appears in two asides):

> Of all Freud's followers, Lacan has, more than others, picked up on the radicality of Freud's pedagogical concern with didactic psychoanalysis, not only as a subsidiary technical, pragmatic question (how should analysts be trained?) but as a major theoretical concern, as a major pedagogical innovation crucial to the very innovation of psychoanalytic insight.[9]

In fact, you could say that it is the genius of this paper to subtract or pull the question of teaching out from under its institutional cover:

> Didactic analysis is thus invested by Lacan not simply with the practical, programmatic value but with the theoretical significance – the allegorical instruction – of a paradigm: a paradigm, precisely, of the interminability not simply of teaching (learning) and of analysing (being analysed) but of the very act of thinking, theorising.[10]

What psychoanalysis has to offer on the subject of teaching is a paradigm for our relationship – precarious, tentative – to knowledge: 'Through Lacan we can understand that the psychoanalytic discipline is an unprecedented one in that its teaching does not just reflect upon itself but turns back upon itself so as to subvert itself, and truly teaches only in so far as it subverts itself.'[11]

But this move, the inverse but symmetrical move to that of the official psychoanalytic institute, relies no less on severing the unconscious from training, leaving a major part of the implications of what Lacan did for teaching unexplored. In the uneasy tension between the pragmatics of training and the theorisation of the unconscious, it is as if official (psychoanalytic) and unofficial (university) knowledge have had to opt primarily for one or the other, as if they have divided up the spoils. University departments of literature would then be guilty, not of separating psychoanalytic theory from its practice or the practice of analysts (the common charge), but far more seriously, from their own. There might be a great deal for teachers involved in certifying and qualifying, in their own form of training as one might say (many of our students enter the teaching profession), to learn from this other history of institutional legitimation. What might the history of psychoanalysis have to say about the way institutions of learning perpetuate and legitimate themselves?[12]

There is a feminist point or rather a point about feminism to be made here. From a position outside or against institutions, many feminists of the 1970s (myself included) have risen up the institutional hierarchy in such a way that it is no longer viable to base any claim for political radicalism on the status of the outsider to the institution, on an uneasy belonging inside its walls. It seems appropriate then to start asking what is wrong with institutions from the inside. There might be much for feminism in an examination of the precise ways in which power entrenches itself in institutions, beyond the more easy disclaimer that makes all institutions necessarily authoritarian, patriar-chal, non-viable. In what ways might an institution constitute a piece of acting out against its own main discovery? What happens when a radical theory, whose radicalness resides at least partly in its unique critique of power as identification, becomes mired in charismatic authority? In this context, failure might be more informative than success. On the first page of *Jacques Lacan and the Question of Psychoanalytic Training*, Moustapha Safouan puts the problem like this:

> the highest echelons of the official psychoanalytic societies acknowledge that it is their unassailable bureaucratic structure which is preventing them from fulfilling their psychoanalytic objectives, the very same structure which allows them to keep going. You could say, then, that Lacan's school was at least graced with a structure able to take on the full consequences of failure instead of being merely sucked into them.[13]

A paradox, then: the IPA fails through the very success with which it reproduces itself; Lacan's school succeeded, at least partially, in its ability to fail.

A more general point about recent theory, to which the discussion to follow could also be said to relate. Following a long period when the politics of psychoanalysis was seen to reside for many in its theory of desire, attention has increasingly shifted to the question of identification, to how the fictive authority of the ego is built out of the bits and pieces of bodies and voices it has felt, seen and heard.[14] An early confidence in the subversive power of sexuality against the delusional stability of the ego has had to reckon with the fact that the ego's intransigence, its conviction in its own identity, is not so easy to shift. It has become more and more important, that is, to ask how subjects come to take up the trappings in which they invest the precarious but no less sacred and often threatening safety of their social identities and selves. 'The ego,' to use Freud's famous formula, is 'the precipitate of its former identifications.' This is how Elizabeth Roudinesco, historian of French psychoanalysis and biographer of Lacan, sums up the key and founding division between the ego psychology underpinning Lacan's analysis with Rudolph Lowenstein, and Lacan's own burgeoning theories as well as those of Melanie Klein:

> After the Freudian revision of 1920, there were effectively two options. One consisted in making the ego the product of a progressive differentiation from the id, acting as a representative of reality with the task of holding the drives in place (Ego psychology); the other, on the contrary, turned its back on any idea of making the ego autonomous so as to study its genesis in terms of identifications. In other words, the first option sought to pull the ego free of the id and turn it into an instrument of the individual's adaptation to external reality, while the second drew the ego back towards the id so as to demonstrate how it was structured in stages as a function of imagos borrowed from the other.[15]

Only the second allows a theorisation of the subject as political subject, because only the second, in its stress on the ego's relation to the other, can account for the ego as radically constituted by the social tie (rather than the more simple opposition between the individual and social norms). It is along these lines that Mikkel Borch-Jacobsen describes the shift to the second topography in Freud's work:

> By the strangest and yet the most logical of paradoxes, with Freud the attention devoted to the ego's narcissism led to the question of the Other, of others . . . This is obviously why the great texts on the second topography are an inextricable mix of 'ego-analysis' and analysis of culture or the social tie: the other is no longer an object, an *Objekt*, whence the need to pay attention to the non-erotic, 'social' relationships, to others; and, inversely, the ego is no longer a subject, whence the need to inscribe this 'sociality' in the ego itself, in the form of identification, superego, etc.[16]

But there is another perhaps more superficial reason why this discussion seems to me to be timely. In the endless discussion of psychoanalysis – now famously known as 'The Freud Wars' – which started with the criticisms of Frederick Crews in the *New York Review of Books*, no one ever raised the question of the psychoanalytic institution, that is of how one gets to be a psychoanalyst.[17] So, in a debate that has turned on – in the words of the title of one book on Freud – what is *wrong* with psychoanalysis, no one seems to have asked whether there might be something wrong, not with psychoanalysis, but with psychoanalysts. Meaning not with them as individuals but with the very process through which they come to define and legitimate themselves as analysts in the first place. Which would suggest that what is wrong with psychoanalysis in its dominant form is not that there is too much of it, but that there is not enough: 'The institutionalisation of psychoanalysis was carried out as if psychoanalysis had not existed.'[18]

Finally, a more personal note. For a long time I have wondered about the disparity between my continuing enthusiasm for many of Lacan's ideas, and the increasing distance I find myself taking from anything that could be described as, or which defines itself as, Lacanianism – something on which I have been challenged more than once. (I was, you might say, perversely delighted when an anxious friend phoned me a number of years ago to say that an article in a new Lacanian journal in England had suggested that my Lacanianism was contaminated by my feminism, a reproach which seemed to me greatly preferable to the reverse.) I have become increasingly aware, since the publication of my translations of Lacan on feminine sexuality in 1982, that I would not have been able to involve myself in such a project – there would of course have been no need – had I been in Paris and as a woman, necessarily embroiled, one way or another, in the conflicts around Lacan's school and his person.[19] I would not, that is to say, have been able to disintricate my passion – and at moments it has had all the qualities of a passion – for Lacan's ideas from my discomfort with the form of charismatic authority which, in his personal and institutional presence, he so dramatically provoked. And, one might say, in the most unexpected quarters. Thus Roland Castro (no relation, I think), the leader of the left group, Vive la révolution:

> I began my analysis with Lacan in 1972 after the dissolution of Vive la révolution. I was a political leader and I wanted to see a leader . . . The concept of the proletariat was collapsing and Lacan was a truth that was still afloat.[20]

Even more unlikely, these words from the feminist Antoinette Fouque: 'From the moment one found oneself before his eyes or ears, one was his.'[21]

Some of Freud's most startling, if not radical, comments about the institution of psychoanalysis were made in *The Question of Lay Analysis*, written as a pamphlet when Theodore Reik was charged in 1926 in Vienna with a breach of an old Austrian law against 'quackery' – a law which made it illegal for a person without a medical degree to treat patients. Subtitling his text 'Conversations with an Impartial Person', Freud formalised on this one occasion the semi-Socratic and defensive rhetoric that characterises so much of what he wrote. In defence of his colleague, Freud insists primarily on the specific nature of the psychoanalytic experience: only someone analysed can analyse, medical education is particularly adept at disqualifying doctors from that role. What is required of an analyst, as he had already clearly stated in his 1912 essay 'Recommendations to Physicians Practising Psycho-Analysis', was an ability on the part of the practitioner, not to interpret the unconscious (with all that implies by way of observing, reasoned, detachment), but to listen to the patient's unconscious with one's own:

To put it in a formula: he must turn his own unconscious like a receptive organ towards the transmitting unconscious of the patient. He must adjust himself to the patient as a telephone receiver to the transmitting microphone. Just as the receiver converts back into sound-waves the electric oscillations in the telephone line which were set up by sound waves, so the doctor's unconscious is able, from the derivatives of the unconscious which are transmitted to him, to reconstruct that unconscious, which has determined the patient's free associations.[22]

Only the unconscious can track the unconscious (Ella Sharpe will use exactly this formula in her 1930 lectures on technique).[23] And on this process, in all its fine-tuned – and one might say slightly deranged-sounding – sensitivity, legality has absolutely no purchase: 'the things that really matter – the possibilities in psychoanalysis for *internal* development – can never be affected by regulations and prohibitions' (the words on which the main text of *The Question of Lay Analysis* ends).[24]

But no less striking is the opposite movement made by Freud's 1926 text, the way he argues that, if psychoanalysis is to survive, it must at the same time expand beyond itself. It may have already become 'indispensable to all the sciences which are concerned with the evolution of human civilisation and its major institutions, such as art, religion and the social order', but this is nothing 'compared with what might be achieved if historians, psychologists of religion, philologists and so on would agree themselves to handle the new instrument of research which is at their disposal': 'The use of analysis for the treatment of the neuroses is only one of its applications: the future will perhaps show that it is not the most important one.'[25] Freud's famous statement – often taken as a dismissal of his own therapeutic aims – has therefore a very precise institutional frame. As much as, or even more than, a point about therapy, it is a comment on the breadth of vision required for psychoanalysis best to institutionalise itself.

In the postscript to his text, Freud reiterates his earlier account of what a training institution – 'an ideal no doubt, but an ideal that can and must be realised' – would look like that corresponded to this double vision: 'it must include elements from the mental sciences, from psychology, from the history of civilisation, from sociology, as well as from anatomy, biology and the study of evolution'. In short, a college based on a university model in which the specificity of the psychoanalytic object – 'it is justifiable to omit anything which has no direct bearing on the practice of analysis' – the stress on the irreducibility of psychoanalysis as experience (one unconscious listening out for another), in no way inhibits the openness of psychoanalysis to the intellectual world outside.[26]

Crucially for Freud, it is in the context of training that the demand on psychoanalysis to exceed its own limits is most strongly made. This in itself should counter the argument that the use of psychoanalysis as a method of intellectual inquiry is a purely external matter. The expansion of psychoanalysis beyond clinical practice cannot be separated from – it arises in direct response to – the founding question of the analytic institution. So what went wrong?

Two moments of psychoanalytic history stand out in relation to the question of training.[27] The first can be dated, according to the 1948 account of Michael Balint, to the 1918 Budapest Congress where Freud warned the delegates that analysis should start preparing itself 'for the coming demand of psychotherapy for the masses both in its technique and its training'. This historic proposition by Freud is worth giving in full:

> Now let us assume that by some kind of organisation we succeeded in increasing our numbers to an extent sufficient for treating a consider-able mass of the population. On the other hand, it is possible to foresee that at some time or other the conscience of society will awake and remind it that the poor man should have just as much right to assistance for his mind as he now has to the life-saving help offered by surgery; and that the neuroses threaten public health no less than tuberculosis, and can be left as little as the latter to the impotent care of individual members of the community. When this happens, institutions or out-patient clinics will be appointed, so that men who would otherwise give way to drink, women who have nearly succumbed under their burden of privations, children for whom there is no choice between running wild or neurosis, may be made capable, by analysis, of resistance and of efficient work. Such treatments will be free. It may be a long time before the State comes to see these things as urgent. Present conditions may delay its arrival even longer. Probably these institutions will first be started by private charity. Some time or other, however, it must come to this.[28]

Anton von Freund had offered to put at Freud's disposal a large sum of money (between £30,000 and £40,000) to organise a tripartite institution: mass psychology, psychoanalytic training, analytic research. It was also at this congress that, in a private discussion, Nunberg formulated the soon-to-become axiomatic principle that no one should practise analysis without undergoing an analysis her or himself.

But a set of contingencies and catastrophes were radically to restrict the field of psychoanalytic endeavour. Massive inflation set off by the Hungarian revolution swallowed von Freund's funds and the Institution set up by Ferenczi in 1919 (the first in the world) came to an end with the counter-revolution. A few weeks after von Freund's death in 1920, Max Eitingon, Karl Abraham and Ernst Simmel opened the Berlin Institute which was to become the key player in what followed. Balint comments: 'Openly and admittedly the aims of the Institute were those indicated by Freud and planned by von Freund: therapy for the broad masses, research and training. In fact what they – and all other institutes – have achieved is only a system of training.'[29]

So behind the first moments of psychoanalytic institutionalisation a dream of access to, and for, the people. As if training, necessarily a form of restriction, could only conceptualise itself through an answering expansion, a counter-movement reaching beyond its own doors (the practical equivalent and anticipation of the intellectual expansion envisaged later by Freud). And then a moment of retreat, so that the institute of training appears as a *residue*, what gets left over when history stifles the politically and intellectually expansive dream. According to Balint, from 1925 to 1938, Eitingon's 'International Training Committee' – a melancholic entity, as he puts it, in contrast with the triumphant, if deadly, history of the Berlin Institute as a whole – produced nothing but futile disputes. But it was Eitingon's favourite creation and the only one that remained to him after the Nazis seized the new Berlin Institute in the 1930s.

Training fossilises, ceases to be a viable object of debate – it loses any character it might have had as a site for controversy and transformation – when history closes around its doors. Between them the Hungarian revolution or rather counter-revolution, and the rise of Hitler, push psychoanalysis back inside its own walls. What arises from these crises is an institution in the image of the ego which Freud himself – borrowing his own metaphors from the First World War – will not hesitate to describe in militaristic terms:

> Think of the difference between 'the front' and 'behind the lines', as things were during the war. We were not surprised then that some things were different at the front from what they were behind the lines, and that many things were permitted behind the lines which had to be forbidden at the front. The determining influence was of course the proximity of the enemy.[30]

Running alongside this history there is another one which, in a famous and controversial essay, the psychoanalyst Siegfried Bernfeld put at the heart of his critique of training.[31] This other history will resurface – grotesque, caricatured – in the 'interminable transference', of François Roustang's formula, which came to attach itself to Lacan (as indeed and no less dramatically will the first). In 1923, the year when Berlin lays down its rules of selection and training – rules which are still largely in operation to this day – Freud was diagnosed with cancer. It took a year before it was clear that the cancer was under control (he had been expected to die within months). Bernfeld comments:

> I need not explain in detail what Freud's 'death and resurrection' within this one year meant to the older psychoanalysts in Vienna and Berlin . . . Some [. . .] grew intensely anxious because of the threatened loss, and became very eager to establish a solid dam against heterodoxy, as they now felt themselves responsible for the future of psychoanalysis. They determined to limit by rigid selection among the newcomers, and by the institution of a coercive, long drawn-out trial period of authoritarian training, any final admission to their societies. In fact, *they punished their students for their own ambivalence.* At the same time, they consolidated the one trend that Freud had wanted to avoid: the shrinkage of psychoanalysis into an annexe of psychiatry.[32]

The institutionalisation of psychoanalysis was therefore, in the words of Safouan, the 'end-point of a set of convergent repressions', a piece of acting-out unconsciously staging the ritual murder and resurrection of the father which, in *Totem and Taboo*, Freud had placed at the origins of the social tie: 'a "fraternal" deal dictated by a murder not so much actual as unable to be acknowledged or able to be so even though it had not actually taken place'.[33] More simply one could say, no child unconsciously forgives a parent her or his mortality; the first generation of analysts handed on their rage against the dying Freud by punishing the next. It is not quite therefore that the psychoanalytic establishment stands in for, or even incarnates itself as, Freud (much more, but also much less, of the body was at stake). What seems to pass into and through the institution of psychoanalysis is the terror which a body, too-present through its mortal frailty, can provoke.

From that moment on, the obligatory aspect of the training analysis won out over the private and personal; it became something to be 'taken' like the introductory course in anatomy you might take in order to qualify as a doctor. 'Such a state of affairs is best judged,' Safouan comments after Bernfeld, 'by its consequences: despite thirty years of experience (to which today we can add another thirty), we still have no idea of what goes on in a training analysis nor in what it consists.'[34] In his report on the 4th Pre-Congress on Training in Vienna in 1971, Victor Calef observed: 'Apparently we do not have definite criteria for assessment at any stage of progression.'[35]

Finally, one has to add to this history the necessary defensiveness of the IPA in response to the Nazi threat. It failed to save the movement from actively collaborating (the takeover of the Deutsche Psychoanalytische Gesellschaft) but not one of its largely Jewish constituency were lost to the concentration camps. When Lacan presents his 1967 'Proposition on the Psychoanalyst of the School', he places this moment at the heart of what he defines as the real (the traumatic kernel of subjectivity), and its consequences for psychoanalysis at the origins of his own history:

> if the IPA of Mitteleuropa showed that it had prepared itself in advance by losing not a single one of its members in the camps, it owed to this same tour de force a post-war stampede, not without its downside in a drastic lowering in quality of candidates (a hundred mediocre analysts, don't forget) for whom the motive of seeking shelter from the red peril, fantasy of the time, was not absent.[36]

This is how Roudinesco sees the inheritance subsequently bequeathed to Lacan:

> From a besieged fortress, the IPA had become a segregationist empire: Hannibal had lost his battle, and Carthage was now beholden to a new Roman Empire [the emigration of a whole generation of analysts to the United States]. The movement turned the persecution whose victim it was into a 'persecution' of a different type: normalisation; the exclusion of the mad, the marginal, the non-conformists. The free Diaspora had devoured its members and constituted itself as a synagogue on the American model of adaptation.[37]

Lacan founds a school because he is expelled from an institution. He becomes 'Lacanian', as opposed to the 'Freudian' on which he had insisted up to then, at the point of his own delegitimation. It was the first time the International Psychoanalytic Association excluded a body of thought defining itself spirit and letter – even if the claim could be contested – in such rigorously Freudian terms (closer in this to Melanie Klein than to Alfred Adler and Jung). The net result would be that the IPA would henceforth avoid any substantive challenge to their own procedures of training. It is one of the ironies of this moment of psychoanalytic history that the IPA's subsequent tolerance of doctrinal differences (excluding Lacan's) would be matched by such technical and institutional rigidity, while it would be in the context of an increasingly rigid Lacanian orthodoxy that the only real experiment in matters of training was allowed to take place ('a genuine Freudian adventure in matters of training analysis').[38] 'The exclusion of Lacan,' Wladimir Granoff comments, 'allowed the IPA to come to agreement in conditions of perfect misunderstanding.' He was speaking in a series, in itself a legacy of this moment, designed to foster Anglo–French psychoanalytic dialogue, which John Forrester – the only non-analyst to succeed in such a venture – organised and hosted at the British Psychoanalytic Society in 1984.

Look at Lacan's founding statement of 1964 and it is this institutional history which it at once anticipates and narrates. The opening declaration is famous: 'I found – alone as I have always been in my relationship to the analytic cause – the école freudienne de Paris', as is the performance of the utterance (a tape recorder of the master's voice played from the back of the room where all his adherents had been summoned). But the rest of the statement, the form of the institution proposed, is rarely mentioned. An institution which despite the arrogation to himself of the directorship and the inclusion by fiat of his own trainees was, in intention at least, designed to operate on the principle of constant self-questioning: 'all those are invited who might contribute in putting the viability of this training to the test' (the translation renders this: 'all those who can contribute to substantiating the *ordeal* of that training', my emphasis – a creative misreading as we shall see).[39] The following clauses are crucial to Lacan's founding gesture of 1964:

> After a certain time in operation, the elements of any one group will be proposed for permutation into another.
>
> The control of the directorship will not constitute a chiefdom ('*une chefferie*') where service rendered will be something to be cashed in against access to a superior rank, and no one should experience work undertaken at the base as a retrograde step.
>
> For the reason that anyone undertaking a personal task will fall within the conditions of critique and control to which any work pursued in the School will be submitted.
>
> Far from implying a hierarchy from top to bottom, what is involved is a circular organisation whose functioning, easy to programme, is to be affirmed by experience.[40]

Three years later, in 1967, on the eve of the barricades, Lacan will propose, at the risk of creating a new empire, an entirely new mode of analytic institutionalisation. It can fairly be described as a radical break with almost everything that had gone before:

> I have never spoken of the formation of analysts; what I have spoken of are the formations of the unconscious. There is no analytic formation [training]. Out of analysis an experience evolves which it is a complete mistake to classify as didactic. Experience is not didactic.[41]

Why would anyone want to become an analyst? You might ask in reply: Why does anyone ever want to become anything at all? But, in relation to psychoanalysis, the question has a particular resonance, since it is a central part of psychoanalysis to ask how you come to recognise and misrecognise yourself in what you are. And since behind, or inside, that question will be the question of desire – the aims, vicissitudes and perversions of our pleasures – 'wanting', no less than 'becoming', is something you cannot take for granted. Wanting to become an analyst cannot be the endpoint of something, like discovering one's vocation, it can only be the start. At the heart of a so-called training analysis there must be, therefore, an 'interminable' questioning of what the prospective analyst is doing there. Only this way can you avoid the risk of analysis turning into a merely professional training; and only if this question is something which a would-be analyst can sustain throughout her or his practice will the qualification of being an analyst avoid becoming a form of institution-alised authority which never has to, because it never had to in the beginning, give an account of itself.

Only along some such lines as these does it seem possible to understand the two cornerstones of Lacan's revolution in training. The *passe* in which the analyst bears witness to what her or his analysis has consisted of; qualifying then becomes, like analysis itself, no more and no less than an act of speech. And the principle for which Lacan became most notorious in the field of training: that the analyst derives authorisation from her or himself alone – the logical consequence of the first, since it is only out of the analysand's experience of their own unconscious, what has shifted in their own relationship to it, that the desire to become an analyst can emerge. 'What,' asks Lacan, 'is this form of madness which drives someone who, by the end of analysis, is aware of what is at stake for the analyst, to choose to practise analysis her or himself?'[42]

When Moustapha Safouan states that psychoanalysis was instituted 'as if psychoanalysis had never existed', or 'that the structure of present day societies is aimed from one end to another at protecting analysts from psychoanalysis', he is therefore arguing that the institutional beginnings of psychoanalysis were set up in such a way as to make it almost impossible for a prospective analyst to ask this question.[43] Nor can this problem be framed in terms of the clash between the free association of the analysand and the authority of the analyst, an opposition too easily translatable into the liberal opposition between the individual and social norms (this is why, as we will see, making the institution more democratic or answerable, albeit crucial, is not enough). What matters at the end of analysis is the relationship of the analysand, not to the analyst, but to analysis. It could not be a matter of trusting to the freedom or autonomy of a self, since the self is precisely what the analysis, through the experience of the unconscious, has thrown into doubt. There is always a danger that the process of becoming an analyst will shift the whole experience backwards, transforming it into an appendage (read: professional qualification) of the self. The unconscious will slip past an institution – perhaps any institution (that was in a sense Lacan's wager) – if it does not enshrine at the heart of its operation the double and constant movement of the unconscious towards, and away from, the act of speech:

> The only principle to be imposed at all costs, all the more for having been misrecognised, is that an analysis is constituted as didactic through the will of the subject and she or he needs to be warned by the analyst to whom the demand is addressed that the analysis will contest this will the more the desire it conceals starts to surface.[44]

Any analytic training which does not make central to the passage from analysand to analyst the former's own testimony, the authority – as it were – of their own experience, can therefore be seen as an act of repression (the two principles – of the *passe* and of the analyst's own authorisation – are therefore inextricable). Why is the prospective analyst never expected, never asked, to speak for her or himself?

What follows is a complete reversal of the relationship normally holding between the institution and any member seeking to become an analyst (anyone, analyst or not, could become a member of the École Freudienne de Paris). Instead of a relationship between candidates and didacticians, it becomes a relationship of testimony in two directions. From School to analyst: the School will vouch that the analyst's own process of training constitutes a sufficient guarantee. From analyst to School: if and when the analyst desires to give an account to the School of her or his own experience of analysis. No hierarchy, no pre-selection of candidates:

> The October proposal undoubtedly constituted one of the most innovative acts, with regard to training, in the history of psychoanalysis. What was at stake was the uncoupling of the training analysis from the

models of instruction which had obscured the passage specific to analytic therapy. Lacan thus wanted to reintroduce what was taught or transmitted by the couch as the *sole* principle of access to a function which until then tended no longer to have anything in common with the specificity of psychoanalysis ... it was a matter, at bottom, of institutionalising a 'third site' for psychoanalysis, partaking neither of exams in the academic sense nor of any doctorate or diploma, but rather of a specifically Freudian politics of training.[45]

Surprisingly then – given how little attention has been paid to the question of training in recent theory – it was in his concept of the institution that Lacan perhaps effected his most radical 'return to Freud'. 'The School must avoid falling into the humourless *tough* talk of a psychoanalyst I met during my last visit to the States who said to me: "The reason I will never attack the instituted forms of analysis is because they ensure me a comfortable and unproblematic routine."' (The words on which Lacan's October 1967 proposition ends.)[46]

And yet Lacan's experiment went wrong. The dissolution of his School is taken, as Safouan puts it on the first page of his book, as a *de facto* judgement. Indeed the moment, or rather form, of dissolution – 'I dissolve you' – can fairly be seen as emblematic of the very authoritarianism of Lacan's own person as it rushed to fill the vacuum of an institutional authority naively trying to liquidate itself.

Once again, as we saw in relation to Freud, too much and too little is made of Lacan's person in this account. That Lacan became a charismatic leader is unquestionable, a charisma that can be situated in the very founding moment of the School: 'I found, alone as I have always been in my relationship to the psychoanalytic cause.' In the first secession from the school, Piera Aulagnier will comment: 'The day an analyst finds himself alone in front of the analytic cause, that cause is dead, over and done.'[47] Lacan was also, to say the least, authoritarian: not only founder but legislator. Even the Roman emperors considered themselves as judges or jurists whose opinion could be sought, but never as an authority enacting and forging the law; and even the so-called pope's infallibility acted as a form of restriction by binding each pope to the dictates – precisely infallible – of the one who went before. We could say that Lacan failed to make the proper distinction between authority and power which Hannah Arendt traces back to the heart of Roman politics: 'The most conspicuous characteristic of those in authority is that they do not have power [. . .] "while power resides in the people, authority rests with the Senate".[48]

Against the seemingly unimpeachable refusal of the IPA of any notion of charismatic leader, Lacan chose instead to displace it, fusing in his own person the 'initiatic function specific to the teaching of psychoanalysis' and the administrative function 'characterising all institutions': 'He would be simultaneously *director* of his school, *master* through his doctrine, and *legislator* of a new mode of training. Through his seminar and the reduction of the length of his sessions, he would also be the *analyst* of all concerned.'[49] Lacan's autocratic function, concludes Roudinesco, 'was impeded by the very fact of its excesses. In arrogating to himself power that absolute, the master was condemning himself not to exercise it and it may paradoxically be wondered whether he had not done so on purpose [. . .] in order to treat himself to the spectacle of the limits of his own training capacities.'[50]

None of this, however, should be used to ignore the extent to which Lacan's School, in its founding moments, was the most open and democratic psychoanalytic institution ever to have existed (there is certainly nothing like it today): 'a single category of members, election of an administrative board through universal suffrage, the same voting rights for every individual'.[51] You only have to compare the Constitution and By-Laws of the IPA to get the point (only subject to minimal alterations since 1976).[52] If Lacan was a monarch, he placed himself at the permanent disposal of his subjects (his door in the rue de Lille was literally always open). Against the barons, Lacan drew his power from the base. His former analysands, trained at the Société française de psychanalyse, the young of the fourth and especially fifth generation came *en masse*: 'so much did the adventure of Lacanianism speak to their own theoretical and anti-institutional aspirationa'.[53] Although we should be cautious about that '*en masse*' – this is not the free psychoanalysis for 'the people' through the State advocated by Freud – we could none the less see this moment of psychoanalytic history as an ironic, caricatured return to Budapest in 1918: a psychoanalysis open to the people while the bureaucratic apparatus which had ousted that founding dream crumbles to the ground. We have to ask then, beyond Lacan's individual person, why this historic opposition: between an institution impeccable in the stifling anonymity of its bureaucratic procedures, and the scandalous edifice of a monarch knowing only his own edicts, at the same time as his multifarious subjects enjoy – almost revel in – the unlimited authority of their own powers.

Which is why the problem with which this essay began – of institutions and their forms – has to exceed the person of Lacan and indeed finally the institution of psychoanalysis itself. In this, Moustapha Safouan's work provides a unique historical and theoretical testimony, because of the way the problem of authority – both as personal history and as theoretical doctrine – marks his particular relationship to Lacan. Safouan's father had been a teacher of rhetoric, a militant nationalist, and first secretary of the first Egyptian workers' union who, for large tracts of Safouan's childhood, was imprisoned for his ideas. By his own account, only the theory of the symbolic father could help him reckon with a father whose absence in prison did nothing to reduce the drama of his felt presence for his son: 'the notion of a non-natural father marked the beginning of my transference to Lacan'.[54] Safouan makes it clear below that what was initiated in this moment, and not only for him, was something fully in the nature of a passion:

> When Lacan introduced his first distinctions between the different registers of paternity at the seminar he initiated in his house – 3, rue de Lille – it resonated with the members of his then minimal audience like a promise to which each and everyone of them was linked with every fibre of their being – even those (or rather: especially those) who were aware that the promise was nothing other than a correct way of working with the unconscious. Thus 'fatally' began the transference to Lacan.[55]

'What have I ever studied,' Lacan is reputed to have once put the question, 'but the motives and methods of power?'[56] For Safouan, more than apprised of the nature of his transference to Lacan, the issue is still not, or not only, Lacan as person, but how institutions, necessarily but variously, constitute themselves in relation to a third. What gives any speech-act its authority? How do two people ever come to, or rather agree to, agree? What matters here is not the resolution of conflict. This is not a Hobbesian view of natural man in need of a law to control the brutality of his desires. Want belongs along the axis of identification: 'man has no immediate relation to nature and he has no fixed goals. What man wants is what the other guy, his neighbour, wants':[57]

> Imagine two subjects. Either they are intimates in which case they have no need of speech; or they can come to agree, something which would be impossible without speech to articulate and decide their course of action and its rules. Now, it is obvious that the only vehicle individually at their disposal for this speech – a true third term – is their own voice; likewise that in and of itself this voice cannot bestow on either of them the authority required to impose agreement between them. Which is why even if the one pronouncing this speech is merely speaking a 'universal' law – one she or he submits to (for example: honour your father and mother) – the only way to gain assent to this law will be to present it – I say *present* since we are not talking about *recognition* – as an utterance emanating from somewhere else. Hence emerges the figure of the Other of the Other, to whom as it were all powers of utterance are referred.[58]

No organisation, no social institution, however democratic can bypass this site of authority. Which is why attempts at liberalisation inside the presently constituted IPA are radically beside the point:

> Despite the pertinence of their criticisms, [these] analysts have gone barely past the point of opposing a more 'democratic' structure to the authoritarianism of psychoanalytic societies. Which means we are still inside the frame of categories belonging to the city, outside whose walls only anarchy or utopia reigns.[59]

These models are tenacious – as Safouan puts it in his 1995 'Témoignage', his personal statement on psychoanalysis today: 'Despite all I have learned about transference love, I still believed in the dignity of the analyst in the same way one believes in the dignity of the citizen.'[60] The quote above continues:

> But we need to stress – remember '68 – that anarchy and utopia define themselves with reference to the same principle operating inside any hierarchy, that of the personified third. No need for this third to be 'big

brother' or the 'father of the people'. It can be a text – constitutional, religious or even scientific. Except that a text is without will. You then have to put in place a 'basic will', along the lines of the 'basic norm', the voice, single or multiple, which settles the matters on which the text is silent, in a word, sovereignty with its essential attribute of 'making and breaking the law'.[61]

To return then, one more time, to 'the' institution (the one that keeps going). The problem with current self-definition of the IPA, laid out in Article 3 of the 1977 Constitution and effectively unchanged to this day, would not therefore be solely its reliance on the proper name of Freud (the point Derrida made in his paper on 'Géopsychanalyse'); nor just, as Safouan puts it, its 'antiseptic, academic character ... void of any reference to the unconscious or desire'; but the 'less obvious link running from a definition of psychoanalysis reliant on the defunct notion of personality to a form of institutionalisation dependent in the final analysis on *statutory* authority':

> The term 'psychoanalysis' refers to a theory of personality structure and function, to the application of this theory to other branches of knowledge, and, finally, to a specific psychotherapeutic technique. This body of knowledge is based on and derived from the fundamental psychological discoveries of Sigmund Freud.[62]

And if the link to stress is the one running from the institution to the concept, or reality, of the unconscious, it is because it is the unconscious which repeatedly empties all utterances of their authority. No one 'can give the reasons for their reasons' (they do not know whether the reasons they give constitute all their reasons, and there is no ultimate reason for their reasons, whether known or unknown).[63] And that also goes – or rather especially goes – for the legislator who lays down the law.

So the question is whether there could be an institution which operates successfully within the terms of such an acknowledgement. What would it look like? 'Could there be,' Safouan asks, 'a conception of sovereignty graspable other than through the social reference to law and to place? [...] there is such a "sovereignty" and it consists of a sovereignty capable of renouncing its own essential or reigning principle.'[64] For Safouan, this is the only basis on which a psychoanalyst could possibly come to be:

> The analytic act is something else. *In principio*, in the beginning was the act. It is born, not of a form of power to be actualised, but of nothing, *ex nihilo*. It is an act which founds itself on nothing whatsoever; it is its own foundation. It rests on, comes with, and brings no guarantee.[65]

In his 'Témoignage', Safouan calls for the opening of a cultural space of dialogue – a new journal in which analysts would present reports on the state, the motivations, and the impasses of their art ('Let's take as one of the first questions whether an analyst should attend her or his analyst's seminars [. . .] as one of the second, the criteria on which a demand for supervision is accepted or refused').[66] Taking his reference from the French philosophical and literary journal *Critique* and the *TLS* in the days when its anonymous writers included Virginia Woolf, T. S. Eliot, Henry James and Ezra Pound, he thus returns the future of psychoanalysis to a non-institutional space and to something of that founding and expansive vision of Freud's (the only way out of the current trap 'between dogmatism and confusion of tongues').[67] What would be the effects if analysts from all over the world, and as part of the process of becoming an analyst, were expected to talk to each other?

Finally, it is not only because there does not seem to be an answer to the questions so graphically posed by this narrative that I choose to end with the story which concludes his most recently translated text, *Speech or Death*, first delivered in English as a lecture, 'Are There Universals in Culture?', at the British Film Institute in London in March 1994:

> The story goes that after a great victory a general camped with his army at the foot of a mountain. Raising his eyes, he saw a man seated above him on the mountain. Wild with anger, he climbed up and hailed the man. 'Who are you,' he asked, 'to make so bold as to sit above me?' 'Sire,' answered the man, 'you are asking me who I am without telling me who you are.' 'I am the head of the army you see down there.' 'And who is above you?' 'The Field Marshal, of course.' 'And above the Field Marshal?' 'Only the King is above the Field Marshal.' 'And above the King?' 'Nothing is above the King!' To which the man

replied: 'I am that nothing,' thereby indicating what makes us all equal.[68]

Perhaps, therefore, it is through this history that psychoanalysis can most productively tell us about something *other* than itself (*applied* psychoanalysis would not therefore be, as is most often assumed, psychoanalysis shorn of its institutional conditions but precisely the reverse). If it is somehow exemplary, it is because it leaves wide open the question of the fate of institutions, of any institution trying to make a space for the unconscious to be recognised inside its walls.

Notes and References

1 Jacques Derrida, 'Géopsychanalyse "and the rest of the world"', *Géopsychanalyse – les souterrains de l'institution, recontre franco–latino– américaine* (Paris: Confrontations, 1981); translated in Chris Lane, *Psychoanalysis and Race* (New York: Columbia University Press, 1998).

2 Freud, *The Question of Lay Analysis: Conversations with an Impartial Person* (1926; *Standard Edition*, 20, London: Hogarth Press), p. 246, cited as epigraph, Jacques Lacan, 'Amendment to Statutes proposed by Dr Sacha Nacht for the Institute of Psychoanalysis: Psychoanalysis and Teaching', January 1953, *La scission de 1953: La communauté psychanalytique en France, I, Ornicar?* (Paris: Seuil, 7, 1976).

3 Lussier, cited Wallerstein, 'Between Chaos and Petrification: A Summary of the Fifth IPA Congress of Training Analysts', *International Journal of Psychoanalysis*, 74 (1993), p. 165.

4 Moustapha Safouan, *Jacques Lacan et la question de la formation des analystes* (Paris: Seuil, 1986); trans. Jacqueline Rose, *Jacques Lacan and the Question of Psychoanalytic Training* (London: Macmillan, 2000).

5 Anna Freud, 'The Problem of Training Analysis' (1938), *The Writings of Anna Freud*, 4: 1945–1956 (New York: International Universities Press, 1968), pp. 420–21. First published in German in *Max Eitingon in Memoriam* (Jerusalem: Israeli Psychoanalytic Society, 1950).

6 Eitingon, Opening Address to the General Meeting of the International Training Commission, Marienbad, 2 August 1936, *International Journal of Psychoanalysis*, 18 (1937), p. 351.

7 Juliet Mitchell, 'Dora: From Hysterical Body to the Dubious Question of Femininity for Psychoanalysis and Feminism', paper delivered to the Seventh International Meeting of the International Association for the History of Psychoanalysis: 'The Role of Women in the History of

Psychoanalysis: Ideas, Practice, Institutions', London, 16 July 1998. Reprinted in *Mad Men and Medusas: Reclaiming Hysteria and the Effect of Sibling Relations on the Human Condition* (London: Allen Lane, 2000).

8   Eitingon, 'Preliminary Discussion of the Question of Analytic Training', 3 September 1925, *International Journal of Psychoanalysis*, 7 (1926), p. 133.

9   Shoshona Felman, 'Psychoanalysis and Education', *Jacques Lacan and the Adventure of Insight: Psychoanalysis in Contemporary Culture* (Cambridge, MA: Harvard University Press, 1987), p. 89.

10   Ibid., p. 91.

11   Ibid., p. 90.

12   Bill Readings make a direct link between the problem of institutionalisation in the universities in an increasingly professionalised world and the analytic scene: 'the sense of incalculable otherness of the student affects the scene of pedagogy [. . .] one of the reasons family relationships are so difficult, as Freud noted, is that neither children nor parents come with instruction manuals. Again, we do not know the nature of our obligations in advance, and any attempt to determine strictly the nature of our mutual obligation, to regulate the reciprocal debt, produces psychotics instead of neurotics. [. . .] an exhaustive knowledge of the nature of [our bonds to other people] is simply not available to us.' *The University in Ruins* (Cambridge, MA: Harvard University Press, 1996), p. 189.

13   Safouan, *Jacques Lacan*, p. 53.

14   In particular Mikkel Borch-Jacobsen's essay, 'The Freudian Subject: From Politics to Ethics', first published in *October*, 39 (Winter 1986); Jean-Luc Nancy and Philippe Lacoue-Labarthe, 'Le peuple juive ne rêve pas', *La psychanalyse est-elle une histoire juive?* Colloque de Montpelier 1980 (Paris: Seuil, 1981); 'The Unconscious is De-structured like an Affect' and 'From Where is Psychoanalysis Possible?' *Stanford Literature Review*, 6 and 8 (1991); Diana Fuss, *Identification Papers* (New York and London: Routledge, 1997).

15   Elizabeth Roudinesco, *Jacques Lacan: Esquisse d'une vie, histoire d'une système de pensée* (Paris: Fayard, 1993), pp. 156–7, trans. Barbara Bray; *Jacques Lacan* (New York: Columbia University Press, 1997), p. 111. (References to the translation, which may have been modified, will be given in parentheses.)

16   Borch-Jacobsen, 'The Freudian Subject', p. 115.

17   Frederick Crews and his critics, *The Memory Wars: Freud's Legacy in Dispute* (New York: New York Review Books, 1995); for a brilliant response to Crews, see John Forrester, 'Dispatches from the Freud Wars', *Dispatches from the Freud Wars: Psychoanalysis and its Passions*

(Cambrige, MA: Harvard University Press, 1997), pp. 208–48; and Jonathan Lear, 'On Killing Freud (Again)', *Open Minded – Working Out the Logic of the Soul* (Cambridge, MA: Harvard University Press, 1998), pp. 16–32.

18 Safouan, *Jacques Lacan*, p. 63.

19 *Feminine Sexuality: Jacques Lacan and the école freudienne*, ed. Juliet Mitchell and Jacqueline Rose, trans. Jacqueline Rose (London: Macmillan; New York: Norton-Pantheon, 1982).

20 Roudinesco, *La bataille de cent ans: Histoire de la psychanalyse en France 2: 1925–1985* (Paris: Fayard, 1994), trans. Jeffrey Mehlman, as *Jacques Lacan & Co* (London: Free Association Books, 1990), p. 431 (p. 423). (References to the translation, which may have been modified, will be given in parentheses.) *Jacques Lacan & Co*, which does not have this title in the French, is the second volume of Roudinesco's study, the only one translated to date. The details of Lacan's presence in French psychoanalysis have therefore been severed from their history.

21 Ibid., p. 430 (p. 422).

22 Sigmund Freud, 'Recommendations to Physicians Practising Psycho-Analysis' (1912; *Papers on Technique*, Standard Edition, 12, London: Hogarth Press), pp. 115–16.

23 Ella Freeman Sharpe, 'The Technique of Psycho-Analysis – Seven Lectures' (1930), 1: 'The Analyst': 'Without this flair it is impossible to acquire technique. This ability depends upon the analysed unconscious mind. It is always strictly in proportion to the freely-moving unconscious mind.' *Collected Papers on Psycho-Analysis* (London: Hogarth Press, 1950), p. 15.

24 Freud, *The Question of Lay Analysis: Conversations with an Impartial Person*, p. 250.

25 Ibid., p. 248.

26 Ibid., 'Postscript', p. 252.

27 Wen-Ji Wang gives a very different account of the earliest history of training as a process of 'purification', purging the unconscious differences of the first generation of analysts to secure didactic transmission, and of training conceived as artisanal craft. By arguing that training necessarily involves subjection to the master's didactic influence, he places the drama of Lacan's institute back at the centre of the training process *per se*. 'Training in Psycho-Analysis', unpublished M. Phil. thesis, Cambridge (1997).

28 Freud, 'Lines of Advance in Psycho-Analytic Therapy', address to the Fifth International Psycho-Analytical Congress, Budapest, September 1918, Standard Edition, 17, p. 167.

29 Michael Balint, 'On the Psycho-Analytic Training System', *International Journal of Psychoanalysis*, 29 (1948), p. 168.

30 Freud, *The Question of Lay Analysis*, p. 196.

31 Siegfried Bernfeld, 'On Psychoanalytic Training', *Psychoanalytic Quarterly* (1962).

32 Ibid., p. 467, cited Safouan, p. 62 (Safouan's emphasis).

33 Safouan, *Jacques Lacan*, p. 63.

34 Ibid., p. 64.

35 Victor Calef, 'A Report on the 4th Pre-Congress on Training to the 27th International Psychoanalytic Congress', *International Journal of Psychoanalysis*, 53 (1972), p. 41.

36 Lacan, 'Proposition du 9 octobre 1967 sur le psychanalyste de l'école', *Scilicet*, 1 (1968), p. 29, cited Safouan, p. 115

37 Roudinesco, *Histoire*, p. 454 (p. 447).

38 Roudinesco, *Histoire*, p. 634 (p. 632). On the issue of IPA pluralism, in a recent website discussion on matters of training, IPA analyst Anne Hayman comments: 'One outcome of the peace is that clarity of the differences in the theoretical models has also diminished . . . there is a paucity of understanding what the differences are, which surely means quite a failure in actually extending the understanding of dissident views.'

39 Lacan, 'Fondation de l'école freudienne de Paris', 21 June 1964, *L'excommunication*, p. 149, cited Roudinesco, *Jacques Lacan*, p. 402 (p. 309).

40 Ibid., pp. 149–50.

41 Jacques Lacan, 'A propos de l'experience de la passe et de sa transmission', November 1973, *Ornicar?*, *Sur la passe* (Paris: Seuil), 12–13, December 1977, p. 121.

42 Safouan, *Jacques Lacan*, pp. 110–11.

43 Ibid., pp. 63, 116.

44 Lacan, Additional Note: on didactic psychoanalysis in its participation in the School', *L'Acte de fondation*, 21 June 1964, cited Safouan.

45 Roudinesco, *Histoire*, pp. 455–6 (p. 449).

46 Lacan, 'Proposition du 9 octobre', 1967, p. 30.

47 Cited, Sophie de Mijolla-Mellor, 'Women Theorists of Psychoanalysis', 'The Role of Women in the History of Psychoanalysis', London, 16 July 1998.

48 Hannah Arendt, 'What is Authority?', *Between Past and Future: Eight Essays in Political Thought* (New York: Viking, 1968), p. 122.

49 Ibid., p. 418.

50 Ibid., pp. 432, 463.

51 Roudinesco, *Histoire*, p. 436 (p. 429). See also p. 632 (p. 634) for Roudinesco's summary of the institutional repercussions of Lacan between 1964 and 1980, and for a fuller account of the experiments that have followed in France in the wake of the école freudienne, 'Cent ans de psychanalyse: état des lieux', the last chapter of *Histoire*, and also 'Heritages' with which she ends *Jacques Lacan*.

52 The International Psychoanalytical Association: Constitution and Bye-laws, ratified June 1994, amended July 1996 (currently under further amendment). One change is of particular note in relation to the critique made by Jacques Derrida of the 1977 Constitution 'Géopsychanalyse et "le reste du monde . . ." '. At that stage, the 'Geographic Areas' named by the Constitution were: America north of the United States–Mexican border; all America south of that border; and the rest of the world (hence Derrida's title). The 1996 Constitution redescribes these areas as follows: 1) North America (America north of the United States–Mexican border); 2) Europe and 3) Latin America (America south of the United States–Mexican border). It then adds: 'For purposes of administering this Article, Japan is allocated to North America, and Australia, Israel and India are allocated to Europe.'

53 *Histoire*, p. 426 (p. 419)

54 Cited, ibid., p. 298 (p. 287).

55 See also the account by the Algerian Houda Aumont of how analysis with Lacan turned on her discovery that her father had executed a member of the FLN, rival of his organisation during the struggle for independence. Roudinesco, *Jacques Lacan*, p. 507 (p. 393).

56 Remark to Jean Lacouture, cited Roudinesco, *Jacques Lacan*, p. 366 (p. 279).

57 Safouan, 'Beyond Society', *Speech or Death*, translated by Martin Thom, typescript, pp. 128–9.

58 Safouan, Philippe Julien and Christian Hoffmann, *Malaise dans la psychanalyse – le tiers dans l'institution et l'analyse de contrôle* (*Psychoanalysis and its Discontents – the third inside the institution and control analysis*), (Paris: Arcanes, 1995), pp. 51–2. Compare Hannah Arendt in her essay 'What is Authority?': 'The essential character of specifically authoritarian forms of government [is] that the source of their authority, which legitimates the exercise of power, must be beyond the sphere of power and, like the law of nature or the commands of God, must not be man-made.' Arendt's account of the authoritarian relation between 'the one who commands and the one who obeys' as resting 'neither on common reason nor on the power of the one who commands' but on 'the hierarchy itself, whose rightness and legitimacy both recognise and

where both have their predetermined stable place' is remarkable for how close it comes to Safouan's analysis of the IPA (Arendt, pp. 111, 93).

59 Ibid., pp. 18–19.

60 Safouan, 'Et maintenant: Témoignage sur la psychanalyse en france depuis 1967', personal communication, 1995, p. 2.

61 Safouan et al. *Malaise*, pp. 18–19.

62 Safouan, *Jacques Lacan*, p. 75.

63 Ibid., p. 35.

64 Ibid., p. 41.

65 Ibid., p. 60.

66 Témoignage', p. 17.

67 Ibid.

68 Safouan, 'Beyond Society', typescript p. 140; Safouan et al., *Malaise*, p. 41. The last line of the translation in fact continues: 'although we may not all be equal in knowing it.' In correspondence with me, Safouan said that he left it to Martin Thom's choice whether to add this clause ('I do not know if he did'). I prefer to omit it, although it beautifully encapsulates the institutional dilemma for analysis which has been the topic here. Does the analyst know better? And if, as subject of the unconscious, what she or he knows is the limit to her or his own knowing, then surely there can be no inequality in the matter? Safouan's addition, as I see it, risks reinstating the analyst's, albeit self-effacing, authority. In correspondence, Safouan replied: 'I do not fear knowledge on sovereignty being transformed into a new source of power; it rather marks the end of all temptation by the latter. This view is probably not unrelated to the traumatic effect of my father's arrest which lay in the fact that I was struck by the cops laying their hands on the One "greater than whom you cannot imagine".'

III: MODERN TIMES

The Cult of Celebrity

The death of Princess Diana in 1997 provoked an overwhelming response among large sections of the British public. In the aftermath, commentators were quick either to diagnose mass hysteria or to greet the outpouring of feeling as a sea change, the sign of a new-found capacity of the British people emotionally to express themselves. I wrote this piece, which was published in the London Review of Books *of 20 August 1998, when its editor Mary-Kay Wilmers asked me to address the topic of celebrity as part of a new series of dialogues between the* LRB *and* New Left Review *launched in 1998. It has become a cliché to say that we live in the age of celebrity. I tried to use the occasion to address its discomforting side. What is it in celebrity that we get so het up – excited and embarrassed – about?*

It is not easy to admit to an interest in celebrity without apology. A passion for celebrity is not something one is meant to talk about. There are worlds, or rather circles, where, if you do, it is somehow assumed that what you are really claiming is a type of intellectual slumming. If, for example, you admit to or even boast of reading *Hello!* magazine, an addiction to which I happily confess, reading *Hello!* could not possibly be what you are really boasting about. 'Is it true that you read *Hello!*?' I am sometimes asked in disbelief – an appropriate enough wording, 'Is it true?', since celebrity depends for its existence on hearsay, innuendo and gossip (although what is distinctive about *Hello!* is that it doesn't, or not quite). Admitting to a passion for celebrity seems to have something in the nature of a shameful secret. So there might be an intimate, even passionate, connection between the cult of celebrity and shame.

Whenever we find a particular rich mix of affective or emotional language, in relation to the cult of celebrity, it might be worth paying close attention. But not in the ways which have followed the public response to the death of princess Diana (our current celebrity *par excellence*). Reactions to that response – the overwhelming, unavoid-able nature of its presence over those famous two weeks and since –

seem to have gone in one of two ways. Either the public was deluded; the emotions expressed were manipulated and/or false (the 'unbelievable!' camp). Or that same public – although at moments it was hard to believe it *was* the same public – was being truer than perhaps it had ever been to itself ('the week that shook the world' camp). For this camp, the very fact of public emotion being expressed by the British was the incontrovertible proof of its authenticity; the emotions were not, therefore, only true but, by dint of that first authenticity, *truer* than anything else about the British psyche (the end of English reserve).

In other words, faced with this public display of feeling, it seemed that we could only cry 'true' or 'false'. From where, we might ask, or on what authority can such a judgement be made? Or is it the need to judge, whether for or against, that is paramount, as if there is nothing more frightening than a public display of emotion – emotion at large, as it were – which refuses to be read immediately and unequivocally; as if public affect must be necessarily either good or bad for us all? What if, instead, we pay attention to the language but also consider ourselves licensed to shift the terms around a bit, to rearrange the dominant vocabularies to see what else they might yield? What happens, that is, if we do two seemingly contradictory things: take wholly seriously public demonstrations of affect without necessarily taking them at their word? If we at one and the same time believe and – to deform the famous formula – suspend our belief?

Consider the celebrity of Mary Bell. How many times did outraged journalists cut straight from their opprobrium at the money she was paid (making profit out of the most hideous of crimes) to the pleasure Bell was purported to have taken in murdering Martin Brown and Brian Howe? Again: how could anyone know? Given the profit that these papers were making out of their horror at the profit (an obvious point), not to say out of the horror they of course re-evoked and drew their readers into at exactly the same time – given we might say their own traffic in the pleasures of horror – we might, again shifting the terms, ask: what is the perverse profit of pleasure? How far is pleasure – the pleasure we take in celebrity, for example – bound up with perversion, or with something we experience as perverse? Is that the bonus which distinguishes celebrity from fame? It depends of course on how you define perversion. If there is a link between shame and celebrity, there is of course also a link between perversion and shame. Shame, or shaming, with its ostentatious morality, might be seen as a form of perversion in itself. Celebrity is often a ritual of public humiliation. Indeed, in relation to celebrity, shaming often appears to be the point, and not just in the shaming of Mary Bell.

Could it be then that celebrity is indeed our guilty secret, a veiled way of putting into public circulation certain things which do not easily admit to public acknowledgement? Hence the pull and the paradox, why it is so exciting and demeaning at the same time. I know that for some it is emphatically neither one nor the other, or perhaps one or the other, but I suspect that for those really grabbed by it, it necessarily partakes of both.

There are, of course, different types of celebrity – celebrities, for example, of the left. You might want to argue that to be a celebrity on the left is 'different' since any self-aggrandisement is offset by the collective good aimed at by their necessarily public commitment. There is a famous psychoanalytic article by Harold Searles called 'The Effort to Drive the Other Person Crazy' in which he lovingly details all the ways people have of driving each other mad, and then continues with the ways people drive each other even madder by denying that that is what they are doing. He then asks: what is the profession in which the denial of the desire to drive the other person crazy is strongest? To which the answer is: psychoanalysis of course. Which suggests that psychoanalysts are the people who most want to drive other people mad (obvious enough some may think). According to that argument, no one would be more passionately committed to the cult of celebrity than those who construct an elaborate façade of public good as the veil for their own need for acclaim.

There is, however, a more historically based way of approaching the drama of display so central to celebrity in the modern world. In his 1986 *Frenzy of Renown: A History of Fame* (the word 'frenzy' will return crucially in relation to Mary Bell), Leo Braudy argues that our uncertainties about the morality of public behaviour and the personalities of public people arise in great part from the 'Judeo-Christian attack against Roman standards of public glory'. In this opposition, to seek or confer fame is either the appropriate manifestation of public valour and dignity, or a self-violation and affront to our true inner worth. It is either civic virtue, the due recognition that our acts are only sanctioned by their staging in the world of men (it was of course mainly men); or spiritually corrupt, performing to the wrong crowd (God is the only true audience of man's worth). 'It is far from honouring him who made us,' writes Montaigne in the Apology for Raymond Sébond, 'to honour him whom we have made.'

For Braudy, Augustine is the key figure. Augustine saw Lucretia's suicide, not as proof of her virtue but the opposite. He called her 'praeclarissa', meaning the most visible, her error being that she commits suicide to make what is in her heart visible; it is the only way, as she sees it, to display her inner worth to the eyes of men. There is of course a tension here, one in which even our secular culture could be said still to be caught. Jesus makes the deaf hear and the mute speak but then enjoins them to silence ('He charged them to tell no one; but the more he charged them, the more zealously they published it'). Augustine, in Braudy's words, 'turned his face against Roman public life and argued that the emptiness that comes from living exclusively in the eyes of others could be filled with God, but even he wrestled with the desire to be praised openly for his denial of worldly values'.

Cut from here to this passage from Mark Twain's 'The Story of a Good Little Boy' (who does this remind you of?):

> Jacob had a noble ambition to be put in a Sunday school book. He wanted to be put in with pictures representing him gloriously declining to lie to his mother . . . and pictures representing him standing on the doorstep giving a penny to a poor beggar-woman with six children . . . and pictures of him magnanimously refusing to tell on the bad boy who always lay in wait for him around the corner as he came from school, and welted him over the head with a lath.

There is a paradox inherent in seeking an audience for one's own worth (which is why discussion of whether Diana's acts of benevolence were hypocritical or sincere are beside the point). The vanity of public life contains its own disavowal. It is not hypocrisy to want to be seen to be doing good; it tells very little about the nature of the act being performed. One definition of a celebrity might then be: celebrities are the people required by us to embody or to carry the weight of the question: who are we meant to be performing to, or what are we doing when performing to an invisible audience? We should never assume that because an audience is present, visible, that there isn't an invisible one, hidden but present too. Among other things, public celebrity might be an elaborate diversion from the complex, often punitive audience, inside the mind (one narcissism as a diversion from another).

Celebrities who affirm with apparent desperation that they do not court publicity, who attempt to wrest their private life from the public gaze on which of course they so totally rely (they are legion – open any paper), are perhaps naive only for failing to realise that this is the paradox or balancing act they are required to perform. They are in fact never performing so appropriately as celebrities, never displaying so perfectly the tension on which it thrives, as in the moments when they make that, as it were, non- or anti-performative claim. A celebrity is someone all too close who also stages something in the nature of a magical disappearing act. In fact, this stunning ambivalence is another thing that celebrity has in common with shame: 'In shame,' writes psychologist Sylvan Tomkins, 'I wish to continue to look and be looked at, but I also do not wish to do so.' This is Richard Gere interviewed – although, as you will see, that is not quite the right word – by Cameron Docherty in the *Independent* in June 1998:

> He is as elusive as smoke. Restless and edgy, he paces around the marble floor of his Malibu home wondering why people are always curious about his private life, and isn't it enough just to talk about his profession. Finally, Richard Gere settles into an armchair and remains motionless, staring straight ahead, his nobleman profile tilted ever so slightly upward, as if he were listening for ethereal music lesser mortals cannot hear. He proceeds to spend the next hour talking to me without ever looking at me. His voice is scarcely audible, even from three feet away; he makes so faint an imprint on his surroundings, I keep fighting the uneasy sensation that he might dematerialise before my eyes.

What I love about *Hello!* (or perhaps I should say – *one* of the things I love about *Hello!*) is the so much more brazen, upfront way, without a tinge of embarrassment, it puts this ambivalence on display. To cite one of my favourite moments: Barbara Taylor Bradford renewing her marriage vows in the total privacy of a completely deserted tropical island on which no tourists step; only black luggage carriers in attendance, as well, of course, as the whole photographic and editorial team of *Hello!*. (She said this day was as good as the first day of her marriage, which made me think the first day probably hadn't been so good.)

So perhaps Princess Diana and Prince Charles broke the rules, boldly crossed the public/private boundary with their television interviews and the intimacies they used them to reveal, but equally perhaps they didn't. More simply, in relation to Diana, we can note the wondrous mixture of forms of celebrity – sacred and secular – which she provokes. This is Andrew Morton on the last page of the revised 1997 edition of his famous book:

> Not only did she capture the spirit of the age, but more than that the manner of her life and death formed part of a religious cycle of sin and redemption, a genuinely good and Christian woman who was martyred for our sins, epitomising our strange appetite for celebrity.

The response to celebrity always harbours a political subtext. It is often assumed, especially on the left, that emotions on public display are politically demeaning and should be put to cultural or political work somewhere else (love against labour, as it were). Or else, more simply, they are a front. As many of the commentators fairly pointed out at the time, the so-called transfiguration of the British psyche at the time of Diana's death left a lot of undesirable components of the British political landscape intact. Those mourning Diana on the Mall do not necessarily want to pay higher taxes to improve the lot of those she sponsored, nor was it hard to hear the undertones of racism in the conspicuous, at moments deafening, silence about Dodi Fayed.

But those most critical of the Diana phenomenon often seem to be expressing, in addition to this, something else. A belief that affect is antagonistic to politics, that if we do not 'reason together', as Mary Wollstonecraft once famously put it, we destroy any chance of collective or individual participation in the fullness of civic life. Politics is emotionally divested reason or it is nothing (emotion eats out the mind). 'September,' Ian Jack kicked off the 'Unbelievable!' issue of *Granta* dedicated in part to Diana's death, 'was not a good month for those who imagined that human society is, or might one day, be governed by reason.' For Elizabeth Wilson, in 'The Unbearable Lightness of Diana' in *New Left Review*, the mythic status of Diana cancels any feminist component of her story (as if both things couldn't be true). The left is the last bastion of a form of reason dangerously discredited in our times, nothing embodying that danger more clearly than the Diana effect:

> Thus grief for Diana privileges the value of feeling over reason and is therefore a good, whereas ideas associated with socialism, such as justice and equality make a fatal claim to rationality and are therefore bad.

Likewise Ross McGibbon in the *London Review of Books*, although much more hesitant about pronouncing on the authenticity of the emotions involved, none the less concluded: 'A democracy which admired her with such intensity is both incomplete and immature.'

For the 'unbelievable' camp, the problem was not, however, just too much emotion, but emotion of the wrong kind. Those participating wholeheartedly in the experience were light-headed ('grief-lite') or even deluded. Grief, this argument goes, is false if it is directed at someone you don't know. Or, if you are not really suffering, the affect is not true. And yet, one of the functions of public figures is, surely, to make you feel you know them, that you have some mysterious but no less powerful link to who they are. More important, what pre-Freudian policing of affect was this? That grief should appear in the right place for the right object at the right time. As if grief comes pat to place, as if it shows up, or only shows up, in the moments when it is due. As if mobilising defences, or even radical dissociation of affect were not one, not uncommon, part of grief. Pain goes underground – the technical name is of course 'repression' – biding its time, waiting for its moment, an occasion when it can catch you unawares. False is the wrong cry. False, in relation to grief, can ring true. (In fact, one of the writers in *Granta* said that what she experienced or relived through the death of Diana was first the death of Kennedy and then her rape as a much younger girl, which Kennedy's death in turn had for the first time re-evoked.)

What this response also ignored was the complex circulation of emotion, not just internally to individual subjects, but more generally in the public realm. If it is unhelpful to think of public trauma (manipulated *or* authentic) as necessarily the veil for more personal, private, trauma, it is because public events can of course do cover for each other. This is from Pat Barker's *The Eye in the Door*, the second of the *Regeneration* trilogy. Siegfried Sassoon is talking about the public obsession with the Pemberton-Billing trial. He was sued for libel by the actress Maud Allan for publishing an article in his newspaper, *The Imperialist*, suggesting that a large number of the audience to her performance of Oscar Wilde's *Salome* were German spies (Lord Alfred Douglas used the occasion of the trial to accuse Wilde's friend, Robert Ross, of being the 'leader of all the sodomites in London'):

> Siegfried's face darkened. 'Do you know we actually sat in dug-outs in France and talked about that trial? The papers were full of it, I think it was the one thing that could have made me *glad* I was out there, I mean, for god's sake, the Germans on the Marne, five thousand prisoners taken and all you read in the papers is who's going to bed with whom and are they being blackmailed? *God.*'

But to say that this trial is an irrelevance in a time of war is of course to overlook the most intimate relation – the whole of the *The Eye in the Door* is in a sense devoted to it – between the persecuting and blackmailing of homosexuals and conscientious objections to the war, between the mental health (or not) of the nation and the public vilification of Oscar Wilde. Or to put it another way, celebrities – the passions they arouse – are rarely only a distraction.

Confronting the 'unbelievable' response, we find celebration, a wholehearted embrace of the new national ethos (that it was not the whole nation, or rather the extent to which mourning Diana was claimed to represent the whole nation, is of course a problem in itself). This is Andrew Morton again expressing a sentiment voiced repeatedly over those two weeks and indeed since:

> While the style was ancient, almost tribal, the substance on that day, 6 September 1997, will be seen by historians as marking the crumbling of the old hierarchical regime and the coming of a more egalitarian era.

The problem with this of course is its complete detachment of the

Diana phenomenon from the surrounding political landscape (the point repeatedly and convincingly made by the other camp). As if the People's Princess made the People's Prime Minister immune to criticism. Suddenly, the worst of what was happening under New Labour – the continuation of Thatcher's economic agenda, minus the ruthlessness (does that make it better or worse?), but with an extra and lethal dose of moralism – seemed to become invisible. Many commentators have made the point that it was only shortly after this so-called egalitarian festival that Blair cuddled up to the monarchy (fifty years of the Queen's marriage) and on the same day declared the end to single-parent benefit (the first, but for many wholly revealing, New Labour fiasco, on which he subsequently had to climb down). As McGibbon puts it, Diana may have also inadvertently allowed the monarchy to survive by obliging it to transform itself. Again, how can we know? I do not think it was the grieving for Diana which severed our public life from political concerns – we know very little about the political affiliations and involvements of the majority of people involved – so much as this strand of celebratory analysis that came after.

But, to stay this time inside the language being used, what is most striking about those who saw the occasion as the expression of a new emotional presence on the part of the British people was the extraordinarily limited, benign, self-congratulatory image of the world of feeling that was evoked. As if, in this analysis, the Diana phenomenon was being used to call up, not just a newly, publicly available form of feeling, but feeling divested of one half of its nature. What we were being offered was more like a vision of the national psyche in the process of purging itself. (Perhaps this is why it all became so coercive – grief must not only be done but must be seen to be done.) This crowd is too knowing, too sure, too politically astute and too pure. It is not really true finally that one camp was 'for' public emotion and one 'against', but rather that in this second case emotion was only permissible as virtue (emotion by virtue of being nice).

Such a vision should surely, however, make us suspicious and nowhere more than in the realm of public acclaim. Oddly, in their uncritical celebration of what happened, this camp reproduce what might be seen as one of the most, if not dubious, certainly precarious components of the phenomenon of celebrity itself. Somebody must be allowed to win for us all; someone must be seen to come out on top; but in defiance of the ruthlessness of their and our ambition – against the psychic odds, as it were – they must survive as pure. In this way self-serving individualism does not have to stop us from feeling, or being, good. This is Braudy:

> The goal is to purge achievement of all negative implications – to strive purely, to win without defeating, to be committed to the life of achieving – while constantly trying to avoid the compromised surrender to a sordid public gaze.

So, what, finally, are the alternatives on offer? (Note the bizarre division of emotional labour involved.) Politics as emotionally divested reason, or alternatively a new politics of feeling divested of one part – the ugly half, to put it crudely – of the mind? Place the two missing portions – affect and psychic violence – back together (or the violent part of affect), and we might get close, we circle back, to the heart of celebrity.

It is easy to list what Diana and Mary Bell have in common, in addition, that is, to the extraordinary public fervour that they provoke. Two innocents, two young girls, too young to know what they were doing when they did what most radically determined their lives, two female figures hounded by the press, two women whose physical attributes seem to be some essential component of their appeal, two women accused of being manipulative. Even Andrew O'Hagan in his *Guardian* review of Gitta Sereny's *Cries Unheard*, in his powerful defence of Bell against what he sees as Sereny's ethical blindness and manipulations, made Bell's own manipulativeness a central part of his case, something Sereny should have been protecting her from: 'Mary Bell is still a very confused and hurt and manipulative person.'

In both cases, the press are seen to have pushed its case to the point of violation, in Diana's case possibly to her death, in Bell's to the destruction of the life she had so carefully built against the legacy of her own crime. Both women try or tried to make use of a public world which exceeds, slips out, overruns their control with devastating consequences. As Diana is purported to have commented on Andrew

Morton's book (her remark is given by Morton in his revised edition): 'He's pretty much written my obituary.' Or in Morton's own words, waiting for its publication was, 'like watching a slowly spreading pool of blood seeping from under a locked door'.

Perhaps this is why these two women embody so dramatically the paradox and the perversion – the passion and loathing – of celebrity. In the first responses to the death of Diana (Earl Spencer evoking the myth of Diana the huntress as hunted); in the dismay at what happened to Mary Bell, subsequent to the publication of *Cries Unheard* – it is as if the violence and sadism of public acclaim have been suddenly laid bare (you are accorded it as a type of punishment). But you might also see how that in-mixing of contraries is just one violent twist away from the more historic one which Leo Braudy describes. There is, we could say, something murderous in our relation to celebrity. On this score, Salman Rushdie would be exceptional only for having had the murderousness precede his status as celebrity rather than the other way around.

There seems to be a general agreement that the attention paid to Mary Bell in the public press has been sadistic, and that it has been sadistic in direct proportion to its vaunting of its own virtue, as if it could be assumed – behind the onslaught of public curiosity – that those pursuing her in the name of that curiosity are totally exempt from any trace of her crime. More interesting, however, and less obvious perhaps than the sadism of the tabloids in pursuit of her, is the ethically complex place in all this of Gitta Sereny herself. Her aim – and this seems to be the strength of her project – is to force the culture to acknowledge the roots of iniquity in an individual life. In the words of Inspector Dobson, chief detective in the investigation of Mary Bell: 'In our system, it is not the business of the police to find out why crimes are committed [. . .] when the perpetrators are children, it doesn't appear that it is anyone's business.' Nobody has bothered to track Mary Bell's childhood, no one in the Bulger case tried to piece together the evidence to understand what the children might have been expressing in the enactment of this monstrous, or frenzied to use Sereny's word, crime. This is the crusading aspect of her writing especially in relation to child criminals whose treatment she wishes to see changed. On this count, what our society suffers from is not too much curiosity, but not enough:

relatives, closing ranks against outsiders, tend to protect their own, unmindful or unaware of the consequences; neighbours close their ears to manifestly serious troubles; over-extended police officers underrate the potential dangers in conflicts between parents and child. [. . .] We are not just discreet in Britain, we make a fetish of privacy. We do not look carefully at our neighbours' children.

On the face of it, Sereny's interest, progressive and socially transformative rather than vicarious, stands at the opposite pole from the sort celebrity feeds.

It is, therefore, all the most disturbing to watch this inquiry slide into the forms of ruthless pursuit of its subject to which it is ostensibly opposed; to observe the violation of ethics at the heart of the ethical moment itself. This might suggest that there is no such thing as virtuous, or pure, curiosity. The formula is an oxymoron, a contradiction in terms. Curiosity does violence to its object. Sereny represents a form of spectatorship that believes in its own virtue and corrupts itself, what we might call the perverting of curiosity in motion. Sereny is a champion of her subjects; she believes in original guiltlessness and she believes in truth ('only the truth will serve the purpose of this book'). They are intimately related since she believes, and not only in relation to Bell but also in relation to Hitler's architect Albert Speer – *Albert Speer: His Battle with Truth* – that if she can bring the subjects of her investigation to acknowledge the truth, then their underlying natures, in all their original innocence, will be released. And so, in the case of Mary Bell, she considers herself, not licensed but *obliged*, to pursue this truth like a quarry, to force Mary Bell (against therapeutic advice) to relive in her presence the moment at which she killed Martin Brown. The violence of this moment in the book – which is its climax and justification – is overwhelming. It has been referred to but not cited in critical responses to the book:

> You cannot bear to remember it as it really was, I told her. But you must try. You must make another, final effort, to tell it honestly. In the final analysis, I told her, only the truth would serve the purpose of this book: which was, on the one hand, to tell her story as completely as it could be told, but also to use what had happened to her, and the reactions of others as an example and a warning. 'I don't know how to do it,' she said. 'I don't know if I can.'

[. . .]

    I told Mary I was going to ask her one more time about the day she killed Martin Brown and that she must concentrate as never before. I had turned off the telephone, the window was closed, and the curtains were half-drawn – not to make the atmosphere overly dramatic, but to underline to Mary, who finds it so difficult, the need to search back in her memory about this day, and relate what had happened as far as it was possible in a sequence of events.

When Mary Bell starts to live the scene in the present tense, Sereny then has to intervene to break the hallucination which she herself has provoked.

Compare that moment with this famous one from Claude Lanzmann's *Shoah* (his 1985 investigation of the Holocaust through interviews with perpetuators and survivors still living at the time). He is interviewing the Treblinka survivor, Abraham Bomba, who had been forced to cut the hair of victims about to enter the gas chambers. As he is interviewed, Bomba is cutting hair, although it transpires that in reality he is no longer a hairdresser.

Bomba: I can't. It's too horrible. Please.
Lanzmann. We have to do it. You know it.
Bomba. I won't be able to do it.
Lanzmann. You have to do it. I know it's very hard. I know and I
    apologise.
Bomba. Don't make me go on please.
Lanzmann. Please. We must go on.
Bomba. I told you today it's going to be very hard.

Why the staging? Why do these moments have to be lived in the present tense?

In his classic book on perversion – *Perversion: The Erotic Form of Hatred* – psychoanalyst Robert Stoller argues that at the heart of perversion is mystery. In the perverse act, a felt and threatening limit to what is knowable, or masterable by knowledge, is repeatedly, coercively and violently subdued. Or to put it another way, whatever the ethical agenda, there is something potentially murderous in our fervour, our frenzied desire to know, as well as in our commitment to a virtuous reckoning of our selves (the belief in innate good turns bad). The simultaneous evoking and annulling of mystery might do as a working definition of celebrity.

Crucially for Stoller, if this is more or less undesirable for the smooth running of our personal erotic affairs, it is no less the pre-condition of our participation in the so-called civilised world. No mind can free itself completely from the aim of mastering the onslaughts of the modern world. No human subject completely escapes perversion:

> For describing an ubiquitous mechanism, 'perversion' is too strong; it cannot rid itself of moral taint. To the point here is a remark of Freud's: 'No healthy person, it appears, can fail to make some addition that might be called perverse to the normal sexual aim; and the universality of this finding is in itself enough to show how inappropriate it is to use the word perversion as a term of reproach.'

Which leaves us with a number of questions in relation both to Diana and to Mary Bell. Can you have public life without idealisation? And then, can you have idealisation without sadism? What would a world look like in which we did not seek out people to carry our own shame? Rather than having celebrities about whom we feel curious, we create celebrities so that our curiosity, or rather curiosity at its most ruthless, can be licensed and maintained.

To return finally to the link between celebrity and shame. There is a historical point, already perhaps suggested by the Lanzmann quote, and that is the covert relationship between the cult of celebrity in British culture and Nazism. Most obviously, the connection is there in the line Gitta Sereny herself makes between her interest in Mary Bell and her work with German children traumatised by their experience as cheap labour in the camps, and again of course by her investigation of Albert Speer. More oddly, it appears in the fact that Leo Braudy chose to open his book on fame with an account of Lindbergh whose belief in his own inviolate isolation (above clouds and crowds) slid into Nazi sympathy; he returned from his tour of the Nazi aircraft industry in 1936 promoting an accommodation with Hitler. He also lived the cruellest aspect of fame through the kidnapping and murder of his child ('Who stole the Lindbergh baby? Was it you? Was it you? Was it you?' went a popular song at the time). Kitty Kelley's *The Royals* describes Princess Margaret flouncing out of a screening of Spielberg's *Schindler's List* on the grounds that she heard too much about the Jews and the Holocaust during the war (Kelley's first – deliberate? – mistake: Margaret may indeed have said it but had anyone in Britain heard too much about the Holocaust during the war?). Reviews of Kelley's book have ignored the extent to which it is an exposé of the royal German connection: it begins at the moment when the royal family come into existence as the Windsors by severing their German heritage in 1917. Given the part the royals have played in the genesis of what it means to be a celebrity in the modern world, why shouldn't that be one of the crucial British secrets behind our present-day preoccupation with celebrity?

To end, however, with Houdini. His daring always left his audience on a knife-edge of sadistic relish: 'Maybe this time he won't escape.' Until the day he let one of his admirers punch him in the stomach to test his muscle control. Just over a week later he was dead of acute appendicitis, too late to operate on after the show which, despite the diagnosis, he had insisted had to go on.

Apathy and Accountability: The Challenge of South Africa's Truth and Reconciliation Commission to the Intellectual in the Modern World

A second essay bringing psychoanalysis directly into the realm of contemporary public life concludes this collection. The South Africa Truth and Reconciliation Commission, coming at the end of the era of apartheid, must rank as one of the most extraordinary and controversial social experiments of modern times. Distinguished from all other such commissions by the fact that it held its hearings in public, it thereby invested itself in the transformative and regenerative power, over the national collective mind, of individual speech. The Chair of the Commission, Archbishop Desmond Tutu, has called for the widest possible dissemination and debate of its Report, a monumental document in itself. In that spirit, I first delivered this essay as a paper at a conference on public intellectual life – 'The Republic of Letters: on the public role of writers and intellectuals' – held in Oxford in 2000, whose papers were published as The Public Intellectual, *edited by Helen Small* (Blackwell, 2002).

> Another man will never be able to know the degree of my suffering, because he is another and not me, and besides a man is rarely willing to acknowledge someone else as a sufferer.
>
> Dostoevsky, *The Brothers Karamazov* (1880)

In perhaps one of the strangest moments in the extraordinary document that makes up the report of the Truth and Reconciliation Commission of South Africa, an application for amnesty, described as 'intriguing', is recorded from an unnamed Indian woman applying for amnesty for what she described as her 'apathy'. The application stated that those appealing for amnesty on these grounds recognised that they:

as individuals can and should be held accountable by history for our lack of necessary action in times of crisis . . . in exercising apathy rather than commitment we allow(ed) others to sacrifice their lives for the sake of our freedom and an increase in our standard of living.[1]

In this case amnesty was not granted. Although the applicants argued that apathy fell within the brief of the Commission as an act of omission, the Commissioners decided that it did 'not disclose an action or omission which amounts to an offence or a delict in respect of which amnesty can be granted'. Amnesty – the most controversial, the last added, and legally challenged clause of the Mandate of the Commission – could only be granted for acts whose motivation was political, which occurred between the Sharpeville massacre of 1960 and the inauguration of Mandela as President in 1994, on the basis of full disclosure of relevant information and if the rubric of proportionality – ends to means – was observed. A declaration or confession of apathy falls at the first of these conditions. No political organisation asked for it. Apathy receives no official sanction. Indeed, only rarely and reluctantly – hence the strangeness of this moment – do people admit to it, although they are very ready to diagnose it in others (it has in fact become one of the favourite recent political diagnoses of the West).

But if apathy does not come on political instruction, one could none the less argue that the system of apartheid, and not only of apartheid, relied on it, or something close. That inhuman political structures depend, for as long as they last, not just on the power of the oppressors and the silent complicity of the beneficiaries, but also on numbers of the oppressed being struck with an inability to connect, or give themselves, to their own cause, as well as on those beneficiaries who may have hated the system but did not – by their own repeated account in the Report – do enough: 'At the very time when we should have continued to speak out clearly for the truth and against injustice,' the spokesperson for the Stellenbosch Presbytery of the Dutch Reformed Church submitted at the human rights violations hearing in Paarl, 'we grew tired and gave up protesting' (5, p. 384). History, the precise formula insists, will hold individuals accountable for 'a lack of necessary action in time of crisis'. For apathy, since the Commission did not recognise the offence, history is the only court.

In fact, the charge falls before the conditions of amnesty on more than the first count. What is the time of apathy? How would you date it? What are the means and what the end? Is it in fact an intention at all? And what could count as full disclosure? Is apathy something communicable, is it something we have a language for talking about? Or does it, more like a disease or shameful secret, rely on doing its work invisibly in the dark? How can you fully disclose something whose chief property is deficiency, to be in some sense absent from history and missing to yourself? In today's political climate, in Great Britain at least, apathy tends to be talked about as something which has been done to civic and political responsibility ('eighteen years of Conservative rule'). As if you could only be *made* apathetic – a kind of double passive, an act of grammatical bad faith which mimics or repeats the problem it is claiming to diagnose. But the idea of apathy as purely passive should make us suspicious – as Freud once famously commented, it requires a great deal of activity to achieve a passive aim.

For anyone reading the Report of the Commission, it is hard not to be 'overwhelmed', to use the word of the Commissioners, not by apathy but by the opposite, that is, by what people are actively capable of. The Commissioners were 'almost overwhelmed', the chapter on Recommendations in the last volume, begins: 'by the capacity of individuals to damage and destroy each other' (5, p. 306). As we look back on the last century, this has become the recurrent and chilling refrain. To use a recent formula of the historian Eric Hobsbawm, we are faced with the paradox that the twentieth century 'has killed more people than any other century, but at its close, there are more people living and living better'.[2] We are faced, that is, with the fact that in the second half of the century we have barely taken leave of, the human capacity for destruction and the human capacity for improvement have – arm in arm as it were – reached new heights. It must be, then, one of the roles of the modern intellectual to try and understand this paradoxical fact of modern times, one half of which must be to try and understand what makes it possible for people to act in this way (it was part of the mandate of the Commission – part of its aim of 'restorative justice' – to understand the 'motives and perspectives' of the perpetrators, 1, p. 130). At what has become a famous moment in the hearings, former Security Branch officer Jeffrey Benzien demonstrated wet-bag suffocation on a dummy in front of the court and when asked by former victim, Tony Yengeni, what kind of man could do this, replied: 'I, Jeff Benzien, have asked that question to such an extent that I voluntarily – and it is not easy for me to say this in a full court with a lot of people who do not know me – approached psychiatrists to have myself evaluated, to find out what type of person am I' (5, p. 370).

Some of the students on a course I teach on South African literature saw this as the supreme moment of fraudulence in the proceedings, whereas – despite the 'pride' Benzien also expressed in his method: 'Mr Yengeni, with my absolutely unorthodox methods and by removing your weaponry from you, I am wholly convinced that I prevented you and your colleagues . . . I may have prevented you from being branded a murderer nowadays' (5, p. 263), and even the chilling repetition only a moment later in court: 'Do you remember, Mr Yengeni, that within thirty minutes you betrayed Jennifer Schreiner?'[3] – I am more inclined to take this question at its word. Not least because it brings us close to one of the defining features of atrocity in the modern world. Something akin to disbelief. In which part of your mind are these testimonies to be stored? How can these narratives be held in the mind at all? – a question which seems to me to go way beyond the issue of remembrance or forgetting. In his extraordinary book on Rwanda – to move for a moment to a very different part of Africa – Phillip Gourevitch writes: 'All at once, as it seemed, something we could only have imagined was upon us – and we could still only imagine it. This is what fascinates me most in existence: the peculiar necessity of imagining what is, in fact, real.'[4]

Among many other things, the Truth and Reconciliation Commission will take up its place historically for its relentless charting of the horrors of our age. Early in the report we are, however, given a warning: 'This focus on the outrageous has drawn the nation's attention away from the more commonplace violations', producing a failure on the part of ordinary South Africans to recognise, 'the "little perpetrator" in each one of us' (1, p. 133). The implication is not only, as the paragraph continues, that 'only by recognising the potential for evil in each one of us [can we] take full responsibility for ensuring that such evil will never be repeated', but also that the hearings themselves, the explicit dwelling on atrocity, have let huge swathes of the white population off the hook, those who in Njabulo Ndebele's words dwell in 'the interstice between power and indifferent and supportive agency': 'Yes, they [the bleeding-heart liberal English-speaking South African] have a story to tell. [. . .] In that interstice the English-speaking South African has conducted the business of his life.'[5]

But what this unnamed Indian woman is talking about is something rather different. She is suggesting, in a way that was clearly baffling to the Commissioners, that what you don't do as a political subject can have effects, might be as important in the transformations of the world as what you do. To read the Report of the Commission is to be confronted on almost every page with how difficult it is to speak of atrocity, whether as victim or perpetrator of the act, although the difficulty is radically different for each. It has been at the centre of the Commission and the source of its greatest difficulty that language – in the words of Antjie Krog, the Afrikaans poet commissioned by the South Africa Broadcasting Association to report on the hearings – does not easily 'bed' the truth'.[6] But we are presented here with the strange suggestion that the ways in which we do not implicate ourselves in the burdens of history might be something which it is even harder to talk about. Intellectuals are of course always accused of talking too much, not acting enough – hence also the relevance of the Commission Report, which presents the problem of speech, and its relation to acting, and failure to act, in such uniquely focused terms.

Although Hobsbawm places most of Africa outside the reach of Western modernity and democratisation – there are, he states boldly, no democracies in Africa – no country perhaps has enacted the paradox he describes as fully as South Africa: the very existence of the Commission is testimony to the violent gestation of a democracy which puts the Western world to shame. Hobsbawm contrasts the mile-long queues of the 1994 election in South Africa with the dwindling numbers of voters in the democracies of the West, and takes this fact to be one of the clearest signs of failure in the polity ('at the cost of the integrity of the political process'[7]; 34–38 per cent of the electorate voted in the last US election). The Chairman of the Commission, Archbishop Desmond Tutu, makes a similar point. 'In normal [his word] countries,' he comments on the second page of his own book on the Commission, trying to convey the exhilaration of April 1994, 'the concern was usually about voter apathy.'[8] What's normal? we might ask. True to the spirit of one strand of modern intellectual life, Tutu has given to abnormality a positive, celebratory, political gloss.

The Indian woman's testimony is given at the end of the report of the Special Hearing for Women which came about when a workshop on gender pressured the Commission to acknowledge that it might be 'missing some of the truth through lack of sensitivity to gender issues' (4, p. 282). This may at a superficial glance seem surprising, for there is a sense in which the Truth and Reconciliation Commission was dominated by the voices of women. It is they who predominantly speak. But they mostly testify as the often sole surviving relatives and dependents of the mainly males who had suffered violations of human rights. The aim of the special hearing, then, was to create a space in which women might talk of the violations they had undergone, might therefore speak for themselves. The Indian woman appears at the very end of this section of the Report concluding the fourth volume – concluding in a sense the whole Report since the fifth and final volume gives the Findings – under a section entitled 'Women as Perpetrators'. Barely five pages long, it is perhaps the most depleted section of the Report (the Report runs to nearly 3,000 pages overall). Of the 7,128 applications for amnesty received by the Commission only fifty-six were known to come from women. Under apartheid, the message seems to be, there is very little women were guilty of.

It is in this blurred and almost empty context – like a frame with no painting – at a moment of the hearings which might, but for pressure from below, have not even existed, that a woman steps forward and claims for apathy a fully political status. Presenting the Commission with something which it had by its own account neglected (it lists apathy as a feature under the 'Neglected Factor' of 'Secrecy and Silence': 'much of the country's population went silent through fear, apathy, indifference or genuine lack of information', 5, pp. 250, 299, although in the chapter on the perpetrators, the Commission does allude to what it defines as 'diminished affective reactivity' 5, p. 259) – something intriguing, unexpected, disturbing perhaps, certainly bizarre. What – her appearance dramatically focuses – are the limits of accountability? How far does it spread? If the idea of apathy is so disquieting in this context, it is because it brings the issue of accountability, for the last person who might seem to be accountable, home to roost. It seems to me that it is not a coincidence – nor the first or last time – that a woman, tucked away almost in the back pages of history, speaks – if not *the* – certainly a truth. One of the things her testimony forces us to acknowledge is that we cannot claim apathy as the exclusive political property of the West.

I always start the course I take on South African literature by asking the students to say, as economically as possible – a word, image, character – what, when they think of South Africa, comes into their minds. It gives us a sense before we begin of an engagement which is going to be, for most people in the room, partial, tentative and refracted in space and time. In one year, the course almost didn't get going when a white student, in response to this query, said 'guilt'. She was challenged by another white student who claimed, outraged, that in relation to South Africa, whites in Britain had nothing whatsoever to feel guilty about. Should this happen again, I will refer the students to the Truth and Reconciliation Report which, in the spirit of fullest reconciliation (hence of course the title), none the less does not mince words when it comes to naming the British. In addition to providing a full historical account for each region whose stories of human rights violations it tells, the Report opens, after the Chairman's foreword, with a chapter on history which regresses accountability for apartheid into South Africa's British-dominated past. This is just one example from the very first pages of the Report:

> It is important to remember that the 1960 Sharpeville massacre (with which the mandate of the Commission begins) was simply the latest in a long line of similar killings of civilian protestors in South African history. It was, for example, not a National Party administration but the South African party government, made up primarily of English-speaking South Africans, that in July 1913 crushed a series of miners' strikes on the Reef – sending in the army and killing just over one hundred strikers and onlookers. Thrice in 1921 and 1922, this same governing party let loose its troops and planes. [. . .] Thus, when the South African Defence force (SADF) killed just over 600 men, women and children, combatant and non-combatant, at Kassinga in Angola in 1978, and when the South African Police (SAP) shot several hundred black protestors in the weeks following the June 16 events at Soweto,

they were operating in terms of a well-established tradition of excessive or unjustifiable use of force against government opponents [1, p. 26].

A simple act of historical recollection which contains a gentle rebuff to the temporal mandate of the TRC (Sharpeville, the start date, was not the start). And while South Africa entered a permanent winter with the Native Land Act of 1913 – 'There is winter in the Native Land Act [. . .] the trees are stripped and leafless' – this too is not the beginning:

> But if this was an act of wholesale dispossession and discrimination, so too was the 1909 South Africa Act which was passed, not by a South African legislature, but by the British Parliament [1, p. 28].

In relation to British accountability, the Report – from its very opening pages – chooses to jog the mind. To use the words of Gerry Hugo, former intelligence officer of the South African Defence Force and torturer (the interview in *Index on Censorship*'s special issue on Truth Commissions and War Tribunals is entitled 'Confession of a Torturer'): 'Accountability doesn't stop' (he is in fact talking about de Klerk).[9]

But it is not as simple as this (you might think that there is nothing easier for the white liberal intellectual in Britain than to point to historical accountability in this sense). For in fact the Report of the Truth and Reconciliation Commission can also be read for the immense difficulty with which it surrounds the issue of accountability – historical and political, collective and individual – in the modern world. The Indian woman's appeal gives one particularly bold, or striking, instance of this. Accountability, the Commission itself and the controversies it has generated clearly demonstrate, is not just a matter of answering the question: who? It is not just a matter of burrowing into corners to find responsibility, or indeed guilt, lurking in the dark – even apathetic – night of the soul. On this issue, although it takes up a strong position, the Commission is not so much judge (it was not of course a criminal hearing) as the active, troubled, sometimes uncertain, not always unified participant in the changing face and climate of what it describes. Hence the 'challenge' of my title: 'The Challenge of the South Africa's Truth and Reconciliation

Commission to the Intellectual in the Modern World'. I read the Report as a document which testifies not only to the horrors of the modern world but to a problem integral to the very recognition of such horror, a recognition which it has perhaps done more than any other modern process to achieve (the only truth commission of our time to have held its hearings in public, no other hearing has managed to combine truth-seeking with quasi-judicial power, 1, p. 54. How do you at once recognise the fullness and extent of historical accountability and draw boundaries around it, how do you let it flow (in the words of Roelf Meyer of the National Party: 'wrongs [. . .] flowed from apartheid', 5, p. 403), while also keeping it in, if not its proper, then at least a definable, precisely *accountable*, place?

To take perhaps the most important and controversial decision of the Commission on this topic. It is only recently in international law that non-state actors have been indictable for gross violations of human rights (1, p. 69). Drawing on decisions of the International Criminal Tribunal in relation to the former Yugoslavia as recent as 1997, the Report states: 'The Act establishing the Commission adopted this more modern position. In other words it did not make a finding of a gross violation of human rights conditional on a finding of state action' (1, p. 70). If this was crucial to pull in all the abuses committed between the release of Mandela and his election in 1994, when 'the great majority of human rights violations were being carried out by persons who were not bound to a political authority' (2, p. 5), it also means that all human rights violations, regardless of their provenance, whether carried out by resistance movements or by the apartheid state, become not ethically, but effectively, equal: 'A gross violation is a gross violation, whoever commits it and for whatever reason' (1, p. 12). What matters is the nature of the act. Justification, the central plank of legal accountability, is therefore set aside:

> the position adopted by the Commission was that any killing, abduction, torture or severe ill-treatment which met the other requirements of the definition, amounted to a gross violation of human rights, regardless of whether or not the perpetrator could be held accountable for the conduct . . . There is legal equivalence between all perpetrators [1, pp. 72, 12].

The Commission therefore holds to the distinction, older in international law, between the justice of the means and the justice of the cause of war: 'The Commission concurred with the international consensus that those who were fighting for a just cause were under an obligation to employ just means in the conduct of this fight' (1, p. 69). On the justice of the cause, the Report is of course unequivocal: apartheid was a crime against humanity, and the struggle against it a just war.

Within these terms, confusing as it may seem, and for some critics unjust, the ANC – in the finding that almost stopped the publication of the Report – becomes wholly accountable. Not legally – legal accountability has been set aside (the Commission is not a court, it is a hearing). Something more like answerable. And ironically, all the more so because, unlike those at the summit of former power, specifically de Klerk, the ANC accepted responsibility for the actions of its members:

> The Commission takes note that the political leadership of the ANC and the command structure of MK have accepted political and moral responsibility for all the actions of its members in the period 1960–1994 and therefore finds that the leadership of the ANC and MK must take responsibility and be accountable for all gross violations of human rights perpetrated by its membership and cadres in the mandate period [2, p. 685].

(All the findings of the Commission are presented in small bold capital letters which makes them look on the page like an inscription on a tomb.)

A great deal of attention has been paid to this finding of the Commission; it is, depending on from where you are looking, the finding on which the ethical viability of the Commission either falls or rests. But there has been less focus on what it says about the issue of accountability, the fraught and fine distinctions, in and out of law, on which it is based. For one set of critics, which includes the present Minister for Education, from the moment the Commission chose to define violations of human rights in terms of individual acts, it ceased – politically and historically – to be viable: 'There is,' write Kader and Louise Asmal and Ronald Suresh Roberts, in a follow-up article to their book on the Commission, 'simply no proportionality between the two sides of the struggle, a fact that is lost in the Commission's decision to individualise its definition of a gross human rights abuse [. . .]' (interestingly, in view of this, all individual explanations of atrocity are rejected in the chapter on 'Causes and Motives' in favour of an analysis in terms of the group). They continue: 'This is a failure deriving from a lack of political and ethical understanding.'[10]

How can everyone be equally answerable when the means available to the opponents, given in advance, are so unequal? How can you hold in the same measure, consider both as perpetrators, an illegal state and the combatants of a just war? For Asmal, Asmal and Roberts, in response to apartheid and as its appropriate legacy for international human rights law, the distinction between just cause and means of war has become – or rather, it *should* become – redundant: 'Given the convention-dependent nature of the morality of war, and apartheid's wholesale breach of those conventions, the question of *jus ad bellum* cannot be arbitrarily separated from the latter question of justice in the conduct of the cause, *jus in bello*.'[11] Ironically, however, if this path had been followed, the Truth and Reconciliation Commission might never have started. Although called into being to effect the transition to democracy (without the possibility of amnesty in some form, the transition could not have been peaceably guaranteed), it none the less had its germ in the decision by the ANC itself to investigate its own human rights abuses. In fact, it was Kader Asmal who mooted the idea, on behalf of the ANC, on his installation as Professor of Human Rights Law at the University of the Western Cape on 25 May 1992.

Spread accountability too wide by flattening out the differences between the state and its opponents, then oddly, symmetrically, it will also start to shrink, as the crimes of apartheid become more and more the acts of individuals, less and less the machinery of the unjust and illegal apartheid state ('the violence of the law' – in the Report's own words – pushed over the legal edge, 1, p. 40). Once it has been individualised, the act stands out in bold, plucked out of its context. In fact, the more inhuman and outrageous the act – remember the Commission's own self-critique for its stress on the 'outrageous' – the more drastically it curtails the Commission. The Report acknowledges as one of its failings its inability to bring under its sway the basic, daily humiliations, inequalities and fundamental social injustice – mostly still unredeemed – of the apartheid state: 'our mandate was not the policies of apartheid' (5, p. 48).[12] When Commissioner Dr Ramashala, referring to those who fall outside the Commission's mandate, especially the orphaned children of the struggle, says to Roelf Meyer of the National Party: 'I really have never heard any discussions from the political parties about these children and our future, because these are our future South Africa,' Meyer responds: 'If we can't find an answer to the very question that you have put, then the work of the Commission, with all respect, is not going to be in the long term worth anything' (5, p. 403).

A similar point was made by Lewis Nkosi when Judge Albie Sachs, also central in the founding of the Commission, came to Queen Mary College at the invitation of the Law Department in 1998 to lecture on the history and justification for the Commission (a lecture he has given worldwide). Nkosi simply asked him what the present government was planning to do about redistribution of land (the issue which has of course emerged so explosively in Zimbabwe in the past year).

So what comes first? Which form of transformation – psychic and subjective, or material and redistributive – will provide the real, sure, foundation for the other? For you could of course argue – as the rationale for the whole Commission and as Asmal himself argued when putting his original proposal for the Commission in 1995 – that a nation aiming to build a new future for its people, whatever concrete measures it enacts, without a reckoning with its own past violence will be building the whole edifice on sand:

> We must take the past seriously as it holds the key to the future. The issues of structural violence, of unjust and inequitable economic social arrangements, of balanced development in the future cannot be properly dealt with unless there is a conscious understanding of the past.

(His words are cited on the first pages of the Mandate chapter, 1, p. 49).

Accountability as an issue is therefore inseparable from that of justice. Justice, of course in the most familiar sense, was set aside by the Act establishing the Commission. 'There would have been no negotiated settlement and so no new democratic South Africa,' Tutu writes, 'had the negotiators on one side insisted that all the perpetrators be brought to trial. While the Allies could pack up and go home after Nuremberg, we in South Africa had to live with one another.' (This chapter of his book is called 'Nuremberg or National Amnesia? A Third Way'.)[13] No trials also because they would simply have been too long and too costly, and because with the burden of absolute proof – 'beyond all reasonable doubt' – falling on the investigators, too many of the guilty would have escaped the net (although the Commission itself was enormously hampered by the Corbett decision, which stipulated that anyone against whom a detrimental finding was being contemplated should be given fore-warning and a reasonable opportunity to respond). 'We discovered in the course of the Commission's investigations,' Tutu observes as part of this case, 'that the supporters of apartheid were ready to lie at the drop of a hat. [. . .] They lied as if it were going out of fashion, brazenly and with very considerable conviction.'[14] He doesn't, however, pause to ask whether his comment casts the whole basis of a Truth Commission into doubt.

But if justice, as in full-scale criminal proceedings, is set aside, it reappears as redistributive justice all the more forcefully through the Commission's back door. I have already given one example in the exchange between Ramashala and Roelf Meyer. This is from the Minister of Justice, cited in a section called 'Amnesty and Social Justice' in the chapter on Concepts and Principles from Volume 1 of the Report:

> We have a nation of victims, and if we are unable to provide complete justice on an individual basis [. . .] it is possible for us . . . to ensure that there is historical and collective justice for the people of our country. If we achieve that, if we achieve social justice and move in that direction [. . .] at that level we will be able to say *that justice has been done* [1, p. 124, original's emphasis].

And on this matter, there is, as it were, a faultline running through the Commission more or less by its own account. For if the Commission, or rather its associated amnesty hearings, has the quasi-judicial power to grant amnesty, on reparation and rehabilitation it has

solely the power to recommend. It was one of the chief principles of
the Commission to restore the dignity of victims (the discussion of
whether indeed they should be called 'victims' turned on this
concern): 'restoring the human and civil *dignity* of [such] victims by
granting them an opportunity to relate their own accounts of the
violations of which they were the victims' (1, p. 55). Dignity in the act
of speech – this the Commission could enact, in this sense the
Commission is one of the great performatives of modern times;
dignity of a continuing life is something else: 'and by recommending
reparation measures in respect of them [. . .] 'the individual reparation
grant provides resources to victims in an effort to restore their *dignity*'
(5, p. 184).[15]

One of these forms of dignity is measurable, calculable; one is not.
The strength and uniqueness of the Commission is to have thrown
itself into the realm of the incalculable, speech upon speech for
victims for whom speech – pained, sometimes reluctant, by no means
always healing – was the only thing left to say. But you could argue
that these two forms of dignity – of speech and of daily life – are not
so much incommensurable as critically reliant on, or even subtractable
from, each other. That the speech of the victim, the speech to which
at one level the whole of the hearings was devoted, cannot reach its
destination, unless economic equality, social justice is achieved (the
minority, dissenting Commissioner, Wynand Malan, even argues that
liberal rights can act as an obstruction to social rights – the granting of
social rights by the previously elite minority costs, as in hurts, more).
The last paragraph of Findings and Conclusions states:

> Ultimately, however, because the work of the Commission includes
> reconciliation, it needs to unleash a process that contributes to
> economic developments that redress past wrongs as a basis for
> promoting lasting reconciliation. This requires *all those who benefited*
> from apartheid, not only those whom the Act defines as perpetrators, to
> commit themselves to the reconciliation process [5, p. 258].

The differential of accountability, lost in one sense in the body of the
Report, returns therefore on the issue of redistributive justice; as does
its infinite, one might say, interminable extensibility: '*all those who
benefited*' is in italics.

Wole Soyinka – in a wonderfully theatrical moment in an already theatrical speech on 'Reparations, Truth, and Reconciliation' – gives the comic – black comic – version:

> Just to let one's fantasy roam a little – what really would be preposterous or ethically inadmissable in imposing a general levy on South Africa's white population? This is not intended as a concrete proposal, but as an exercise in pure speculation [. . .] such an offer could originate from the beneficiaries of Apartheid themselves, in a voluntary gesture of atonement – it need not be a project of the state. Is such a genesis – from within the indicted group itself – truly beyond conception? [. . .] [should] some external prodding prove necessary, the initiative could be taken up by someone of the non-establishment stature of Archbishop Desmond Tutu. The respected cleric and mediator mounts his pulpit one day and addresses his compatriots on that very theme: 'White brothers and sisters in the Lord, you have sinned, but we are willing to forgive. The scriptures warn us that the wages of sin are death but, in your case, they seem to be wealth. If therefore you chose to shed a little of that sinful wealth as a first step towards atonement . . . etc. etc.'[16]

The suggestion that perpetrators should make a financial contribution to the families of victims is also made by Cynthia Ngewu, mother of one of the Gugulethu Seven, at the forum on Reconciliation, Reconstruction and Economic Justice in Cape Town in March 1997 ('the best way to demonstrate a truthful commitment to peace and a truthful commitment to repentance', 5, p. 402). But it says something that outside that context, Soyinka can only conjure up the possibility of such material accountability on the part of the white community as fantasy.

There is therefore, by its own account, a hiatus in the Commission, a double deal on either side of the truth in which one justice is exchanged for another, neither of which are exactly there. Justice, as in criminal proceedings, set aside for the Commission to do its work; justice as in social justice suspended beyond its remit into an unknowable future. In the middle sits 'restorative justice', the foundation of the Commission's daily work, but only 'if the emerging truth unleashes a social dynamic that includes redressing the suffering of victims will it meet the ideal of restorative justice' (1, p. 131). If the

Commission presents us more starkly than any other modern document with the difficult relationship between truth and language it also forces a no less crucial and fraught connection between the registers of justice and truth. As Wole Soyinka puts the question: 'Is knowledge on its own of lasting effect?'[17]

It is not then, quite, that making accountability a matter of individual acts fails to discriminate appropriately, veiling the state behind its agents; if anything it is the opposite, as each individual act described, along with all the acts which surrounded it and made it possible – the 'interstice between power and indifferent or supportive agency' – are, in a still unredeemed future, held to indefinite account. To read the Report is to watch accountability contract and expand, pulsing under the pressure of a set of crucial but barely sustainable distinctions. 'Accountability doesn't stop.' There is no upper limit – hence the devastating effect on the Commissioners of the denials and fudges of de Klerk; there is no outer limit – the interstice between 'power and indifferent or supportive agency' is very, very wide; not before, not after – the Commission makes its recommendations, halfway between a pledge and a plea.

To end, therefore, by bringing these matters a little closer to home, to the university back door. 'The Commission should' – this from a final section on the Commission's shortcomings – 'for example, have investigated [. . .] educational institutions (in particular universities) . . .' (5, p. 207, also p. 434). Universities are named as one of the institutions of civil society into which the Commission did not reach: they did not appear at any of the Institutional and Special Hearings, which included Business and Labour, the Faith and Legal Communities, the Health Sector, Media and Prisons. The University was then, one could almost say, the only institution that escapes.

It cannot, I think, be wholly coincidental that J. M. Coetzee situates or at least opens his much acclaimed and much critiqued novel, *Disgrace*, in the setting of a university.[18] That he chose, to the objections of many critics, to write this novel, at this particular moment in South Africa's slow emergence from the night of apartheid, about someone who could be taken for himself (Susan Barton in *Foe* couldn't be, nor Magda in *The Heart of the Country*, nor the old lady in *The Age of Iron*, nor even, although this one doesn't require a gender leap of the same order, *Michael K.*)

I read *Disgrace* as Coetzee's response to the Truth and Reconciliation Commission. David Lurie, a semi-depressed university professor sexually harasses a young female student, is charged, refuses to justify himself, refuses to speak. Disgraced, he goes to live with his daughter Lucy on a white farm where they are subjected to a violent assault by a group of black youths, she is raped, he is severely beaten. The novel then charts the psychic trajectory of both of them, as she decides to keep the baby who will result from the abuse and to accept the marriage proposal of her black co-manager into whose hands the farm, the baby and herself will then fall, while he takes up work at a clinic where he devotes himself – with a humanity which neither he nor the reader can at first imagine him capable of – to the comfort of a succession of stray, sick and finally condemned dogs. In 'the interstice between power and indifferent agency', Lurie lives outside the mainstream of a history which gradually engulfs him. Opening his novel at the university, Coetzee brings his character closer than any other to his own world (Lurie is a university professor of literature). At the same time – while Lurie does acquire the partial status of trauma victim, and he is, or at least it could be argued that he is, partially redeemed at the end of the novel – in this novel, Coetzee seems to have gone out of his way to create a character with whom it is almost impossible for his reader to sympathise or identify. Lurie is repellent – simply, literally, people withdraw from him – incapable of intimacy with the women he sexually approaches, and repellent to himself.

Like a perpetrator, Lurie is someone who suffers, in the Commission's words, from 'diminished affective reactivity' ('Causes, Motives and Perspectives of Perpetrators', 5, p. 259), even before he is the subject of an assault which robs him of all feeling. This is perhaps the only moment, in a novel which in fact constantly forces unexpected and unwelcome moments of identification between its protagonists, when we are drawn into something like empathy for what Lurie has experienced. It is after the assault:

> Aimlessly he roams about the garden. A grey mood is settling on him.
> It is not just that he does not know what to do with himself. The events
> of yesterday have shocked him to the depths. The trembling, the
> weakness are only the first and most superficial signs of that shock. He

has a sense that, inside him, a vital organ has been bruised, abused – perhaps even his heart. For the first time he has a taste of what it will be like to be an old man, tired to the bone, without hopes, without desires, indifferent to the future. Slumped on a plastic chair amid the stench of chicken feathers and rotting apples, he feels his interest in the world draining from him drop by drop.[19]

He is already disconnected before the assault, which his daughter will take on as the burden of atonement for the past wrongs of South Africa, drains him of all connection to the world. 'Indifferent', his interest in the world 'draining from him drop by drop' – the terms embedded in this passage hover between diagnosis and accusation; as the effect of trauma, Lurie enters a state of mind – indifference, lack of interest, failure to connect – for which, in terms of the history of his country to which he has paid such scant regard, he could also be held accountable. In *Disgrace*, the psychic consequences of trauma are also being offered as their own cause.

In *The Lives of Animals* (Coetzee's last publication before *Disgrace*), which consists of his Tanner lectures, written by choice in fictional form, Elizabeth Costello, feminist fiction writer and campaigning vegetarian, uses the occasion of two public lectures (not unlike the Tanner lectures) to make the case against the slaughter of animals: 'There is no limit to which we can think ourselves into the being of another.'[20] In the discussion papers which followed (also included in the book), by literary critic Marjorie Garber, ethical and religious philosophers Peter Singer and Wendy Doniger, and anthropologist Barbara Smuts, South Africa is not mentioned once, despite this moment from Elizabeth Costello in which she is, surely, making the link:

'To me, a philosopher who says that the distinction between human and nonhuman depends on whether you have a white or a black skin, and a philosopher who says that the distinction between human and nonhuman depends on whether or not you know the difference between a subject and a predicate, are more alike than they are unlike.'[21]

And yet it does seem to me that these two texts by Coetzee share a question. How do you get from dissociation, a consciously or unconsciously willed refusal to connect to the horrors going on around you, a drastic failure of historical imagination as we might call it, to empathy with – being able to think yourself into the being of – a dog? (An aside, or perhaps not an aside: Marlene Van Niekerk's prize-winning Afrikaans novel, *Triomf*, which centres on another group which falls out of the remit of the Truth Commission, South Africa's white trash, not only, like *Disgrace*, has a dog on its cover, not only opens with a chapter called 'Dogs', not only at a key point signals its catastrophically dysfunctional family's humanity through their tele-pathic awareness of the death of their dog, but also at several points is written from the point of view of a dog.)[22] 'They just buried him like a dog,' in the words of one testimony to the Commission (5, p. 152). Lucy replies to Lurie: 'Yes, I agree, it is humiliating. But perhaps that is a good point from which to start again. [. . .] With nothing. No cards, no weapons, no property, no rights, no dignity.' 'Like a dog.' 'Yes, like a dog.'[23]

Accountability halts at the barrier of identification. As does atrocity. All the evidence suggests that people do not kill if they can imagine themselves in the other person's shoes. 'The horror,' Costello states in a deliberately shocking analogy between animal slaughter and the Nazi death camps, 'is that the killers refused to think themselves into the place of their victims, as did everyone else.'[24] Another way of putting this would be to say that we should never underestimate people's ability – internal as well as external – to ward off bad news (a victim is of course someone for whom this has ceased to be an option). There are exceptions: 'I thought,' said the Afrikaans Johan Smit talking of the death of his eight-year-old son in a bomb blast in 1985: 'I thought that if I placed myself in the other person's shoes, how would I have felt about it [. . .] I realised I would not have liked it [. . .] I realised how it must have felt for them' (5, p. 377). After he had spoken, Tutu stopped the proceedings to express his appreciation.

One of the things for which the Truth Commission has become famous is the concept of '*ubuntu*', a traditional Zulu term which is placed by the Commission at the basis of restorative justice: '*Ubuntu* generally translated as "humaneness", expresses itself metaphorically in *umuntu ngumuntu ngabantu* – "people are people through other people"' (1, p. 127). 'A person,' Tutu expanded at his inauguration as Archbishop of Cape Town in 1986, 'is a person because he recognises others as persons.'[25] As Mark Sanders argues in a recent article in *diacritics*, the term involves more than a call to collective solidarity, and more than a recognition from a safe place; for such a recognition to occur, you have fundamentally to lose or disappropriate yourself. Sanders retranslates: 'a human being is a human being through human beings', 'a human being is realised through his or her being (human) through human beings'.[26] Perhaps, however, even this does not go far enough. Perhaps, Coetzee is suggesting in *The Lives of Animals*, the human is the block. So how about animals? Or, even, a corpse. Pushing her analogy and her audience to the limit, Elizabeth Costello announces in the middle of her lecture: 'For instants at a time, I know what it is like to be a corpse.'[27]

The original meaning of the word 'apathy' was to be without 'pathos', insensibility to suffering, the highest virtue for the Stoics, only gradually degrading itself to listless, stolid indifference. It could be, however, that in the setting of South Africa, apathy includes something of the earlier meaning, in which suffering – actively – is held at bay. A state of mind racing away from itself. Apathy in the modern sense would then contain, working away inside it, the germ of its own undoing, a kind of internal dissent. The implication would be that, for anyone struck with apathy in a situation of historic injustice, there is a partial recognition, not just of the suffering of others, but of what it would do to you, just how far you might have to go, to make the link. If making those links is, as I see it, one of the tasks of modern intellectual life, one of the things South Africa's Truth and Reconciliation Commission teaches me is that it has never been more important or harder to do so.

Notes and References

Many people have contributed to my engagement with South African politics and literature, but the person whose writings have most consistently inspired and informed my understanding are those of Gillian Slovo. My special thanks to her.

1 *Truth and Reconciliation Commission of South Africa Report*, 5 volumes (London: Macmillan, 1998, 1999), 4, p. 313. Hereafter cited in the text.

2 Eric Hobsbawm with Antonio Pollio, *The New Century*, trans. Allan Cameron (London, New York: Little Brown, 2000), p. 86.

3 Antjie Krog, *Country of My Skull* (Johannesburg: Random House, 1998), p. 73.

4 Phillip Gourevitch, *We Wish to Inform You that Tomorrow We Will be Killed with Our Families: Stories from Rwanda* (London: Picador, 1999), p. 7.

5 Njabulo Ndebele, 'Memory, Metaphor and the Triumph of Narrative', in Sarah Nuttall and Carli Coetzee (eds), *Negotiating the Past: The Making of Memory in South Africa* (Cape Town: Oxford University Press, 1998), p. 26.

6 Krog, p. 36. I discuss Krog and the question of representation and language in relation to the Truth Commission more fully in 'Aux marges du littéraire: justice, verité, reconciliation', *Où é en est la théorie litteraire?*, edited by Julia Kristeva and Evelyne Grossman, Actes du Colloque organisé à l'Université Paris 7, May 1999, *Textuel*, 37 (2000).

7 Hobsbawm, p. 115.

8 Desmond Tutu, *No Future Without Forgiveness* (London: Rider, 1999), p. 2.

9 Gerry Hugo, 'Confession of a Torturer', *Wounded Nations, Broken Lives: Truth Commissions and War Tribunals, Index on Censorship*, 5, 1996, p. 66.

10 Kader Asmal, Louise Asmal, Ronald Suresh Roberts, 'When the assassin cries foul: modern Just War doctrines', in Charles Villa-Vicencio and Wilhelm Verwoerd (eds), *Looking Back, Reaching Forward: Reflections on the Truth and Reconciliation Commission of South Africa* (Cape Town: University of Cape Town Press/London: Zed Books, 2000), p. 93; see also their *Reconciliation Through Truth: A Reckoning of Apartheid's Criminal Governance* (Cape Town: David Philip, 1997). Compare Neville Alexander: 'The fundamental flaw in the conceptualisation of the TRC as a mechanism for "dealing with the past" lies in the fact that the question of moral debt (Habermas) is judged by both trying to "share" it between victim and perpetrator and by individualising it, i.e., removing it from systematic embedment.' 'The Politics of Reconciliation', unpublished mimeo of chapter of book forthcoming from University of Natal Press. My thanks to Benita Parry for making this available to me.

11 Asmal et al., p. 92.

12 For fuller discussion, see Neville Alexander and Deborah Posel, *The Making of Apartheid 1948–1961: Conflict and Compromise* (Oxford: Clarendon, 1991).

13 Tutu, p. 25.

14 Ibid., p. 28.

15 See Arthur Chaskalson, 'Human Dignity as a Foundational Value for our Constitutional Order', Third Bram Fischer lecture. My thanks to Stephen Clingman for making this text available to me.

16 Wole Soyinka, *The Burden of Memory, The Muse of Forgiveness* (New

York: Oxford University Press, 1999), pp. 25–6.

17 Ibid., p. 9. See Janet Cherry, 'Historical Truth: Something to Fight For', in Villa-Vicencio and Verwoerd. For me the best critique of the Commission in relation to the category of truth is contained in Gillian Slovo's extraordinary novel, *Red Dust* (London: Virago, 2000). See also Richard Wilson's critique of the TRC in terms of the distinction between retribution and revenge in *The Politics of Truth and Reconciliation in South Africa: Legitimising the Post-Apartheid State* (Cambridge: Cambridge University Press, 2001). I do not, however, agree with those critiques of the Commission which see it as 'an officially instituted memory-loss' (Benita Parry, 'Reconciliation and Remembrance', *Pretexts*, 5, 1–2, 1995) or which suggest, as Alexander does at points in his chapter on the Commission, that the truth offered by the Commission was simply unexamined truth, or rather that this was a problem of which the Commissioners were unaware. See, for example, this statement by Professor Simpson, a psychiatrist specialising in post-traumatic stress disorder, cited in the final volume chapter on Reconciliation (Oxford: 'Truth is one essential component of the needed social antiseptic which could cleanse the social fabric of the systematised habit of disregard for human rights, but it needs to be an *examined truth; it needs to be considered, thought about, debated and digested and metabolised by individuals and society*' (5, p. 356, my emphasis); and the statement from Bishop David Beetge at the follow-up hearing workshop in Reiger Park: 'We retell our painful stories so that we shall remember . . .', 5, p. 350).

18 For a summary of these critiques see Anthony Sampson, 'The Gloom and the Glory', *Prospect* (April 2000), p. 58.

19 J. M. Coetzee, *Disgrace* (London: Secker & Warburg, 1999), pp. 106–7.

20 J. M. Coetzee, *The Lives of Animals* (Princeton NJ: Princeton University Press, 1999), p. 35.

21 Ibid., p. 66.

22 Marlene Van Niekerk, *Triomf*, trans. Leon de Kock (London, New York: Little Brown, 1999; first published in Afrikaans, Quellerie, 1994).

23 Coetzee, *Disgrace*, p. 205.

24 Coetzee, *The Lives of Animals*, p. 34.

25 Cited in Mark Sanders, reviewing the *TRC Report*, and Thomas Keenan, *Fables of Responsibility*, *diacritics* (Fall 1999), p. 12.

26 Ibid., p. 13.

27 Coetzee, *The Lives of Animals*, p. 32.

Index